M000294769

Teach...
Inspire...
Lead...

With REA's FTCE Social Science test prep, you'll be in a class all your own.

We'd like to hear from you!
*Visit **www.rea.com** to send us your comments*
*or e-mail us at **info@rea.com**.*

Research & Education Association

The Best Teachers' Test Preparation for the

FTCE
Social Science
6-12

Thomas E. Murray, Ph.D.
University of Central Florida
Orlando, Florida

Visit our Educator Support Center at:
www.REA.com/teacher

The competencies presented in this book were created and implemented by the Florida Department of Education in conjunction with National Evaluation Systems, Inc. For further information visit the FTCE website at *www.fldoe.org/asp/ftce*.

Research & Education Association
61 Ethel Road West
Piscataway, New Jersey 08854
E-mail: info@rea.com

The Best Teachers' Test Preparation for the Florida FTCE® Social Science 6-12 Test

Printed in the United States of America

Library of Congress Control Number 2007943340

ISBN-13: 978-0-7386-0206-6
ISBN-10: 0-7386-0206-X

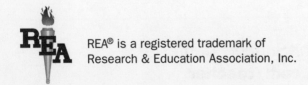

REA® is a registered trademark of Research & Education Association, Inc.

About Research & Education Association

Founded in 1959, Research & Education Association is dedicated to publishing the finest and most effective educational materials—including software, study guides, and test preps—for students in middle school, high school, college, graduate school, and beyond.

REA's Test Preparation series includes books and software for all academic levels in almost all disciplines. Research & Education Association publishes test preps for students who have not yet entered high school, as well as for high school students preparing to enter college. Students from countries around the world seeking to attend college in the United States will find the assistance they need in REA's publications. For college students seeking advanced degrees, REA publishes test preps for many major graduate school admission examinations in a wide variety of disciplines, including engineering, law, and medicine. Students at every level, in every field, with every ambition can find what they are looking for among REA's publications.

REA's practice tests are always based upon the most recently administered exams and include every type of question that you can expect on the actual exams.

REA's publications and educational materials are highly regarded and continually receive an unprecedented amount of praise from professionals, instructors, librarians, parents, and students. Our authors are as diverse as the fields represented in the books we publish. They are well-known in their respective disciplines and serve on the faculties of prestigious high schools, colleges, and universities throughout the United States and Canada.

Today, REA's wide-ranging catalog is a leading resource for teachers, students, and professionals.

We invite you to visit us at *www.rea.com* to find out how REA is making the world smarter.

Acknowledgments

We would like to thank Larry Kling, Vice President, Editorial, for his editorial direction; Pam Weston, Vice President, Publishing, for setting the quality standards for production integrity and managing the publication to completion; Alice Leonard, Senior Editor, for project management and preflight editorial review; Diane Goldschmidt, Senior Editor, for post-production quality assurance; Christine Saul, Senior Graphic Artist, for cover design; Rachel DiMatteo, Graphic Artist, for test design; and Jeff LoBalbo, Senior Graphic Artist, for post-production file mapping.

We also gratefully acknowledge Malla Kolhoff for technical editing, Barbara McGowran for copyediting, Aquent Publishing Services for typesetting, Ellen Gong for proofreading, and Brooke Graves for indexing the manuscript.

About the Author

Author Tom Murray earned his Ph.D. in Curriculum and Instruction, Secondary Education Concentration: Social Science Education, from the University of South Florida. He also holds an M.B.A. from the University of Dayton, and B.S. from Xavier University in Cincinnati. Currently teaching in the Educational Studies Department at the University of Central Florida, Tom has also taught at the College of Charleston, Charleston, South Carolina, and Bayside High School in Pinellas County, Florida. He has his teaching certification in the teaching of Secondary Education 6-12 in Social Science. Through his foundation, *Think About the Children,* Tom has devoted much of his personal time to working with the children who live in remote villages in Vietnam.

Contents

CONTENTS

CONTENTS

Introduction
Passing the FTCE Social Science 6–12 Test

ABOUT THIS BOOK

REA's *The Best Teachers' Preparation for the FTCE Social Science 6–12 Test* is a comprehensive guide designed to assist you in preparing to take the FTCE required for teaching social sciences in grades 6–12. To enhance your chances of success in this important step toward your career as a teacher in Florida schools, this test guide:

- presents an accurate and complete overview of the FTCE Social Science 6–12 Test

- identifies all of the important information and its representation on the exam

- provides a comprehensive review of every competency and skill

- presents sample questions in the actual test format

- suggests tips and strategies for successfully completing standardized tests

- provides diagnostic tools to identify areas of strength and weakness

- provides two full-length practice tests based on the most recently administered FTCE

- replicates the format of the official exam, including levels of difficulty

- provides the correct answer and detailed explanations for each question on the practice tests, which enables you to identify correct answers and understand why they are correct and, just as important, why the other answers are incorrect

This guide is based on the best research and resources. The editors considered the most recent test administrations and professional standards. They also researched information from the Florida Department of Education, professional journals, textbooks, and educators in the field. This guide includes the best test preparation materials based on the latest information available. Nonetheless, it is always wise to check for any late updates from the test administrator.

ABOUT THE TEST

Since 1980 the state of Florida has used the Florida Teacher Certification Examinations as a requirement for teacher certification. In 1986 the legislature added the requirement to pass a test in the content area in which the teacher desires to be certified. The purpose of this preparation guide is to help you successfully prepare for the test by providing you with a clear overview of what content is considered essential in the social science curricula for grades 6–12. The guide is not designed to be an all-inclusive source for social science content.

There are two versions of the social science test in Florida. Be sure you are registered for the proper test. The version for grades 5–9 is what you should take if you want to be a middle school teacher. The version for grades 6–12 requires greater depth of knowledge. This guide is designed to prepare you for the grades 6–12 test.

Below are the competencies used as the basis for the FTCE Social Science grades 6–12 examination, as well as the approximate percentage of the total test that each competency occupies. These competencies represent the knowledge that teams of teachers, subject area specialists, and district-level educators have determined to be important for beginning teachers. This book contains a thorough review of these competencies, as well as the specific skills that demonstrate mastery of each area.

Competencies	Percentage
1. Knowledge of Geography	15%
2. Knowledge of Economics	15%
3. Knowledge of Political Science	15%
4. Knowledge of World History	20%
5. Knowledge of American History	30%
6. Knowledge of Social Science and its Methodology	5%

Who Administers the Test?

The Florida Department of Education develops this test. Subject area knowledge tested on the Social Science 6–12 examination of the FTCE was identified and validated by committees of content specialists from the state of Florida. Public school teachers made up the majority of the committee members, but the committees also included district supervisors and college faculty. Selection of committee members was based on recommendations by professional associations, experts, and teachers' unions. Development of the appropriate content and difficulty levels of the exam involved literature review, teacher interviews, beta tests, and professional judgment. Testing services, including test administrations, for the FTCE are provided by National Evaluation Systems, Inc.

Can I Retake the Test?

If you do not achieve a passing grade on the FTCE, don't panic. The test can be taken again after 31 days, so you can seriously work on improving your score in preparation for your next FTCE. A score on the FTCE that does not match your expectations does not mean you should change your plans about teaching.

When Should the FTCE Be Taken?

Florida law requires that teachers demonstrate mastery of basic skills, professional knowledge, and content area of specialization. If you've graduated from a Florida state-approved teacher preparation program and made the decision to teach Social Science 6–12, you need to begin the process by applying for a Florida Temporary Certificate in that subject. The Bureau of Educator Certification will only evaluate your eligibility in the subject(s) you request on your application form. The Temporary Certificate is valid for three school years, which allows you time to complete the certification tests while teaching full-time.

For high school graduates and out-of-state educators, the Bureau of Educator Certification will provide you with official information about which test(s) to take to complete requirements for the Professional Certificate. The FTCE is usually administered four times a year in several locations throughout Florida. The usual testing day is Saturday, but the test may be taken on an alternate day if a conflict exists, such as a religious obligation. Special accommodations can also be made for applicants who are visually impaired, hearing impaired, physically disabled, or specific learning disabled.

To receive information on upcoming administrations of the FTCE you should consult the FTCE Registration Bulletin, which can be obtained by contacting:

Florida Department of Education
325 West Gaines Street, Suite 414
Tallahassee, FL 32399-0400
Phone: (413) 256-2893
Website: *www.fldoe.org/asp/ftce* or *www.fl.nesinc.com*
Bureau of Educator Certification: *www.fl doe.org/edcert*

The FTCE Registration Bulletin also includes information regarding test retakes and score reports.

Is There a Registration Fee?

To take the FTCE, you must pay a registration fee. You may pay by personal check, money order, cashier's check, or Visa or MasterCard. Cash is not accepted. Utilize the contact information above for any questions.

HOW TO USE THIS BOOK

How Do I Begin Studying?

1. Review the organization of this test preparation guide.

2. To best utilize your study time, follow our FTCE Independent Study Schedule. The schedule is based on a six-week program, but can be condensed to four weeks if necessary by combining a few weekly periods.

3. Take the first Practice Test and score it according to directions.

4. Review the format of the FTCE.

5. Review the test-taking advice and suggestions presented later in this chapter.

6. Pay attention to the information about competencies and skills, content, and topics on the test.

7. Spend time reviewing topics that stand out as needing more study.

8. Take the second Practice Test, review the explanations to your answers carefully, study the competencies that your scores indicate need further review.

9. Follow the suggestions at the end of this chapter for the day before and the day of the test.

When Should I Start Studying?

It is never too early to start studying for the FTCE. The earlier you begin, the more time you will have to sharpen your skills. Do not procrastinate! Cramming is not an effective way to study, since it does not allow you the time to think about the content, review the competencies, and take the practice tests. It is important, however, to review the material one last time the night before the test administration.

STUDYING FOR THE FTCE SOCIAL SCIENCE TEST

It is very important for you to choose the time and place for studying that works best for you. Some individuals may set aside a certain number of hours every morning to study, while others may choose to study at night before going to sleep. Other people may study during the day, while waiting in line, or even while eating lunch. Only you can determine when and where your study time will be most effective. Be consistent and use your time wisely. Work out a study routine and stick to it.

When you take the practice tests, simulate the conditions of the actual test as closely as possible. Turn your television and radio off, and sit down at a quiet table free from distraction. As you complete each practice test, score your test and thoroughly review the explanations to the questions you answered incorrectly; however, do not review too much at any one time. Concentrate on one problem area at a time by reviewing the question and explanation, and by studying our review until you are confident that you have mastered the material.

Keep track of your scores. By doing so, you will be able to gauge your progress and discover general weaknesses in particular sections. Give extra attention to the reviews that cover your areas of difficulty, as this will build your skills in those areas.

FORMAT OF THE FTCE SOCIAL SCIENCE TEST

The FTCE Social Science Grades 6–12 addresses six main areas of competency identified by the Florida Department of Education as foundational to effective teaching. Divided among the six competencies are 53 skill areas on which you will be tested to assess your mastery of Social Science 6–12. Individual test items require a variety of different thinking levels, ranging from simple recall to evaluation and problem solving.

The competencies are broad statements written in a way to reflect the information that an entry-level educator needs in order to be a truly effective teacher. The competencies themselves will not be discussed in the actual FTCE test, only the skills.

All the questions on the FTCE are in multiple-choice format. Each question will have four options, lettered A through D, from which to choose. You should have plenty of time in which to complete the FTCE, but be aware of the amount of time you are spending on each question so that you allow yourself time to complete the test. Although speed is not very important, a steady pace should be maintained when answering the questions. Using the practice tests will help you prepare for this task.

Computer-Based Testing

As of this writing, computer-based testing is available for the FTCE Subject Area Examination, Social Science Grades 6–12. To verify, go to *www.cefe.usf.edu* and click on "FTCE Computer-Based Testing." Exams on the computer have the advantage of providing you with a notice of Pass/Fail immediately after completing the exam, which can be scheduled at a time that is convenient for you.

About the Review Sections

The reviews in this book are designed to help you sharpen the basic skills needed to approach the FTCE, as well as provide strategies for attacking the questions.

Each teaching competency is examined in a separate chapter. The skills required for all six competencies are extensively discussed to optimize your understanding of what the FTCE covers.

Your schooling has taught you most of what you need to answer the questions on the test. The education classes you took should have provided you with the know-how to make important decisions about situations you will face as a teacher. Our review is designed to help you fit the information you have acquired into specific competency components. Reviewing your class notes and textbooks together with our competency reviews will give you an excellent springboard for passing the FTCE.

SCORING THE FTCE SOCIAL SCIENCE TEST

How Do I Score My Practice Test?

There are approximately 120 multiple-choice questions on the FTCE Social Science 6–12. This is a pass or fail test. You must get 67% of the 120 questions correct to pass. NOTE: Because the number of items on the FTCE is approximate, we have provided 125 questions in each of our practice tests.

If you do not achieve a passing score on the practice test, review the detailed explanations for the questions you answered incorrectly. Note which types of questions you answered wrong and re-examine the corresponding review. After further review, you may want to re-take the practice tests.

When Will I Receive My Score

Approximately one month after you take the test, your score report will be mailed to you. Your scores will be submitted electronically to the Bureau of Educator Certification. A copy of your score report is provided to one Florida college or university and one Florida school district. You should have requested this information on your registration application.

When you receive your score report and have passed, only the word "PASS" will be reported. If you do not pass, you will receive a numeric score and will have to retake the test.

Test-Taking Tips

Although you may not be familiar with tests like the FTCE, this book will help acquaint you with this type of exam and help alleviate your test-taking anxieties. Listed below are ways to help you become accustomed to the FTCE.

Tip 1. Become comfortable with the format of the FTCE. When you are practicing, stay calm and pace yourself. After simulating the test only once, you will boost your chances of doing well, and you will be able to sit down for the actual FTCE with much more confidence.

Tip 2. Read all of the possible answers. Just because you think you have found the correct response, do not automatically assume that it is the best answer. Read through each choice to be sure that you are not making a mistake by jumping to conclusions.

Tip 3. Use the process of elimination. Go through each answer to a question and eliminate as many of the answer choices as possible. By eliminating two answer choices, you have given yourself a better chance of getting the item correct since there will only be two choices left from which to make your guess. Do not leave an answer blank; it is better to guess than to not answer a question on the FTCE test.

Tip 4. Place a question mark in your answer booklet next to answers you guessed, then recheck them later if you have time.

Tip 5. Work quickly and steadily. You will have two and one-half hours to complete the test, so work quickly and steadily to avoid focusing on any one problem too long. Taking the practice tests in this book will help you learn to budget your precious time.

Tip 6. Learn the directions and format of the test. This will not only save time, but will also help you avoid anxiety (and the mistakes caused by getting anxious).

Tip 7. Be sure that the answer circle you are marking corresponds to the number of the question in the test booklet. Since the test is multiple-choice, it is graded by machine, and marking one wrong answer can throw off your answer key and your score. Be extremely careful.

THE DAY OF THE TEST

Before the Test

On the day of the test, make sure to dress comfortably, so that you are not distracted by being too hot or too cold while taking the test. Plan to arrive at the test center early. This will allow you to collect your thoughts and relax before the test, and will also spare you the anguish that comes with being late.

You should check your FTCE Registration Bulletin to find out what time to arrive at the testing center.

Before you leave for the test center, make sure that you have your admission ticket and two forms of identification, one of which must contain a recent photograph, your name, and signature (i.e., driver's license). You will not be admitted to the test center if you do not have proper identification.

You must bring several sharpened No. 2 pencils with erasers, as none will be provided at the test center.

If you would like, you may wear a watch to the test center. However, you may not wear one that makes noise, because it may disturb the other test takers. Dictionaries, textbooks, notebooks, calculators, briefcases, or packages will not be permitted. The testing center suggests that you lock your cell phone in your car, as it is not allowed in the exam room. Drinking, smoking, and eating are prohibited.

During the Test

The FTCE is given in one sitting with no breaks. Procedures will be followed to maintain test security. Once you enter the test center, follow all of the rules and instructions given by the test supervisor. If you do not, you risk being dismissed from the test and having your scores cancelled.

When all of the materials have been distributed, the test instructor will give you directions for filling out your answer sheet. Fill out this sheet carefully since this information will be printed on your score report.

Once the test begins, mark only one answer per question, completely erase unwanted answers and marks, and fill in answers darkly and neatly.

After the Test

When you finish your test, hand in your materials and you will be dismissed. Then, go home and relax—you deserve it!

FTCE STUDY SCHEDULE

The following study schedule allows for thorough preparation for the FTCE. The course of study here is six weeks, but you can condense or expand the timeline to suit your personal schedule. It is vital that you adhere to a structured plan and set aside ample time each day to study. The more time you devote to studying, the more prepared and confident you will be on the day of the test.

Week	Activity
1	**Take the first practice test.** The score will indicate your strengths and weaknesses. Make sure you simulate real exam conditions when you take the test. Afterwards, score it and review the explanations, especially for questions you answered incorrectly.
2	**Review the explanations for the questions you missed, and review the appropriate chapter sections.** Useful study techniques include highlighting key terms and information, taking notes as you review the book's sections, and putting new terms and information on note cards to help retain the information.
3 and 4	**Reread all your note cards, refresh your understanding of the exam's competencies and skills, review your college textbooks, and read over class notes you've previously taken.** This is also the time to consider any other supplementary materials that your counselor or the Florida State Department of Education suggests. Review the Department's website at *www.fldoe.org*.
5	**Have someone quiz you using the index cards you created.** Take the second practice test, adhering to the time limits and simulated test-day conditions.
6	**Review your areas of weakness using all study materials.** This is a good time to re-take both practice tests.

Knowledge of Geography

The following skills are used as a basis to determine your competency for the geography portion of the FTCE Social Science Grades 6–12:

- Identify and apply the five themes of geography.

- Identify the natural processes that shape the earth's physical and human systems.

- Identify physical and cultural features (e.g., communities, language, and political and economic institutions).

- Analyze and interpret geographic information from maps, charts, and graphs.

Identify and apply the five themes of geography.

The five themes of geography are location, place, human–environmental interaction, movement, and regions.

Location can be described in relative or absolute terms. An example of a relative location is "on the beaches of Florida." An example of an absolute location is "Clearwater is located in Pinellas County on the west coast of Florida in the United States. It is on the

Pinellas Peninsula between the Gulf of Mexico on the west and Tampa Bay on the east. The geographic latitude is 27°57′ N and longitude 82°48′ W."

Place has both human and physical characteristics. Physical characteristics include mountains, rivers, soil, beaches, and wildlife. Human characteristics are derived from the ideas and actions of people that result in changes to the environment, such as buildings, roads, clothing, and food habits.

Human–environmental interaction comprises three concepts:

- Humans adapt to the environment.

- Humans modify the environment.

- Humans depend on the environment.

An example of humans **adapting to the environment** can be as simple as wearing warm clothing in a cold climate. Humans **modify the environment** in many ways, but a simple example is that humans heat and cool buildings to adjust the climate to their comfort. People also **depend on the environment** in many ways. For example, they depend on the forest to provide wood to build shelter, and they depend on the environment for food and water.

The theme of **movement** involves many concepts. People move and interact with each other. Products or raw materials move as imports and exports. Many people in the United States move from the Northeast or Midwest to Florida for vacation or to retire. Communication is a form of movement. In today's era of highly technical electronics, communication plays a major role in our lives.

FTCE Fact

Communication is a form of movement.

Regions are areas that have unifying characteristics. These characteristics can be a common language, culture, or government. There are three main types of regions:

- **Formal regions** are defined by governmental or administrative boundaries. Examples are the United States; Birmingham, Alabama; and Brazil. Formal regional boundaries can also be physical, such as the Rockies and the Great Lakes.

- **Functional regions** are defined by a function. An example is a cell phone service area or an area served by bank branches. If the function ceases to exist, the region no longer exists.

- **Vernacular regions** are loosely defined by people's perceptions. Examples of vernacular regions are the Deep South, Eastern Europe, and the Middle East.

Identify the natural processes that shape the earth's physical and human systems.

One of the characteristics of physical systems is **weather**. Weather can be defined as the day-to-day conditions of the atmosphere. These conditions include precipitation, temperature, and wind. With television news and 24-hour weather channels, weather may be the most widely understood geographic feature.

Climate is weather averaged over time for a specific region or location. There are five factors that affect climate:

- **Latitude:** Temperature range increases with distance from the equator. Also, temperatures decrease as you move away from the equator. The variations occur because the sun's rays are dispersed over a larger area of land as you move away from the equator. This is owing to the curved surface of the earth. In addition, polar regions are colder because the sun's rays have further to travel to reach them than they do to reach places on the equator. (The sun's rays are more direct on the equator.) Any discussion of climate must reference the latitudes.

- **Altitude:** Temperatures decrease with height. The air is less dense and cannot hold heat as easily.

- **Winds:** If winds are warm, they have been blown from a hot area and will raise temperatures. If winds have been blown from cold areas, they will lower temperatures.

- **Distance from the sea, or continentality:** Land heats and cools faster than does the sea. Therefore, coastal areas have a lower temperature range than do inland areas. On the coast, winters are mild and summers are cool. In inland areas, temperatures are high in the summer and cold in the winter.

- **Aspect:** Slopes facing the sun are warmer than those that are not. Thus, south-facing slopes in the Northern Hemisphere are usually warm. However, slopes facing north in the Southern Hemisphere are warmest.

Climate can be displayed on a graph. A climate graph contains two pieces of information: the amount of rainfall and the temperature of an area. The temperature is shown as a line, and the rainfall is displayed as bars. The figures are usually calculated as an average over a number of years. This reduces the impact of any anomalies in the weather affecting the statistics.

People are central to geography and make up the component of **human systems.** Human activities help shape the earth's surface; human settlements and structures are part of the earth's surface; and humans compete for control of the earth's surface. This competition for control has positive and negative outcomes.

Maybe the most common element of human systems throughout history has been war. Wars are fought by nations, and in today's world they are fought by nation-states. Wars may be fought for resources, territory, race, or religion. On a smaller scale, there can be competition in neighborhoods, school districts, or cities for resources, land, or trade. As our world turns more to a global economy, changes in our lifestyle and the way we perceive the world around us are shifting dramatically.

Identify physical and cultural features (e.g., communities, language, and political and economic institutions).

The world can be divided into **four major hemispheres:** Eastern, Western, Northern, and Southern. It can also be divided into seven continents: Australia, Africa, Asia, Europe, North America, South America, and Antarctica. Political and physical boundaries can be determined precisely by either surveying or using longitude and latitude.

A relatively new geographic tool is the **geographic information system (GIS)**. This is a technology that combines the advantages of computer-assisted cartography with those of spatial database management. It facilitates the storage, retrieval, and analysis of spatial information in the form of digital map "overlays," each representing a differ-

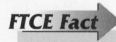

ent landscape component such as terrain, roads, or vegetation. Each of these data layers can be digitally fit to the same map scale and map projection, in any combination, permitting the analysis of relationships among any combination of environmental variables for which data have been input into the geographic information systems.

Seventy percent of the earth's surface is water. Physical features of the earth include mountains, hills, plateaus, valleys, and plains. Other landforms are deserts, deltas, canyons, mesas, and swamps. The earth's water features are rivers, lakes, oceans, seas, intercoastal waterways, and canals.

Cultural geography is the study of a country's culture, customs, foods, clothing, music, architecture, traditions, religions, and languages. The world has about 200 different nations and more than 6,000 distinct languages. Language is the basis for forming a culture, which means that the world has more than 6,000 distinct cultures. Of the thousands of languages in the world, most are spoken by small tribal groups, and only about 12 to 15 are common in international trade and politics. In the recent past, English has become the accepted international language of trade.

Analyze and interpret geographic information from maps, charts, and graphs.

Illustrations allow us to better visualize geography. It is critical for students to be able to use maps, charts, and graphs productively.

Every map has a title and a legend that describes the symbols used. Most maps use a longitude and latitude grid. During the FTCE Social Science 6–12, you will have to use maps, charts, and graphs. Familiarize yourself with the information provided before reading the questions. Typically, a map, chart, or graph will be displayed with a set of questions following it. Be sure you understand what the data reveal before proceeding to the questions. The practice tests in this guide will give you the opportunity to use some of these items.

Knowledge of Economics

The following skills are used as a basis to determine your competency for the economics portion of the FTCE Social Science Grades 6–12:

- Analyze how scarcity and opportunity cost impact choices about how to allocate resources.

- Identify how economic systems answer the three basic economic questions.

- Analyze the role of supply and demand in coordinating consumption, production, and distribution in a market system.

- Analyze fundamental macroeconomic concepts such as inflation, employment, money supply, the components of gross domestic product, and the role of the stock market.

- Analyze the role of government in market and nonmarket economies.

- Apply the principle of comparative advantage to local, state, national, and international trade.

- Evaluate the role of credit in a consumer economy.

Analyze how scarcity and opportunity cost impact choices about how to allocate resources.

A **market economy** relies largely on market forces to allocate resources and goods and to determine the price and quantity of each good that will be produced. Capitalist economies are market economies, while planned economies, like a socialist economy, are antithetical to it. Market economies typically are free of government control. Although taxes are a form of government influence, they are not considered control. Government control is seen in a planned economy within which the government has substantial influence.

Market economies work on the assumption that market forces, such as supply and demand, are the best determinants of what is right for a nation's well being. These economies rarely engage in government interventions such as price fixing, license quotas, and industry subsidies.

In a market economy individuals are free to do whatever they want as a career. If they are willing to take a risk and see an opportunity, they may start a business. It is these financial opportunities that motivate small businesses. Additionally, businesses are free to produce whatever they want. They can invest their resources in whatever they choose. This competitiveness and freedom are the essence of a market economy.

FTCE Fact

Competitiveness and freedom are the essence of a market economy.

Economics is the science that deals with the production, allocation, and use of goods and services. **Resources** refer to the four factors of **production**: **labor, capital, land,** and **entrepreneurship**. The supply of these four factors is finite. A resource is considered scarce when its availability is not enough to meet its demand. **Scarcity** happens when a limited supply of goods or services comes up against an ever-increasing demand for it. Faced with scarcity, an economy must make every effort to ensure the proper utilization and distribution of resources to avoid inefficiency. Most goods and services can be considered scarce because individuals desire more of them than they already possess (scarcity is maintained by demand). Resources that are readily abundant are referred to as free goods.

Opportunity cost is the cost we pay when we give up something to get something else. Although we may sacrifice many alternatives to get something, the opportunity cost of a decision is the most desirable alternative we give up to get what we want.

Identify how economic systems answer the three basic economic questions.

The **three basic economic questions** are the questions all nations must ask when dealing with scarcity and efficiently allocating their resources.

1. What to produce

2. How to produce

3. For whom to produce

Consumers decide what products they want to buy and then spend their money on them. Those products generate enough demand to be profitable and answer the "what" question. The lower a firm's cost for a given product, the higher the profit. The profit motive answers the "how" question. The "for whom" question is really a question of distribution. Once a commodity is produced, some mechanism must exist to distribute finished products to the ultimate consumers of the product. The mechanism of distribution for those products depends on the economic system.

The opposite of a market economy is a **planned economy**. Many examples of this system exist in Asian countries, such as Japan, China, and Vietnam.

The term **mixed economy** was coined to identify economic systems that stray from the ideals of either the market economy or the planned economy and "mix" elements of each.

Analyze the role of supply and demand in coordinating consumption, production, and distribution in a market system.

Microeconomics, the study of the economic behavior of small economic groups such as firms and families, is one of the largest fields in economics. **Macroeconomics** is the study of the elements of economics on the national level. Macroeconomics is possibly the largest field in economics and includes output, consumption, investment, government, spending, and net exports.

FTCE Fact

Microeconomics is the study of the economic behavior of small groups; macroeconomics is the study of economics on the national level.

There are four kinds of market structures: **perfect competition, monopoly, monopolistic competition,** and **oligopoly. Perfect competition** is largely a theoretical extreme most closely found in agriculture. Under perfect competition, products are relatively identical and sellers have no control over the price. There are no barriers to entry. A **barrier to entry** is anything that makes it difficult for firms to enter the industry. The opposite of perfect competition is a **monopoly**. In a monopoly one firm controls the price, that firm is equal to an industry, and barriers to entry are very high. Monopolies are illegal in the United States.

Between perfect competition and the monopoly are the two economic structures into which all U.S. firms fall. An **oligopoly** is a market form in which a market or industry is dominated by a small number of sellers (oligopolists). The word *oligopoly* is derived from the Greek for "few sellers." The steel and automobile industries are examples. An oligopoly has high barriers to entry. The other structure is monopolistic competition. **Monopolistic competition** is a common market form. Many markets can be considered as monopolistically competitive, including the markets for restaurants, books, clothing, and the film and service industries in large cities.

Monopolistically competitive markets have the following characteristics:

- There are many producers and many consumers in a given market.

- Consumers have clearly defined preferences, and sellers attempt to differentiate their products from those of their competitors. The goods and services are heterogeneous, usually (though not always) intrinsically so.

- There are few barriers to entry and exit.

- Firms have a degree of control over price.

The characteristics of a monopolistically competitive market are almost the same as those of perfect competition, with the exception of the heterogeneous products and non-price competition (based on subtle product differentiation) of monopolistic competition.

Analyze fundamental macroeconomic concepts such as inflation, employment, money supply, the components of gross domestic product, and the role of the stock market.

Macroeconomists study and seek to understand the determinants of aggregate trends in the economy with particular focus on national income, unemployment, inflation, investment, and international trade. The four broad sectors of macroeconomics are consumers, businesses, government, and the foreign sector.

Gross domestic product (GDP) is an important component of macroeconomics. GDP is the monetary value of all the finished goods and services produced within a country's borders in a specific period, though GDP is usually calculated on an annual basis. It includes all of private and public consumption, government outlays, investments, and exports, less imports that occur within a defined territory.

Government-spending policies can influence macroeconomic conditions and are intended to control the economy through measures like taxation and interest rates. The other tool available to the government is **monetary**. Monetary policy is the process by which the government, central bank, or monetary authority manages the money supply to achieve specific goals, such as constraining inflation, maintaining an exchange rate, achieving full employment, and sustaining economic growth. The overall goal of monetary policy is to accommodate economic growth in an environment of stable prices.

The monetary policy actions of the **Federal Reserve System (Fed)** affect prices, employment, and economic growth by influencing the availability and cost of money and credit in the economy. This in turn influences consumers' and businesses' willingness to spend money on goods and services.

The Fed uses three monetary policy tools to influence the availability and cost of money and credit: **open-market operations,** the **discount rate,** and **reserve requirements.** The Fed's most flexible and often-used tool of monetary policy is its open-market operations for buying or selling government securities.

The **Federal Open Market Committee (FOMC)** sets the Fed's monetary policy, which is carried out through the trading desk of the Federal Reserve Bank of New York. If the FOMC decides that more money and credit should be available, it directs the trading desk in New York to buy securities from the open market.

The Fed pays for those securities by crediting the reserve accounts of banks involved with the sale. With more money in their reserve accounts, banks have more money to lend, interest rates may fall, and consumer and business spending may increase, encouraging economic expansion.

To tighten money and credit in the economy, the FOMC directs the New York trading desk to sell government securities, collecting payments from banks by reducing their reserve accounts. With less money in their reserve accounts, banks have less money to lend, interest rates may increase, consumer and business spending may decrease, and economic activity may slow down.

The discount rate is the interest rate a Federal Reserve Bank charges eligible financial institutions to borrow funds on a short-term basis. Unlike open-market operations, which interact with financial market forces to influence short-term interest rates, the discount rate is set by the boards of directors of the Federal Reserve Banks, and it is subject to approval by the Fed's board of governors. Under some circumstances, changes in the discount rate can affect other open-market interest rates in the economy. Changes in the discount rate also can have an announcement effect, causing financial markets to respond to a potential change in the direction of monetary policy. A higher discount rate can indicate a more restrictive policy, while a lower rate may be used to signal a more expansive policy.

By law, financial institutions, whether or not they are members of the Federal Reserve System, must set aside a percentage of their deposits as reserves to be held either as cash on hand or as reserve account balances at a Federal Reserve Bank. The Fed sets reserve requirements for all commercial banks, savings banks, savings and loans, credit unions, and U.S. branches and agencies of foreign banks. Depository institutions use their reserve accounts at Federal Reserve Banks not only to satisfy reserve requirements but also to process many financial transactions through the Fed, such as check and electronic payments and currency and coin services.

Altering reserve requirements is rarely used as a monetary policy tool. However, reserve requirements support the implementation of monetary policy by providing a more predictable demand for bank reserves, which increases the Fed's influence over short-term interest rate changes when implementing open-market operations.

Analyze the role of government in market and nonmarket economies.

This concept gets back to the discussion of the form of government and its influence on the economy. A market economy is characterized by free-market forces; in a planned economy, government influence and control are dominant; and a mixed economy has government regulation in some areas but also allows the markets to flow freely. These economies may seem simple, but the reality can be quite complex. For instance, a communist government in general is expected to control the economy, but no two communist governments are alike. North Korea is far different from Cuba, and China is different from Vietnam. All these countries exert very different influences on their economies. It is far more common to find mixed economies. In the real world it is best to analyze specific situations rather than to generalize by government types.

FTCE Fact

No two communist governments are alike.

Apply the principle of comparative advantage to local, state, national, and international trade.

Much conversation surrounds the current dichotomy between a global economy and the new trend in the United States to buy local. As technology develops, our world gets smaller and the push to think globally becomes stronger. However, many U.S. consumers want to support local merchants, especially farmers. This is a simple analysis that can get complicated when the discussion turns to jobs being shifted overseas and U.S. workers losing job opportunities to low-cost workers in Mexico, Asia, and other countries.

Evaluate the role of credit in a consumer economy.

Credit has become a very important part of life today. Instead of waiting until they have saved cash, consumers often use credit, buying the goods and services they desire now and paying later using future income. Credit can have both positive and negative outcomes. The **Federal Trade Commission** deals with issues that touch the economic life of every American. It is the only federal agency with both consumer protection and competition jurisdiction in broad sectors of the economy.

The **stock market** is the mechanism that enables the trading of company stocks (collective shares), other securities, and derivatives. A derivative is a financial instrument whose value is derived from the value of something else. Generally, a derivative takes the form of a contract under which the parties agree to payments between them based on the value of an underlying asset or other data at a particular time. An example of a derivitive is a future or an option. Bonds are still traditionally traded in an informal, over-the-counter market known as the bond market. Commodities are traded in commodities markets, and derivatives are traded in a variety of markets (but, like bonds, mostly over the counter).

In Europe the European Union (EU) created a single market that seeks to guarantee the freedom of movement of people, goods, services, and capital between member states.

CHAPTER

Knowledge of Political Science

4

Political science is the study of the processes, principles, and structure of government and of political institutions. The following skills are used as a basis to determine your competency for the political science portion of the FTCE Social Science Grades 6–12:

- Identify the features and principles of the United States Constitution, including the Bill of Rights, the separation of powers, checks and balances, and federalism.

- Identify the functions of U.S. political institutions, including the executive, legislative, and judicial branches.

- Identify the functions of political parties, elections, interest groups, public opinion, and mass media in the United States.

- Identify the elements and functions of state and local governments in the United States.

- Analyze the guiding concepts, principles, and consequences of U.S. foreign policy.

- Compare the elements, structures, and functions of various political systems.

- Analyze the key elements of U.S. citizenship, including rights, privileges, and responsibilities within the legal system.

Identify the features and principles of the United States Constitution, including the Bill of Rights, the separation of powers, checks and balances, and federalism.

It is well established that the United States was born from the idea of individual freedoms and responsibilities. These freedoms can be described as civil liberties and civil rights. Civil liberties are freedoms that completely protect the individual from government. Civil liberties set limits on the government to prevent it from abusing its power and interfering with the lives of its citizens. Civil rights are the protections and privileges of personal power given to all citizens by law. Distinct from civil rights are human rights or natural rights, which are basic rights and freedoms to which everyone is entitled morally, legally, or officially.

FTCE Fact

Civil liberties prevent the government from abusing its citizens.

The **Declaration of Independence** and the **Constitution** embody the ideals of individual freedom that define the United States. The United States was initially formed under the **Articles of Confederation**. Within months the defects of that system of government became obvious. The need for change was recognized, and a congressional convention was organized. It took four months to write the fundamental document of law within the republic, the Constitution of the United States. The Constitution not only binds the states in areas that affect the welfare of all states but also recognizes the rights of the people in individual states to determine their own laws.

Many differences of opinion were resolved by compromise during the country's infancy. Was there to be a strong or weak presidency? Large states and small states were in conflict. Slavery was an issue. The final conflict was how the president would be chosen. The **electoral college** was created. The president and vice president of the United States are really elected by the votes of only 538 citizens, the electors of the electoral college.

When you vote for a presidential candidate, you are really voting to instruct the electors from your state to cast their votes for that candidate. The candidate who wins the popular vote in a state wins all the pledged votes of the state's electors.

The electoral college system was established in Article II of the Constitution and amended by the Twelfth Amendment in 1804. Each state gets a number of electors equal to the number of representatives it has in the U.S. House of Representatives plus one for each of its two U.S. senators. The District of Columbia gets three electors. State laws determine how electors are chosen. The political party committees within the states generally select electors.

Each elector gets one vote. Thus, a state with eight electors can cast eight votes. There are currently 538 electors, and a majority (270 votes) is required to be elected. Since electoral college representation is based on congressional representation, states with larger populations get more electoral college votes.

Identify the functions of U.S. political institutions, including the executive, legislative, and judicial branches.

The **three branches** of the U.S. government form a system of **checks and balances** that prevents any one branch from having the power to override the others and protects the people from an oppressive form of government.

Article I of the Constitution defines the **legislative branch**, the law-making branch. The **House of Representatives** (or simply the House) is one of the two chambers of **Congress**; the other is the **Senate**. Each state is represented in the House proportionally by its population and is entitled to at least one representative. The total number of representatives is currently fixed at 435 by Public Law 62-5 of 1911, although Congress has the authority to change that number. Each representative serves for a two-year term and may be reelected an unlimited number of times. The presiding officer of the House is known as the Speaker and is elected by the members.

The **bicameral** (two-house) Congress arose from the desire of the founders to create a House "of the people" that would represent public opinion, balanced by a more deliberative Senate that would represent the governments of the individual states, and would be less susceptible to variations of mass sentiment. The House is often called the lower house and the Senate the upper house, although the Constitution does not use those terms. The Constitution provides that the approval of both houses is necessary for the passage of legislation.

Because its members are generally elected from smaller districts (each has approximately 693,000 residents as of 2007) that typically are more homogenous than Senate districts, the House is generally considered a more partisan chamber. Many of the Founding Fathers intended the Senate (whose members were originally chosen by the state legislatures) to be a check on the popularly elected House, just as the House was to be a check on the Senate. The **advice and consent** powers (such as the power to approve treaties) are therefore granted to the Senate alone. The House has its own exclusive powers: the power to initiate revenue bills, impeach officials, and elect the president in electoral college deadlocks. The Senate, however, can propose amendments to spending bills and has exclusive authority to try impeached officials and choose the vice president in an electoral college deadlock. Members of the Senate generally have greater prestige than House members because senators serve longer terms (six years) in a smaller body and represent larger constituencies than representatives.

Article II establishes the second of the three branches of government, the **executive branch**. Section 1 establishes the offices of the president and vice president and sets their terms to be four years. Originally, the president was the candidate with the most votes and the vice president was the person who came in second, but that system later changed to the use of the electoral college explained earlier.

The power of the **executive branch** is vested in the **president**, who also serves as **commander in chief of the armed forces**. The president appoints the **cabinet** and oversees the various agencies and departments of the federal government.

For a person to become president, he or she must be a natural-born citizen of the United States, be at least 35 years of age, and have resided in the United States for at least 14 years. Once elected, the president serves a term of four years and may be reelected only once. The two-term limit on the presidency was not originally in the Constitution but was established in the Twenty-Second Amendment after Franklin D. Roosevelt was elected to four terms.

FTCE Fact

The 22ⁿᵈ amendment placed a limit on the number of terms a president may serve.

Article III defines the **judicial branch** of government. The judicial branch hears cases that challenge or require interpretation of the legislation passed by Congress and signed by the president. It consists of the Supreme Court and the lower federal courts. Appointees to the federal bench serve for life or until they voluntarily resign or retire.

The **Supreme Court** is the most visible of all the federal courts. The number of justices is determined by Congress rather than the Constitution, and since 1869 the Court has been composed of one chief justice and eight associate justices. Justices are nominated by the president and confirmed by the Senate.

The 85 essays in the *Federalist Papers* were written and published between 1787 and 1788 in several New York newspapers to persuade voters in that state to ratify the proposed constitution. The essays outline how the newly formed government operated and why it would be the best type of government for the United States. All the essays were signed "**Publius**," and although the actual authors of some essays are under dispute, the general consensus is that Alexander Hamilton wrote 52, James Madison wrote 28, and John Jay contributed the remaining 5. The *Federalist Papers* remains an excellent reference for anyone who wants to understand the U.S. Constitution.

The **Bill of Rights** consists of the first 10 amendments to the U.S. Constitution. These amendments limit the powers of the federal government, protecting the rights of all citizens, residents, and visitors on United States territory. Among the enumerated rights these amendments guarantee are the freedoms of speech, press, and religion; the people's right to keep and bear arms; the freedom of assembly; the freedom to petition; and the rights to be free of unreasonable search and seizure, cruel and unusual punishment, and compelled self-incrimination. The Bill of Rights prohibits Congress from making any law concerning the establishment of a religion and prohibits the federal government from depriving any person of life, liberty, or property without due process of law. Additionally, the Bill of Rights requires indictment by grand jury for any capital crime, guarantees a speedy public trial with an impartial and local jury, and prohibits double jeopardy. The Bill of Rights also states that "the enumeration in the Constitution, of certain rights, shall not be construed to deny or disparage others retained by the people" and reserves all powers not granted to the federal government to the citizenry or states.

The first 10 amendments of the Constitution came into effect on December 15, 1791, when ratified by three-fourths of the states. Most were applied to the states by a series of decisions applying the due process clause of the Fourteenth Amendment, which was adopted after the American Civil War.

Initially drafted by **James Madison** in 1789, the Bill of Rights was written at a time when ideological conflict between Federalists and Antifederalists, dating from the Philadelphia Convention in 1787, threatened the Constitution's ratification. The Bill of Rights was largely a response to the Constitution's influential opponents, including prominent Founding Fathers, who argued that it failed to protect the basic principles of human liberty. As a key element of American law and government, the Bill of Rights remains a fundamental symbol of the freedoms and culture of the nation.

Identify the functions of political parties, elections, interest groups, public opinion, and mass media in the United States.

The Constitution does not mention **political parties**. In fact, "factions" with "jealousies and false alarms" were feared to cause damage to the country. Political parties were thought of as searching for profit, not providing for the common good. However, two of President Washington's chief advisors, Thomas Jefferson and Alexander Hamilton, formed the first two parties. It is interesting to remember the Founding Fathers' fears in the light of politics today.

Topics such as voter turnout, election forecasting, campaign strategies and financing, campaign effects, strategic candidate behavior, election reform, and electoral laws are all part of political science. The vote is the most basic right of a citizen, but it is a right not exercised by all. There has been much discussion in modern times of transforming the electoral college, but no change seems forthcoming.

Interest groups have a strong hold on politics today. Lobbyists are an ever-growing part of today's politics. Interest groups are not exclusively found in the Senate, but since each state has only two senators, it is the place where lobbyists spend a lot of time and money when a bill needs to be defeated.

The **media** is another element of political science in which influence has exploded with the appearance of the Internet. A large segment of our society, our oldest citizens, grew up without television and depended instead on newspapers and radio for information on current events. Now cable television's 24-hour news channels and the Internet with YouTube and blogs (many offering opinions disguised as news) have changed our perception of media. A free press is essential to maintaining a responsible, ethical government.

The Constitution not only defines the structure and powers of the federal government but also contains general provisions regarding **state government**. Each state, in turn, has its own constitution that contains provisions for local governments within that state. Local governments include cities, counties, towns, school districts, and special-purpose districts, which govern such matters as local natural resources and transportation networks.

The federal government is limited to the powers and responsibilities specifically granted to it by the U.S. Constitution. Some of the powers listed in the Constitution include regulating commerce between the states, providing for national defense, creating money, regulating immigration and naturalization, and entering into treaties with foreign countries.

Over time, however, the Constitution has been interpreted and amended to adapt to changing circumstances, and the powers exercised by the federal government have changed with it. Working with the states, the federal government creates certain laws and programs that are funded federally but administered by the states. Education, social welfare, housing and nutritional assistance, homeland security, transportation, and emergency response are key services that states deliver using federal funds and thus are subject to federal guidelines.

FTCE Fact

The powers of the federal government have changed as the Constitution has been interpreted and amended.

This gives the federal government the power to influence the states. For example, in the 1970s the federal government wanted to lower highway speed limits to reduce energy consumption. Rather than simply legislate a lower speed limit, the federal government threatened to withhold money for road projects from states that did not lower the speed limit on their state highways. In many cases the states must also partially fund the programs to qualify for federal funds.

Identify the elements and functions of state and local governments in the United States.

A **local government** is chartered according to its state's constitution. Just as the policies enacted by the state government must not conflict with federal law, a local government is subject to the legal environment created by the state constitution and statutes.

As sovereign entities within the framework of the U.S. federal system, each state has its own constitution, elected officials, and governmental organization. States have the power to make and enforce laws, levy taxes, and conduct their affairs largely free from intervention from the federal government or other states.

State governments have primary responsibility for providing many important services that affect the everyday lives of their residents. These include the following:

- Setting educational standards and establishing methods for funding public education

- Building and maintaining transportation networks

- Establishing state-sponsored colleges and universities

- Licensing and regulating businesses and professions

- Creating and overseeing nonfederal courts and the criminal justice system

- Generally providing for the public safety

- Issuing marriage licenses and driver's licenses

- Issuing and recording birth and death certificates

- Administering publicly funded health, housing, and nutrition programs for low-income and disabled residents

- Managing state parks and other lands for recreation and environmental conservation purposes

- Administering and certifying elections, including elections for federal officials

- Commanding the state National Guard, except when it is called to national service

Some of these responsibilities are delegated to or shared with local governments in many states. For example, in most states, marriage licenses are issued by city or county governments.

Analyze the guiding concepts, principles, and consequences of U.S. foreign policy.

Realism has been one of the dominant forces guiding international relations theory and influencing foreign policy, especially since the end of World War II. Realism is an international theory that holds that the nation-state is the basic governmental unit and there is no authority above individual nations.

International relations are normally carried out through diplomacy. **Diplomacy** is the art and practice of conducting negotiations between representatives of groups or states. **Nations** conduct international relations through the intercession of professional diplomats with regard to issues of peace making, trade, war, economics, and culture. International treaties are usually negotiated by diplomats before they are endorsed by national politicians.

Liberalism is often thought to be opposed to realism because it holds that nations do not act in their own interest but cooperate for their common interest. Realists believe that states act based on their capabilities, and liberalism holds that states act on their preferences.

The **United Nations (UN)** was initially created with diplomacy in mind. It comprises 191 member countries (nearly every country in the world) and works toward maintaining international peace and security and finding solutions for global economic and humanitarian problems. The UN conducts its mission through six main organs, the Economic and Social Council, the General Assembly, the International Court of Justice, the Secretariat, the Security Council, and the Trusteeship Council. The United Nations was founded in 1945 when the UN Charter was ratified by China, France, the Soviet Union, the United Kingdom, the United States, and most of the other signatory countries. The UN is headquartered in New York and has offices in Geneva and Vienna.

Compare the elements, structures, and functions of various political systems.

There are many **forms of government**. The ancient Greek philosopher Aristotle (384–322 B.C.E.) said, "The true forms of government . . . are those in which the one, or the few, or the many govern, with a view to the common interest."

As defined by Aristotle, a government run by one person is a **monarchy**, a government by the few is an **aristocracy**, and a government by the many is a polity—what is now called a constitutional **democracy**.

A monarchy that rules only for the purpose of increasing the monarch's wealth and power can become a **tyranny** and the ruler a tyrant. When the ruling few in an aristocracy rule only for their own benefit, they become an oligarchy. **Oligarchic** governments were more common in ancient times than they are today.

Like many other terms used in government, **autocracy** is derived from Greek roots, in this case the words for "self" and "rule." An autocrat is a ruler with unlimited authority. Absolute monarchy, a related term, refers to a monarch who rules without checks on his or her power. Absolute monarchies exist today only in some of the states of the Arabian Peninsula. Another term for autocracy, more commonly used in the past, is **despotism**, or rule by a despot.

Present-day democratic government differs significantly from the democracy practiced in ancient Greece, particularly in the city-state of Athens, where democracy reached its height. All male Athenian citizens were expected to participate directly in their government, in the making of laws, and in choosing officials.

The modern democratic state is usually a **republic**, in which the people do not take a direct role in legislating or governing but elect representatives to express their views and wants. A democratic government exists when citizens freely choose representatives who then ensure that their constituencies' demands are recognized by the duly elected government.

FTCE Fact

A peaceful and orderly transfer of power is a standard of a democratic government.

In addition to **free elections**, a true democratic government has other standards by which it can be measured. One is **freedom of speech**, which means that people can criticize their government without fear of persecution. Another standard of a democratic government is the peaceful and orderly transfer of political power when new leaders are elected to office.

A **constitutional monarchy** is a democratic government in which the monarch is retained as the ceremonial head of state but has little or no political power. Constitutional monarchies evolved from absolute monarchies, whose powers were gradually reduced and whose functions are now limited by a constitution. Probably the best-known constitutional monarchy is that of the United Kingdom, which has an unwritten constitution.

As a form of government, **totalitarianism** is of fairly recent origin. The term came into use in the 1920s and 1930s to describe the regimes of fascist Italy and Nazi Germany, until their destruction in World War II. Following the end of the war in 1945, the term *totalitarianism* was increasingly used in reference to the governments of the Soviet Union and the newly created communist states of Eastern Europe.

A **totalitarian government**, as its name implies, is characterized by its total control over all aspects of its citizens' political and economic activities. Although often used interchangeably with the term *dictatorship* to indicate an undemocratic form of government, totalitarianism is even more rigorous in its controls. It is also marked by a distinct ideology, or set of beliefs, as in Fascism, Nazism, or Communism. The term *authoritarian government* is sometimes used for a form of government similar to a totalitarian government but one that does not exert such absolute control over its peoples' lives.

The disintegration of the Soviet Union in late 1991 brought about the collapse of the Eastern European communist governments. The result was their replacement by more genuinely democratic ones.

Socialism is a system of social organization in which property and the distribution of income are subject to social control rather than individual determination or market forces. Socialism refers to both a set of doctrines and the political movements that aspire to put those doctrines into practice. Examples are the Soviet Union under Lenin and Stalin and China under Mao.

Analyze the key elements of U.S. citizenship, including rights, privileges, and responsibilities within the legal system.

At the heart of this final skill as it's tested in the FTCE is the Bill of Rights. Here are the 10 amendments that comprise that document:

THE BILL OF RIGHTS

- Congress shall make no law respecting an establishment of religion, or prohibiting the free exercise thereof; or abridging the freedom of speech, or of the press; or the right of the people peaceably to assemble, and to petition the government for a redress of grievances.

- A well regulated militia, being necessary to the security of a free state, the right of the people to keep and bear arms, shall not be infringed.

- No soldier shall, in time of peace be quartered in any house, without the consent of the owner, nor in time of war, but in a manner to be prescribed by law.

- The right of the people to be secure in their persons, houses, papers, and effects, against unreasonable searches and seizures, shall not be violated, and no warrants shall issue, but upon probable cause, supported by oath or affirmation, and particularly describing the place to be searched, and the persons or things to be seized.

- No person shall be held to answer for a capital, or otherwise infamous crime, unless on a presentment or indictment of a grand jury, except in cases arising in the land or naval forces, or in the militia, when in actual service in time of war or public danger; nor shall any person be subject for the same offense to be twice put in jeopardy of life or limb; nor shall be compelled in any criminal case to be a witness against himself, nor be deprived of life, liberty, or property, without due process of law; nor shall private property be taken for public use, without just compensation.

- In all criminal prosecutions, the accused shall enjoy the right to a speedy and public trial, by an impartial jury of the state and district wherein the crime shall have been committed, which district shall have been previously ascertained by law, and to be informed of the nature and cause of the accusation; to be confronted with the witnesses against him; to have compulsory process for obtaining witnesses in his favor, and to have the assistance of counsel for his defense.

• In suits at common law, where the value in controversy shall exceed twenty dollars, the right of trial by jury shall be preserved, and no fact tried by a jury, shall be otherwise reexamined in any court of the United States, than according to the rules of the common law.

• Excessive bail shall not be required, nor excessive fines imposed, nor cruel and unusual punishments inflicted.

• The enumeration in the Constitution, of certain rights, shall not be construed to deny or disparage others retained by the people.

• The powers not delegated to the United States by the Constitution, nor prohibited by it to the states, are reserved to the states respectively, or to the people.

Citizens of the United States can participate in their government. This process ensures that power will always remain where it belongs, with the people.

The most important right U.S. citizens have is the **right to vote**. By voting, the people have a voice in the government. The people decide who will represent them in the government. Before voting in an election, each citizen should be well informed about the issues and candidates.

The government may call on citizens to serve on a jury. In the United States every person is expected to obey the laws of the community and state in which he or she lives as well as the laws of the nation. All Americans are expected to respect the rights of others. All persons living in the United States are expected to pay the income taxes and other taxes honestly and on time.

Knowledge of World History

The two major areas examined by the FTCE are world history and American history. The world history section comprises 20 percent of the test. The following skills are used as a basis to determine your competency for the world history portion of the FTCE Social Science Grades 6–12:

- Compare prehistoric cultures and early civilizations (e.g., Mesopotamia, Egypt, Indus Valley, China).

- Compare ancient civilizations (e.g., Greek, Roman) and their impact on Western civilization.

- Identify the cultural, political, and economic developments of African, Asian, and Mesoamerican societies.

- Differentiate between the Middle Ages, Renaissance, and Reformation periods.

- Identify the major contributions of Western and non-Western civilizations during the Middle Ages, Renaissance, and Reformation periods.

- Identify the significant scientific and social changes from the Age of Reason through the Age of Enlightenment.

- Identify the causes, events, consequences, and significant individuals associated with the Age of Exploration and global civilization.

- Evaluate the causes, events, consequences, and significant individuals associated with the development of the nation-state and capitalism.

- Assess the Industrial Revolution in terms of cultural, political, and economic effects in both Western and non-Western civilizations.

- Identify the causes, events, consequences, and significant individuals associated with the Age of Revolution, including independence movements in France, Africa, Asia, and Latin America.

- Assess the growth of nationalism and its impact on the world's social, political, and geographic development.

- Analyze the causes and consequences of wars and military conflicts related to the world's social, political, and geographic development in the twentieth century, including pogroms and genocide.

- Analyze major contemporary world issues and trends in terms of their political, social, economic, and geographic characteristics.

- Identify major world religions and ideologies and their impact on world events.

Compare prehistoric cultures and early civilizations (e.g., Mesopotamia, Egypt, Indus Valley, China).

Prehistoric refers to the time during the development of human culture before the appearance of the written word. Since writing developed at different times for different cultures, the prehistoric period is not exactly defined. The era is divided into three stages based on what tools dominated the era: Stone Age, Bronze Age, and Iron Age. The following chart puts these periods in perspective.

Archaeological and Historical Periods Chart

Period		Years
Stone Age	**Paleolithic** (Old Stone Age)	Before 10,000 B.C.E.
	Mesolithic (Middle Stone Age)	10,000–8000 B.C.E.
	Neolithic (New Stone Age)	
	Prepottery	8000–5500 B.C.E.
	Pottery	5500–4000 B.C.E.
	Chalcolithic (Copper Age)	4000–3000 B.C.E.
Bronze Age	**Early Bronze Age** (EB)	
	EB I	3000–2800 B.C.E.
	EB II	2800–2500 B.C.E.
	EB III	2500–2200 B.C.E.
	EB IV	2200–2000 B.C.E.
	Middle Bronze Age (MB)	
	MB I	2000–1800 B.C.E.
	MB II	1800–1500 B.C.E.
	Late Bronze Age (LB)	
	LB I	1500–1400 B.C.E.
	LB II	1400–1200 B.C.E.
Iron Age	Iron I	1200–1000 B.C.E.
	Iron II	1000–600 B.C.E.
Babylonian and Persian Periods		586–332 B.C.E.
Hellenistic Period		332–37 B.C.E.
Roman Period		37 B.C.E.–325 C.E.

The **Stone Age** is the time early in the development of human cultures, before the use of metals, when tools and weapons were made of stone. The dates of the Stone Age vary considerably for different parts of the world. In Europe, Asia, and Africa, it began about 2 million years ago.

In the most advanced parts of the Middle East and Southeast Asia, it ended about 6000 B.C.E., but it lingered until 4000 B.C.E. or later in Europe, the rest of Asia, and Africa. The Stone Age in the Americas began when human beings first arrived in the New World, some 30,000 years ago, and ended in some areas about 2500 B.C.E., at the earliest.

FTCE Fact

During the Stone Age vast changes in climate affected human culture.

Throughout the immense time span of the Stone Age, vast changes occurred in climate and in other conditions affecting human culture. Humans themselves evolved into their modern form during the latter part of it. The Stone Age has been divided accordingly into three periods: the Paleolithic, Mesolithic, and Neolithic.

The Paleolithic, or Old Stone Age, was the longest. It began about 2 million years ago, when stone tools were first used by humanoid creatures, and ended with the close of the last ice age about 13,000 B.C.E.

Obtaining food required hunting and gathering. At first, single tools, such as chipped pebbles or flaked stone implements, were used for all purposes. Over time various tools were made for specific purposes. By about 100,000 years ago, Neanderthal cultures had several types of tools and were using bone implements.

At the end of the Paleolithic period, modern humans (*Homo sapiens*) made such specialized tools as needles and harpoons. In the Cro-Magnon caves of Europe, wall paintings and evidence of both religious cults and possible social stratification point to the complexity of the cultures.

After 13,000 B.C.E. more clement weather patterns resulted in the greater availability of food. In tropical and temperate forest regions, Paleolithic tools, still chipped, were adapted to the new conditions. This period is known as the Mesolithic, or Middle Stone Age.

In both the Middle East and Mesoamerica, however, agricultural villages had begun to develop by 8000 B.C.E. This is known as the Neolithic period, or New Stone Age. Animals were domesticated for man's use starting with cattle and pigs. Stone tools became highly polished and varied. By 6000 B.C.E. pottery appeared in the ancient Middle East, and copper was used for the first time in some regions. Across the world at this time, significant developments and changes coincided with one another. In Europe the Stone Age was coming to an end, in the Middle East the pyramid culture of the Egyptians was to dominate, and in the Americas the Maya came to prominence.

The development of written languages, styles of building techniques, and forms of pottery and the expansion of agriculture occurred almost everywhere at the same time. The existence of trading and commercial traffic between all the major centers from Europe to the Maya cultures was a significant development. The remains of silk uncovered in the tombs of the Pharaohs and the similarity of the Egyptian and Maya cultures is no coincidence. The style of pottery and the emergence of bronze occurred in the Americas at the same time as in Europe. Developments in agriculture produced a change from hunter-gatherer societies to ones based on a settled way of life.

The **Bronze Age** is the time in the development of any human culture, before the introduction of iron, when most tools and weapons were made of bronze. Chronologically, the term is of strictly local value, because bronze came into use and eventually was replaced by iron at different times in different parts of the world. In most cultures the Bronze Age succeeded the Copper Age.

Archaeological discoveries since 1960 have upset traditional theories concerning the origins of copper and bronze technologies. It had been thought that the use of bronze originated in the Middle East, but discoveries near Ban Chiang, Thailand, indicate that bronze technology was known there as early as 4500 B.C.E. This precedes by several hundred years the earliest evidence of bronze work found in the Middle East. Bronze objects have been found in Asia Minor that date from before 3000 B.C.E. At first this alloy was used sparingly, mostly for decorative purposes; the tin needed to make it was not available in the region.

Regular imports of tin from Cornwall in Britain during the second millennium B.C.E., however, made possible wider use of bronze in the Middle East, and it was eventually used for tools and weapons. Raw copper was being pounded into tools and ornaments as early as 10,000 B.C.E. Later discoveries at Rudna Glava in Yugoslavia show that copper was in use there in 4000 B.C.E., although bronze was not made at that time.

By 3000 B.C.E. bronze began to be used in Greece. In China the Bronze Age did not begin until 1800 B.C.E. The pre-Columbian civilizations of the Americas had no bronze technology until about 1000 C.E.

The Bronze Age in the Middle East and the eastern Mediterranean has been divided into three phases: early, middle, and late. The early phase is characterized by increased use of the metal, from the sporadic to the common. It was the time of the Sumerian civilization, the rise of the Akkad region to prominence in Mesopotamia, and the spectacular treasures of Troy. Babylon reached its height of glory during the middle Bronze Age. Minoan Crete and Mycenaean Greece were major civilizations of the Late Bronze Age. The Bronze Age there ended about 1200 B.C.E., after which iron technology became common.

FTCE Fact

The development of writing as communication was a basic step in the advancement of civilization.

The invention of writing was one of the great advances in civilization. Writing helps ensure the continuity of civilization by establishing a tangible record of the human race from generation to generation.

The earliest writing can be traced to Sumer in Mesopotamia. The Sumerian system did not use an alphabet but instead used pictographs, which are symbols representing familiar objects. This type of writing was called cuneiform, or wedge-shaped writing. Egyptians used hieroglyphics, another pictographic system.

The use of an alphabet probably originated among the Phoenicians sometime between 1700 and 1500 B.C.E. This Semitic writing had only consonants; the ancient Greeks later came up with the idea of vowels. The Chinese writing system, also very ancient, maintained its pictograph characters instead of developing an alphabet.

The history and prehistory of writing are as long as the history of civilization itself. Indeed, the development of communication by writing was a basic step in the advancement of civilization.

Yet writing is little more than 5,000 years old. The oldest writings that have come down to the present day are inscriptions on clay tablets made by the Sumerians in about 3100 B.C.E. The Sumerians lived in Mesopotamia, between the Tigris and Euphrates rivers. The Egyptians in the Nile River Valley developed writing about 100 to 200 years later.

Writing is sometimes spoken of as humankind's greatest invention. It was developed by many people, in many places, and over a long period. The identity of the individuals responsible for the major steps in the development of writing is not known. Their names, like those of the inventors of the wheel, are lost forever in the dimness of the past.

Based on diagrams on ancient clay tablets, the earliest known use of the wheel was a potter's wheel used at Ur in Mesopotamia (part of modern-day Iraq) as early as 3500 B.C.E. The first use of the wheel for transportation was probably on Mesopotamian chariots in 3200 B.C.E. It is interesting to note that wheels may have had industrial or manufacturing applications before they were used on vehicles.

A wheel with spokes first appeared on Egyptian chariots around 2000 B.C.E., and wheels seem to have developed in Europe by 1400 B.C.E. without any influence from the Middle East. Because the idea of the wheel appears so simple, it is easy to assume that the wheel would have just "happened" in every culture when it reached a particular level of sophistication. However, that is not the case. The great Inca, Aztec, and Maya civilizations reached an extremely high level of development, yet they never used the wheel. In fact, there is no evidence that the use of the wheel existed among native people anywhere in the Western Hemisphere until well after contact with Europeans.

Compare ancient civilizations (e.g., Greek, Roman) and their impact on Western civilization.

The origins of Western culture are often referred to as **three pillars**: ancient Greece (Greek philosophy), the Roman Empire (Roman law), and Catholic and Protestant Christianity. Broadly, these foundations are referred to as the Greco-Roman and Judeo-Christian roots of Western civilization. Germanic, Slavic, and Celtic popular cultures also took part in the formation of the culture of medieval Europe, and the influence of secular humanism has been profound since the European Renaissance. Western culture has developed many themes and traditions, but the following are among the most prominent:

- Christian theology and philosophy, with an abundant tradition in the philosophical discipline of ethics

- Humanism, secularism, rationalism, and empiricism in contrast and reaction to Catholicism and Protestant Christianity

- A very rich tradition and understanding of law, which has been followed by practically all other cultures

- Scholasticism

- Renaissance arts and letters

- The scientific method

- The Western canon

- The Enlightenment and the Age of Reason

The **ancient Greek civilization**, marked by many significant political, philosophical, artistic, and scientific achievements, formed a legacy with unparalleled influence on Western civilization. Ancient Greece is considered the **cradle of Western civilization**. The dates for the beginning and end of the ancient Greek period are not fixed or universally agreed on. In common usage *ancient* refers to all Greek history before the Roman Empire. In Greek schoolbooks, "ancient times" is a period of about 900 years, from the catastrophe of Mycenae until the conquest of the country by the Romans, divided into four periods based on styles of art, culture, and politics.

Traditionally, the ancient Greek period was taken to begin with the date of the first recorded Olympic Games in 776 B.C.E., but many historians now extend the term back to about 1000 B.C.E. The traditional date for the end of the ancient Greek period is the death of Alexander the Great in 323 B.C.E. The following period, called the Hellenistic period, lasted until the integration of Greece into the Roman Republic in 146 B.C.E. These dates are historians' conventions, and some writers treat the ancient Greek civilization as a continuum running until the advent of Christianity.

The timeline of ancient Greece starts with the **Greek Dark Ages** (1100–800 B.C.E.). In this period artists used geometrical schemes such as squares, circles, and lines to decorate amphora and other pottery. The **archaic period** (800–490 B.C.E.) represents those years when the artists made larger freestanding sculptures in stiff, hieratic poses with the dreamlike "archaic smile." In the classical period (490–323 B.C.E.) artists perfected the style that since has been taken as exemplary, or "classical," such as that of the Parthenon. The years following the conquests of Alexander are referred to as the **Hellenistic** or **Alexandrian** period (332–37 B.C.E.). Aspects of Hellenic civilization expanded to Egypt, the Levant, Mesopotamia, Persia, and beyond.

The **Persian Wars** ushered in a century of Athenian dominance of Greek affairs. Athens was the unchallenged master of the sea and the leading commercial power, although Corinth remained a serious rival.

The wealth of Athens attracted talented people from all over Greece and created a wealthy leisure class whose members became patrons of the arts. The Athenian state also sponsored learning and the arts, particularly architecture. Athens became the center of Greek literature, philosophy, and art. Some of the greatest figures of Western cultural and intellectual history lived in Athens during this period. Among these were the dramatists **Aeschylus, Aristophanes, Euripides,** and **Sophocles**; the philosophers **Aristotle, Plato,** and **Socrates**; and the historians **Herodotus, Thucydides,** and **Xenophon**.

No other texts in the Western imagination occupy as central a position in the self-definition of Western culture as the two epic poems of **Homer**, the *Iliad* and the *Odyssey*. They both concern the great defining moment of Greek culture, the **Trojan War**. Whether or not this war really occurred, or occurred as the Greeks narrate it, is a relatively unanswerable question. We know that such a war did take place around a city that quite likely was Troy, and we know that Troy was destroyed utterly, but all other information is mere speculation. The war fired the imaginations of the Greeks and became the defining cultural moment in their history. Technically, the war was not fought by Greeks in the classical sense. It was fought by the Mycenaeans; the Greek culture that we call "classical" is actually derived from two other groups of Greeks, the Dorians and the Ionians.

However, the Greeks saw the Trojan War as the first moment in history when the diverse groups in Greece came together as one people with a common purpose. This unification, whether it was myth or not, gave the later Greeks a sense of national or cultural identity, even though their governments were small, disunified city-states. Since the Greeks regarded the Trojan War as the defining moment in the establishment of "Greek character," they were obsessed about the events of the war and told them repeatedly with great variety. As the Greek idea of cultural identity changed, so did their stories about the Trojan War.

The **Roman Empire**, centered at the city of Rome, in what is now Italy, is the most extensive Western civilization of ancient times. According to legend, the empire was founded in 753 B.C.E. by two brothers, Romulus and Remus; they were distant descendants of **Aeneas**, one of the few Trojan survivors of the Trojan War. Rome was first ruled by kings. Then, in about 500 B.C.E., the Roman republic was established, with two annually elected consuls at its head, guided by a senate. The republic eventually weakened, and the Senate decided that Rome should be ruled by one man. The first emperor was Julius Caesar, who was assassinated in 44 B.C.E. and was succeeded by Augustus. Over the next few centuries, Rome had a succession of emperors. The whole Western world eventually became subject to Rome and was at peace for roughly the first four centuries after the birth of Christ. The empire was known for its strong centralized government and for massive public works, such as roads and aqueducts, that helped maintain its power and efficiency. As the years passed, the Roman Empire was divided into eastern and western portions, developed internal weaknesses, was invaded by outside tribes, and eventually ceased to exist.

FTCE Fact

The Roman Empire was known for its strong central government and public works.

In the history of mathematics, the contributions of the Roman Empire are sometimes overlooked. Roman numerals are considered cumbersome. Their number system lacked the concept of the zero. One could also infer that they were aware of the concept of a negative number. How else would Roman merchants understand and manipulate liabilities against assets and loans versus investments? The Romans developed a handheld abacus as a portable counting board, the first portable calculating device for both engineers and businessmen.

The **decline of the Roman Empire**, also referred to as the fall of the Roman Empire, is a historical term of periodization for the end of the Western Roman Empire. The Roman Empire's collapse remains one of the greatest historical questions and has a tradition rich in scholarly interest.

The traditional date of the fall of the Roman Empire is September 4, 476, when Romulus Augustus, the emperor of the Western Roman Empire, was deposed by Odoacer. Some historians question this date, noting that the Eastern Roman Empire continued until the fall of Constantinople in May 29, 1453. Many scholars maintain that rather than a simplistic "fall," what occurred can more accurately be described as a complex transformation. Over time, numerous theories have been proposed as to why the empire fell, or whether indeed it fell at all.

The reasons for the fall, or transformation, of the Roman Empire are numerous and intertwined. Some scholars suggest that as Christianity spread throughout the empire, Roman citizens became pacifists, making it more difficult to defend against barbarian attackers. Also, money used to build churches could have been used to maintain the empire. On the other hand, some historians argue that Christianity may have provided some morals and values for a declining civilization and therefore may have actually prolonged the imperial era. Following are some generally accepted reasons for the fall of the Roman Empire:

- Decline in morals and values

- Public health and environmental issues

- Political corruption and no clear way to choose a new emperor

- Unemployment resulting from wealthy landowners taking over small farms

- Inflation caused by an insufficient flow of gold to use for coins

- Urban decay

- Inferior technology

- Military spending

- Civil war in Italy that brought many soldiers home from battling outside invaders

During this time China was reunited under the rule of the **Han Dynasty**, which is divided into two major divisions: the Western or Former Han (206 B.C.E.–9 C.E.) and the Eastern or Later Han (25–220 C.E.). The boundaries established by the Qin and maintained by the Han have more or less defined the nation of China to the present day. The Western Han capital, Xi'an in present-day Shaanxi Province—a monumental urban center laid out on a north–south axis with palaces, residential wards, and two bustling market areas—was one of the two largest cities in the ancient world (Rome was the other).

Poetry, literature, and philosophy flourished during the reign of **Emperor Wudi** (141–86 B.C.E.). The monumental *Shiji*, written by **Sima Qian** (145–80 B.C.E.), set the standard for later government-sponsored histories. Among many other things, it recorded information about the various peoples, invariably described as "barbarian," who lived on the empire's borders. Wudi also established **Confucianism** as the basis for correct official and individual conduct and for the educational curriculum. The reliance of the bureaucracy on members of a highly educated class grounded in Confucian writings and other classics defined China's statecraft for many centuries.

Identify the cultural, political, and economic developments of African, Asian, and Mesoamerican societies.

Africa is one continent with several worlds. Covering an area of around 30 million square kilometers, Africa comprises one-fifth of the earth's landmass and more than 50 countries. Its geographical features are diverse, ranging from tropical rain forests with rainfall of 100 to 150 inches annually, to tropical dry areas. **Mount Kilimanjaro** (elevation 19,340 feet) remains capped with snow year round, whereas the **Sahara** is the largest and the hottest desert on the earth. The continent's plant life is as varied as its landscape, with vegetation that includes mountain scrub, savanna grasses, desert shrubs, and deciduous forests.

Like the flora and fauna of Africa, the continent's 800 million people have evolved into a cultural milieu that is a study in contrast and has several dimensions. Africa is home to innumerable tribes, or ethnic and social groups, some consisting of millions of people and others with populations of only a few thousand. The mosaic of cultural diversity represented by these many groups is part of what makes Africa unique among the world's continents.

FTCE Fact

Africa has more diverse cultural groups than any other continent.

The different African peoples speak hundreds of different languages, and if dialects spoken by various ethnic groups are included, the number is much higher. Some languages and dialects are spoken by only a few hundred persons, while others are spoken by millions. Among the most prominent languages spoken are **Arabic, Swahili,** and **Hausa.** Very few countries of Africa use a single language, and therefore several official languages coexist, African and European.

East Asia is usually thought to consist of China, Japan, and Korea but can also include Mongolia and Vietnam. Rarely, it is said to include the rest of Southeast Asia. The dominant influence on this region historically has been China. Major characteristics that East Asia shares with China are Chinese-derived languages and religions, especially Buddhism. The two regions also share a social and moral philosophy derived from Confucianism.

The **Chinese script** is generally agreed to be a unifying force between China and East Asia. The pictorial method of writing was historically used throughout East Asia and is still used to some extent in most countries of the region. In most cases the meanings of the characters remain unchanged, but the pronunciations differ between countries. Even within China, a Cantonese person and a person from northern China probably cannot hold a conversation, but they can certainly understand each other by passing notes. The Chinese writing system is the oldest continuous writing system in the world (but by no means is it primitive). It was passed on first to Korea, where it was the main writing system until the end of World War II, and then to Japan, where it now forms a major component of the Japanese writing system. In Vietnam, classical Chinese (Han Tu) was used during the millennium of Chinese rule, with the vernacular Chu Nom script replacing it later. However, this has now been replaced completely by the Latin alphabet-based Quocngu writing system. In these cultures, especially in China, the educational level of a person is traditionally measured by the quality of his or her calligraphy, rather than diction, as is sometimes the case in the West.

Although Korea, Japan, and Vietnam are not Chinese-speaking regions, their languages have been heavily influenced by Chinese. Although the writing systems in these countries have changed over time, the Chinese script is still found in the historical roots of many borrowed words, especially technical terms.

Apart from the unifying influence of Confucianism, Buddhism, Chinese characters, and other Chinese cultural influences, much diversity among the countries of the region is evident.

The nations of **India, Pakistan, Bangladesh, Bhutan, Nepal,** and **Sri Lanka** share an ethnic background and have similar cultures. This commonality is largely the result of Pakistan and Bangladesh being within India's borders before the 1947 partition. The countries separated because of their varying religious compositions.

The **Indus Valley civilization** began on the Indus River (now in Pakistan). In time, however, Aryans from the north settled in the Indian subcontinent. The Aryans also invaded the island of Sri Lanka and set up the Sinhala Kingdom. The island people eventually mingled with the invaders to form a common culture.

Hinduism, Buddhism, Jainism, and **Sikhism,** the four major world religions founded in modern-day India, are spread throughout the subcontinent. While 80 percent of Indians are Hindus and Nepal is a Hindu-majority state, Sri Lanka has a majority of Buddhists. South Asian culture was influenced somewhat by the arrival of Islam, which based itself in the northwest of India (now Pakistan), near the border with Afghanistan.

In 1947 India was split as a result of the Indian independence movement. The partition was the result of religious differences, although the Pakistani and Indian peoples have similar spoken languages (Urdu and Hindi, respectively). Many Hindus and Sikhs still live in Pakistan, while 10 percent of the Bangladesh population is Hindu.

Despite their religious differences, the ways of life in India and Pakistan are similar because of the history the two countries share. Foods such as **chapatis** (unleavened bread) are common in both nations. South Indian foods (from the states of Kerala and Tamil Nadu) can be found in Sri Lanka. Bangladeshi ways of living are similar to those of people in West Bengal, a state in eastern India.

The **Maya** developed one of the most astonishing early civilizations in the Americas. They did so under challenging conditions. Scholars believe that the Mayans developed the most advanced of all the ancient **Mesoamerican** cultures. The Maya lived mostly in the **Yucatan Peninsula** of Mexico. As farming practices improved, the many small Mayan villages could support larger populations, and city-states began to emerge. Some city-states, such as Tikal, had nearly 40,000 inhabitants.

The Maya saw an explosion of cultural creativity throughout the region. They derived many cultural forms from the north, but also devised many cultural innovations that profoundly influenced all subsequent cultures throughout Mesoamerica. Much of Maya culture, particularly the religious reckoning of time, is still a vital aspect of life in Guatemala and Honduras.

Mayan culture developed in three regions in Mesoamerica. The most important and most complete urban developments were in the lowlands of the central region of southern Guatemala. This region is a drainage basin about 60 miles long and 20 miles wide and is covered by tropical rain forest; in fact the Mayans are one of only two peoples to develop an urban culture in a tropical rain forest. The principal city in this region was **Tikal**, but the spread of urbanization extended south to Honduras; the southernmost Mayan city was **Copán** in northern Honduras. In the Guatemalan highlands to the north, Mayan culture developed less fully. The highlands are more temperate and seem to have been the main suppliers of raw materials to the central urban centers. The largest and most complete urban center was Palenque. The other major region of Mayan development was the Yucatan Peninsula, making up the southern and eastern portions of modern-day Mexico. This is a dry region and, although urban centers were built there, including Chichén Itzá and Uxmal, most scholars believe that this was a culturally marginal area.

The cities Mayan built were ceremonial centers. A priestly class lived in the cities, while most of the rest of the Mayan population lived in small farming villages. The priestly class would carry out daily religious duties, particularly sacrifices, and the peasants would periodically gather for religious ceremonies and festivals. For reasons that historians do not fully understand, the Maya abandoned their cities around 900 C.E. There is evidence of invasion from the outside, and it is possible that economic difficulties led them to abandon the cities. The greatest change seems to be the disappearance of the priestly class; with this disappearance, the Maya stopped working on the cities. The peasants seem to have continued to use the cities for a time, but that eventually came to a halt as well. Life for the Maya did not really change drastically after the decline of the cities, because the cities were central only in their ceremonial life.

It is interesting to explore the interrelationships of cultures. We can gain an appreciation of the evolution of civilization as a cross-fertilization of many cultures over the few thousand years of recorded history. Trade contributed to the spread of technology around the world. One critical component of this is the **Silk Road**. Calling this route to the West the Silk Road is somewhat misleading. First, no single route was taken; crossing Central Asia, several different branches developed, passing through different oasis settlements. Second, the Silk Road was not a trade route that existed solely for the purpose of trading in silk; many other commodities were also traded, from gold and ivory to exotic animals and plants. Of all the precious goods crossing this area, silk was perhaps the most remarkable for the people of the West. The movement of people along the Silk Road can also be traced to the movement of religion and the development of languages.

FTCE Fact

Civilization has evolved from the cross-fertilization of many cultures.

It is important to understand the importance of the **Hammurabi Code**. This code of laws is the earliest-known example of a ruler proclaiming publicly to his people an entire body of laws. It was arranged in orderly groups so that all men might read and know what was required of them. The code was carved on a black stone monument eight feet high and was clearly intended to be read in public view.

The Hammurabi Code regulates in clear and definite strokes the organization of society. The judge who blunders in a law case is to be expelled from his judgeship forever and heavily fined. The witness who testifies falsely is to be slain. Indeed, all the heavier crimes are made punishable with death. Even if a man builds a house badly and it falls and kills the owner, the builder is to be slain. If the owner's son was killed, then the builder's son is slain. These grim retaliatory punishments take no note of excuses or explanations but only of the facts—with one striking exception. An accused man was allowed to cast himself into the Euphrates River. Apparently the art of swimming was unknown, because according to the code, if the current bore him to the shore alive, he was declared innocent, and if he drowned, he was guilty. This aspect of the Hammurabi Code shows that faith in the justice of the ruling gods was firmly established in the minds of men.

> **FTCE Fact**
>
> The Hammurabi Code clearly outlines the organization of society.

Differentiate between the Middle Ages, Renaissance, and Reformation periods.

The **Middle Ages** is the middle period in a traditional schematic division of European history into three ages: the classical civilization of antiquity, the Middle Ages, and modern times. A period of great cultural, political, and economic change in Europe, the Middle Ages witnessed the first sustained urbanization of northern and western Europe. Modern European states owe their origins to the Middle Ages, and their political boundaries as we know them are essentially the result of the military and dynastic achievements in this tumultuous period. Science, technology, agricultural production, and social identity changed drastically. The Middle Ages are commonly dated from the fifth-century fall of the Western Roman Empire until the end of the fifteenth century.

The **Carolingian Renaissance** was a period of intellectual and cultural revival occurring in the late eighth and ninth centuries, with the peak of the activities occurring during the reigns of the Carolingian rulers Charlemagne and Louis the Pious. During this period literature, the arts, architecture, jurisprudence, and liturgical and scriptural studies made significant advances. The period also saw the development of the medieval Latin language and the Carolingian minuscule writing style, which helped to unify communication across most of Europe.

During the twelfth century the civilization of the **Byzantine Empire** experienced a period of intense change and development. This has led some historians to refer to a twelfth-century Renaissance in Byzantine cultural and intellectual achievement. These changes were particularly significant in two areas of Byzantine civilization: its economic prosperity and its artistic output.

The **Renaissance**, which means "rebirth" in French, was a cultural movement that spanned roughly the fourteenth through seventeenth centuries, beginning in Italy in the late Middle Ages and later spreading to the rest of Europe. It encompassed the revival of learning based on classical sources, the rise of courtly and papal patronage, the development of perspective in painting, and advancements in science. The Renaissance had wide-ranging consequences in all intellectual pursuits but is perhaps best known for its artistic aspect and the contributions of such polymaths as Leonardo da Vinci and Michelangelo, who have inspired the term "Renaissance men."

The **Protestant Reformation** was a movement in the sixteenth century to reform the Catholic Church in western Europe. Many western Christians were troubled by what they saw as false doctrines and malpractices within the Catholic Church. This particularly involved the teaching and sale of indulgences. Another major contention was the tremendous corruption within the church's hierarchy, all the way up to the pope, who appointed individuals to various positions within the church (e.g., bishops, cardinals) on the basis of financial contributions.

Martin Luther (1483–1546) was a German monk, theologian, and church reformer. He is also considered to be the founder of Protestantism. In 1517, Martin Luther published his *Ninety-five Theses on the Power of Indulgences* criticizing the Catholic Church, including its practice of selling indulgences and their policy on purgatory. Martin Luther built his thesis on work done by John Wycliffe and Jan Hus, and other reformers. Reformation Day is an important liturgical festival that is celebrated by Lutherans and Christians of many Protestant denominations. It commemorates Martin Luther's posting of his *Ninety-five Theses* on the door of the Castle Church in Wittenberg, Germany, on October 31, 1517. This act triggered the Protestant Reformation.

Church beliefs and practices under attack by Protestant reformers included purgatory, particular judgment, devotion to Mary, the intercession of saints, most of the sacraments, and the authority of the pope.

The Protestant zeal for translating the Bible and getting it into the hands of the laity was empowered by the invention of the movable-type printing press by Gutenberg, which advanced the culture of biblical literacy.

The most important Protestant groups to emerge directly from the Reformation were the Lutherans, Calvinists, Presbyterians, Anabaptists, and Anglicans. Subsequent Protestant denominations generally trace their roots back to the initial Reformation traditions. It also led to the Counter-Reformation within the Roman Catholic Church.

Identify the major contributions of Western and non-Western civilizations during the Middle Ages, Renaissance, and Reformation periods.

Following are the major contributions to the Western world during the Renaissance and Reformation:

- **Artists**
  - Giotto: painter and architect from Florence, generally considered the first in a line of great artists who contributed to the Italian Renaissance
  - Leonardo da Vinci: artist, inventor, and scientist
  - Michelangelo: sculptor, painter, and architect

- **Philosophy**: Machiavelli, Thomas Moore, and Francis Bacon

- **Literature**: Shakespeare, Chaucer, Petrarch, and Boccaccio

- **Science**: Galileo

- **Medicine**: Andrea Vesalius and William Harvey

The invention of the printing press allowed for the rapid spread of the ideas, writings, and innovations of the times.

Identify the significant scientific and social changes from the Age of Reason through the Age of Enlightenment.

The **Age of Reason** is considered to succeed the **Renaissance** and precede the **Age of Enlightenment**. In Western philosophy the modern period is usually taken to start with the seventeenth century—specifically, with the work of René Descartes, who set much of the agenda as well as much of the methodology for those who came after him. The period is typified in Europe by the great system builders—philosophers who present unified systems of epistemology, metaphysics, logic, and ethics, and often politics and the physical sciences. The work of this era is often characterized as either rationalist or empiricist.

The three main **rationalists** are **Descartes, Baruch Spinoza,** and **Gottfried Leibniz**. Building on their English predecessors **Francis Bacon** and **Thomas Hobbes,** the three main **empiricists** were **John Locke, George Berkeley,** and **David Hume**. The rationalists believed that, in principle (though not in practice), all knowledge can be gained by the power of reason alone. The empiricists rejected that idea, believing that all knowledge comes through the senses, from experience. Thus the rationalists took mathematics as their model for knowledge, and the empiricists took the physical sciences.

FTCE Fact

> The rationalists thought that knowledge was gained by reason; the empiricists believed knowledge came through the senses.

This period also saw the birth of some of the classics of political thought, especially Thomas Hobbes's *Leviathan* and John Locke's *Two Treatises of Government*.

The seventeenth century in Europe witnessed the culmination of the slow process of detachment of philosophy from theology. Thus, while philosophers still talked about—and even offered arguments for the existence of—a deity, this was done in the service of philosophical argument and thought. (Philosophers of the Enlightenment would go still further, leaving theology and religion behind altogether.)

The **Age of Enlightenment** refers to eighteenth-century European and American philosophy. It can more narrowly refer to the historical intellectual movement that advocated reason as the primary basis of authority. As a movement it occurred solely in Germany, France, Britain, and Spain, but its influence spread beyond those boundaries. Many of the Founding Fathers of the United States were also heavily influenced by Enlightenment-era ideas, particularly in the religious sphere and, in parallel to the French Declaration of the Rights of Man and the Citizen, in the governmental sphere with the U.S. Bill of Rights.

Jean-Jacques Rousseau (1712–78) was a philosopher of the Enlightenment whose political ideas influenced the French Revolution, the development of both liberal and socialist theory, and the growth of nationalism. With his *Confessions* and other writings, he practically invented modern autobiography and encouraged a new focus on the building of subjectivity that would bear fruit in the work of thinkers as diverse as Hegel and Freud. His novel *Julie, ou la nouvelle Héloïse* was one of the best-selling fictional works of the eighteenth century and was important to the development of romanticism. Rousseau also made important contributions to music, both as a theorist and a composer.

The Enlightenment is often closely linked with the scientific revolution. Both movements emphasized reason, science, and rationality, but the Enlightenment also sought their application in comprehension of divine or natural law. Inspired by the revolution of knowledge begun by Galileo and Newton, and in a climate of increasing disaffection with repressive rule, Enlightenment thinkers believed that systematic thinking might be applied to all areas of human activity, carried into the governmental sphere in their explorations of the individual, society, and the state. Its leaders believed they could lead their states to progress after a long period of tradition, irrationality, superstition, and tyranny, which they imputed to the Middle Ages, while many were religious. The movement helped create the intellectual framework for the American and French revolutions, the Latin American independence movement, and the Polish constitution of May 3, 1791, and led to the rise of classical liberalism, democracy, and capitalism.

The Enlightenment is matched with the high baroque and classical eras in music and the neoclassical period in the arts. The era receives modern attention as being one of the central models for many movements in the modern period.

The Enlightenment influenced the Jewish Haskalah, a movement that in western Europe and particularly in Germany resulted in the elevation and eventual replacement of Yiddish by Hebrew, as well as the Jewish reform movement.

Immanuel Kant is regarded as one of the most influential thinkers of modern Europe and the last major philosopher of the Enlightenment.

Identify the causes, events, consequences, and significant individuals associated with the Age of Exploration and global civilization.

The **Age of Exploration,** also called the **Age of Discovery**, was a period from the early fifteenth century and continuing into the early seventeenth century when European ships traveled around the world in search of new trading routes and partners to feed burgeoning capitalism in Europe. They also were looking for trading goods like gold, silver, and spices. In the process, Europeans encountered peoples and mapped lands previously unknown to them. Among the most famous explorers of the period were Christopher Columbus, Vasco da Gama, Pedro Álvares Cabral, John Cabot, Yermak Timofeyevich, Juan Ponce de León, Francisco Coronado, Juan Sebastián de Elcano, Bartolomeu Dias, Ferdinand Magellan, Willem Barents, Abel Tasman, Jean Alfonse, Jacques Cartier, Samuel de Champlain, Willem Janszoon, James Cook, Henry Hudson, and Giovanni da Verrazano.

The Age of Exploration was rooted in new technologies and ideas growing out of the Renaissance. These included advances in cartography, navigation, firepower, and ship-building. Many people wanted to find a route to Asia through the west of Europe. The most important inventions came out of Iberia: the carrack and the caravel. These vessels evolved from medieval European designs, reflecting Mediterranean and North Sea influences and some Arabic elements. They were the first ships that could leave the relatively placid and calm Mediterranean and sail safely on the open Atlantic.

A **carrack** was a three- or four-mast sailing ship developed in the Mediterranean in the fifteenth century. Carracks were among the first proper oceangoing ships in Europe: large enough to be stable in heavy seas and roomy enough to carry provisions for long voyages. They were the ships in which the Portuguese and Spanish explored the world in the fifteenth and sixteenth centuries.

Evaluate the causes, events, consequences, and significant individuals associated with the development of the nation-state and capitalism.

The word **capitalism** can be applied to the economies of very diverse countries, including the United States, Japan, Russia, Brazil, and South Africa. Although these countries are in many ways very different, they have in common certain basic social forms and economic laws. In a system called global capitalism, national capitalist economies are interconnected within a global system driven by the same capitalist laws of motion. In this system economic crises and prolonged downturns are not national in origin but are rooted in the general dynamics that drive the whole global economy and in the relations that bind all capitalist economies together.

In Europe in the eighteenth century, the **classic non-national states** were the multi-ethnic empires: the Austro-Hungarian Empire, the Russian Empire, and the Ottoman Empire. **Nation-states** have characteristics different from those of these non-national states. For example, unlike dynastic monarchies, nation-states view their territories as nearly sacred and nontransferable. No nation-state would swap territories with other states simply, for example, because the king's daughter got married. A nation-state has a border that, in principle, is defined only by the area of settlement of the national group, although many nation-states also seek natural borders (rivers, mountain ranges). The most notable characteristic is the degree to which a nation-state uses the state as an instrument of national unity in economic, social, and cultural life.

The early nation-states promoted economic unity by abolishing internal customs and tolls. Nation-states typically have a policy to create and maintain a national transportation infrastructure, facilitating trade and travel. In nineteenth-century Europe the expansion of the rail transport networks was at first largely a matter for private railway companies but gradually came under the control of the national governments. The French rail network, with its main lines radiating from Paris to all corners of France, is often seen as a reflection of the centralized French nation-state that directed its construction. Nation-states continue to build national motorway networks. Transnational infrastructure programs, such as the Trans-European Networks, are a recent innovation.

The nation-states typically had a more centralized and uniform public administration than their imperial predecessors; compared with empires, nation-states were smaller and their populations were less diverse. (The internal diversity of, for instance, the Ottoman Empire was great.) After the triumph of the nation-state in Europe, regional identity was subordinate to national identity in regions such as Alsace-Lorraine, Catalonia, Brittany, Sicily, Sardinia, and Corsica. In many cases the regional administration was also subordinated to central (national) government.

However, the most obvious impact of the nation-state was **the creation of a uniform national culture through state policy**. The model of the nation-state implies that its population constitutes a nation, united by a common descent, a common language, and many forms of shared culture. When the implied unity was absent, the nation-state often tried to create it. It promoted a uniform national language through language policy. The creation of national systems of compulsory primary education and a relatively uniform curriculum in secondary schools was the most effective instrument in the spread of national languages. The schools also taught the national history, often in a propagandistic and mythologized version. Language and cultural policy was sometimes negative, aimed at the suppression of non-national elements. Language prohibitions were sometimes used to accelerate the adoption of national languages and the decline of minority languages.

In some cases the policies of nation-states triggered bitter conflicts and separatism. Where it worked, the cultural uniformity and homogeneity of the population increased. Conversely, cultural divergence at the borders became sharper. In theory a uniform French identity extends from the Atlantic coast to the Rhine, and on the other bank of the Rhine, a uniform German identity begins. To enforce that model, both sides have divergent language policies and educational systems.

The **Peace of Westphalia** was the result of a pair of treaties—the **Treaty of Münster** and the **Treaty of Osnabrück**, signed on October 24 and May 15, 1648, respectively—that ended both the Thirty Years' War and the Eighty Years' War. In more than a hundred articles, the largely identical treaties deal with the internal affairs of the Holy Roman Empire. Thus the treaties involved the Holy Roman Emperor Ferdinand III of Habsburg, but other German princes, Spain, France, Sweden, and representatives of the Dutch Republic also participated. Often the **Treaty of the Pyrenees**, signed in 1659, ending the war between France and Spain, is also considered part of the overall accord. Many historians use the Peace of Westphalia to mark the beginning of the modern era in **international relations**.

Assess the Industrial Revolution in terms of cultural, political, and economic effects in both Western and non-Western civilizations.

The **Industrial Revolution** was a major shift of technological, socioeconomic, and cultural conditions that occurred in the late eighteenth century and early nineteenth century in some Western countries. It began in Britain and spread throughout the world in a process that continues today as industrialization. During that time an economy based on manual labor was replaced by one dominated by industry and the manufacture of machinery. It began with the mechanization of the textile industries, the development of iron-making techniques, and the increased use of refined coal. Trade expansion was enabled by the introduction of canals, improved roads, and railways. The introduction of steam power and powered machinery, mainly in textile manufacturing, was the foundation of dramatic increases in production capacity. The development of all-metal machine tools in the first two decades of the nineteenth century facilitated the manufacture of more production machines for other industries.

The period covered by the Industrial Revolution began in approximately 1760 to 1780 and lasted until 1930 to 1940. In this case the term *revolution* does not indicate an explosive change but more of a gradual change over many decades. The effects spread throughout western Europe and North America during the nineteenth century, eventually affecting most of the world. The impact of this change on society was enormous.

FTCE Fact

The Industrial Revolution was not violent, but rather a gradual change over many years.

The first Industrial Revolution merged into the second Industrial Revolution around 1850, when technological and economic progress gained momentum with the development of steam-powered ships, railways, and later in the nineteenth century the internal combustion engine and electrical power generation.

It has been argued that gross domestic product per capita was much more stable and progressed at a much slower rate before the Industrial Revolution and the emergence of the modern capitalist economy, and that it has since increased rapidly in capitalist countries.

The technological changes of the Industrial Revolution included the following:

- The use of new basic materials, chiefly iron and steel

- The use of new energy sources, including both fuel and motor power, such as coal, the steam engine, electricity, petroleum, and the internal combustion engine

- The invention of new machines, such as the spinning jenny and the power loom, that permitted increased production with a smaller expenditure of human energy

- A new organization of work known as the factory system, which entailed increased division of labor and specialization of function

- Important developments in transportation and communication, including the steam locomotive, steamship, automobile, airplane, telegraph, and radio

- The increasing application of science to industry

These technological changes made possible a tremendously increased use of natural resources and the mass production of manufactured goods.

The Industrial Revolution also resulted in new developments in nonindustrial spheres, including the following:

- Agricultural improvements that provided food for a larger nonagricultural population

- Economic changes that resulted in a wider distribution of wealth, the decline of land as a source of wealth in the face of rising industrial production, and increased international trade

- Political changes that reflected the shift in economic power and new state policies corresponding to the needs of an industrialized society

- Sweeping social changes, including the growth of cities, the development of working-class movements, and the emergence of new patterns of authority

- Cultural transformations of a broad order: workers acquired new and distinctive skills, and their relation to their tasks shifted; instead of being craftspeople working with hand tools, they became machine operators, subject to factory discipline

Finally, there was a psychological change: people gained confidence in their ability to use resources and to master nature. Political theories also changed: instead of the laissez-faire ideas that had dominated economic and social thought, governments generally moved into the social and economic realm to meet the needs of their more complex industrial societies.

Identify the causes, events, consequences, and significant individuals associated with the Age of Revolution, including independence movements in France, Africa, Asia, and Latin America.

The **French** and **American revolutions** were the most important political events of the eighteenth century. They were also a dramatic conclusion to the Enlightenment, and both revolutions, taken together, form a major turning point in human history. This **Age of Revolution** was the period (from roughly 1750 to 1800) after most of the European countries changed their governments to absolutist states or constitutional states. The Age of Revolution specifically includes the American Revolution, the French Revolution, and the Russian Revolution.

The **American Revolution** occurred in the last half of the eighteenth century, when the 13 colonies that became the United States of America gained independence from the British Empire. In that period the colonies rebelled against the British Empire and launched the American Revolutionary War, also referred to as the American War of Independence. The war began in 1775 when the revolutionaries seized control of the colonies, established the Second Continental Congress, and formed the Continental Army. The American Declaration of Independence was signed in 1776, and Americans won the final victory on the battlefield in 1781, forcing the surrender of the British army. A peace treaty, the Treaty of Paris, was signed in 1783.

France played a key role in aiding the new nation of Americans by providing money and munitions, organizing a coalition against Britain, and sending an army and a fleet that played a decisive role at the battle that effectively ended the war at Yorktown. The Americans, however, were revolting against royalty and aristocracy and consequently did not look to France as a model.

The American Revolution included a series of broad intellectual and social shifts that occurred in the early American society, such as the new republican ideals that took hold in the American population. In some states sharp political debates broke out over the role of democracy in government. The American shift to republicanism, as well as the gradually expanding democracy, caused an upheaval of the traditional social hierarchy and created the ethic that formed the core of American political values.

FTCE Fact

The French and American revolutions had a huge effect on human history.

The revolutionary era began in 1763, when the military threat to the American colonies from France ended. Adopting the view that the colonies should pay a substantial portion of the costs of defending them, Britain imposed a series of taxes that proved highly unpopular and, because the colonies lacked elected representation in the governing British Parliament, many colonists considered to be illegal. After protests in Boston, the British sent combat troops, the Americans mobilized their militia, and fighting broke out in 1775. Although Loyalists were about 15 percent to 20 percent of the population, throughout the war the Patriots generally controlled 80 percent to 90 percent of the territory. The British could only hold a few coastal cities. In 1776 representatives of the 13 colonies voted unanimously to adopt a Declaration of Independence, by which they established the United States of America. The Americans formed an alliance with France in 1778 that evened the military and naval strengths. Two main British armies were captured at Saratoga in 1777 and at Yorktown in 1781, leading to peace with the Treaty of Paris in 1783. The United States was bounded by British Canada on the north, Spanish Florida on the south, and the Mississippi River on the west.

The **French Revolution** (1789–99) was not only a crucial event in the broad context of Western history but also perhaps the single most crucial influence on British intellectual, philosophical, and political life in the nineteenth century. In the early stages of the revolution, its proponents considered it a triumph of the forces of reason over those of superstition and privilege, and as such it was welcomed by English radicals like Thomas Paine, William Godwin, and William Blake.

The old regime in England, on the other hand, had from the first allied itself closely with Locke and Newton, great advocates of reason and order. Edmund Burke maintained that the radicals who had begun the French Revolution by releasing the pent-up quasi-religious energies of the common people of France were interested first in the conquest of their own country and then in the conquest of Europe and the rest of the world, which would be "liberated" whether it wished to be or not. Thomas Paine responded to Burke, and the debate between conservatives and radicals raged on for many years and certainly influenced, directly or indirectly, the thought and the work of every major English author for the remainder of the century and beyond.

The **Russian Revolution** of 1917 was a series of political and social upheavals involving first the overthrow of the tsarist autocracy and then the overthrow of the liberal and moderate socialist provisional government, resulting in the establishment of Soviet power under the control of the Bolshevik party. This eventually led to the establishment of the Union of Soviet Socialist Republics (USSR, or Soviet Union), which lasted until its dissolution in 1991.

The February Revolution led directly to the fall of the autocracy of Tsar Nicholas II of Russia, the last tsar of Russia, and sought to establish in its place a democratic republic. A period of dual power followed, with the provisional government holding state power and the national network of Soviets, led by socialists, holding the allegiance of the lower classes and the political left.

In the October Revolution, the Bolshevik party, led by Vladimir Lenin, and the Soviet workers, overthrew the provisional government and brought about a dramatic change in the social structure of Russia, as well as paving the way for the formation of the Soviet

Union. While many notable historical events occurred in Moscow and Saint Petersburg, there was also a broad-based movement in cities throughout the country, among national minorities throughout the empire, and in the rural areas, where peasants seized and redistributed land.

At the start of 1917, a turning point in Russian history, the country was ripe for revolution. Peasant villagers more and more often migrated between agrarian and industrial work environments, and many relocated entirely, creating a growing urban labor force. A middle class of white-collar employees, businessmen, and professionals like doctors, lawyers, teachers, journalists, and engineers was on the rise. Even nobles had to find new ways to subsist in this changing economy, and contemporaries spoke of new classes forming (proletarians and capitalists, for example), although these classes were also divided along crisscrossing lines of status, gender, age, ethnicity, and belief. If anything, it was becoming less and less simple to speak of clearly defined social groups or boundaries. Not only were groups fractured in various ways, but also their defining boundaries were increasingly blurred by migrating peasants, intellectual workers, gentry professionals, and the like. Almost everyone felt that the very texture of their lives was being transformed by a spreading commercial culture that was remaking the surfaces of material life (buildings, storefronts, advertisements, fashion, clocks, and machines) and nurtured new objects of desire.

By 1917 the growth of political consciousness, the impact of revolutionary ideas, and the weak and inefficient system of government (which had been debilitated further by its participation in the First World War), should have convinced the tsar, Nicholas II, to take the necessary steps toward reform. In January 1917, in fact, Sir George Buchanan, the British ambassador to Russia, advised the emperor to break down the barrier that separates the tsar from his people to regain their confidence. The ambassador received little response from Tsar Nicholas.

The people of Russia resented the autocracy of Nicholas II and the corrupt and anachronistic elements in his government. He was out of touch with the needs and aspirations of the Russian people, most of whom were victims of the wretched socioeconomic conditions that prevailed. Socially, tsarist Russia stood well behind the rest of Europe in its industry and farming, resulting in few opportunities for fair advancement on the part of peasants and industrial workers. Economically, widespread inflation and food shortages in Russia contributed to the revolution. Militarily, inadequate supplies, logistics, and weaponry led to heavy Russian losses during World War I, losses that strengthened the prevailing view of Nicholas II as weak and unfit to rule. Ultimately, those factors, coupled with the development of revolutionary ideas and movements, led to the Russian Revolution.

Jean-Jacques Rousseau's profound insights can be found in almost every trace of modern philosophy today. He was one of the most influential political theorists of the French Revolution. Somewhat complicated and ambiguous, Rousseau's general philosophy tried to grasp an emotional and passionate side of man, which he felt was left out of most previous philosophical thinking.

His essay titled "**Discourse on the Arts and Sciences**," published in 1750, argued that the advancement of art and science had not been beneficial to mankind. He proposed that the progress of knowledge had made governments more powerful and had crushed individual liberty. He concluded that material progress had actually undermined the possibility of sincere friendship, replacing it with jealousy, fear, and suspicion.

Perhaps Rousseau's most important work is *The Social Contract*, which describes the relationship of man with society. In contrast with his earlier work, the book set out Rousseau's idea that the state of nature is a brutish condition without law or morality and that good people exist only as a result of society's presence. In the state of nature, people are prone to be in frequent competition with their fellow human beings. A person can be more successful facing threats by joining with other people and thus has the impetus to do so. People join together to form the collective human presence known as society. The social contract is the compact agreed to among people that sets the conditions for membership in society.

Rousseau was one of the first modern writers to seriously attack the institution of private property and therefore is considered a forefather of modern socialism and communism. Rousseau also questioned the assumption that the will of the majority is always correct. He argued that the goal of government should be to secure freedom, equality, and justice for all within the state, regardless of the will of the majority.

FTCE Fact

Rousseau is considered a forefather of modern socialism and communism.

One of the primary principles of Rousseau's political philosophy is that politics and morality should not be separated. When a state fails to act in a moral fashion, it ceases to function in the proper manner and ceases to exert genuine authority over the individual. The second important principle is freedom, which the state is created to preserve.

Rousseau's ideas about education have profoundly influenced modern educational theory. He minimized the importance of book learning and recommended that children's emotions be educated before their reason. He placed a special emphasis on learning by experience.

The **Declaration of the Rights of Man and of the Citizen** is one of the fundamental documents of the French Revolution, defining a set of individual and universal rights that are valid at all times, in all places, and for all people. On August 26, 1789, the National Constituent Assembly adopted the declaration and subsequently used it as the preamble to the constitution of 1791. In the opening paragraph, the declaration states that "the ignorance, neglect, or contempt of the rights of man are the sole cause of public calamities and of the corruption of governments." In setting forth fundamental rights, the declaration is considered a precursor to international human rights instruments.

The American **Declaration of Independence** drafted by **Thomas Jefferson** between June 11 and June 28, 1776, is our nation's most cherished symbol of liberty and Jefferson's most enduring monument. In exalted and unforgettable phrases, Jefferson expressed the convictions in the minds and hearts of the American people. The political philosophy of the Declaration was not new; its ideals of individual liberty had already been expressed by John Locke and the Enlightenment philosophers. What Jefferson did was to summarize this philosophy in "self-evident truths" and set forth a list of grievances against the king to justify before the world the breaking of ties between the colonies and the United Kingdom.

Assess the growth of nationalism and its impact on the world's social, political, and geographic development.

The term **nationalism** is generally used to describe two phenomena: the attitude that members of a nation have when they care about their national identity and the actions that the members of a nation take when seeking to achieve or sustain self-determination. Nationalism has had an enormous influence on world history. The quest for national hegemony has inspired millennia of imperialism and colonization, while struggles for national liberation have resulted in many revolutions. In modern times the nation-state has become the dominant form of societal organization. Historians use the term *nationalism* to refer to this historical transition and to the emergence and predominance of nationalist ideology.

When nationalism turns ugly, the results are war, military conflict, and even genocide. Possibly the most dominant concept in world history is war. War is a constant. It can be said that in human history there have been very few, if any, times when war was not being waged somewhere on the globe. In today's world of terrorism, the concepts of war and genocide are no longer found only within nation-states, making the elimination of war and genocide even more of a challenge.

Analyze the causes and consequences of wars and military conflicts related to the world's social, political, and geographic development in the twentieth century, including pogroms and genocide.

Genocide is the mass killing of a group of people. According to **Article 2** of the **Convention on the Prevention and Punishment of the Crime of Genocide** (CPPCG), genocide is

> any of the following acts committed with intent to destroy, in whole or in part, a national, ethnical, racial or religious group, as such: killing members of the group; causing serious bodily or mental harm to members of the group; deliberately inflicting on the group conditions of life, calculated to bring about its physical destruction in whole or in part; imposing measures intended to prevent births within the group; and forcibly transferring children of the group to another group.

To claim the territory now known as the United States, Americans fought battles against indigenous peoples that resulted in the systematic removal of Native Americans from their territories. A time line of the Indian Wars might begin in 1622 in Virginia and end in 1890 at the battle of Wounded Knee, but some Native Americans contend that conflicts between indigenous people and the U.S. government have not ended.

After World War I hundreds of Armenian leaders were murdered in Istanbul after being summoned and gathered by the Turkish government. The mass murder of the then-leaderless Armenian people followed. Across the Ottoman Empire (with the exception of Constantinople, presumably owing to a large foreign presence), the same events transpired from village to village, from province to province.

The Holocaust is the term generally used to describe the killing of approximately 6 million European Jews during World War II, as part of a program of deliberate extermination planned and executed by the National Socialist regime in Germany led by Adolf Hitler. Other groups were persecuted and killed by the regime, including Soviet POWs, disabled people, gay men, Jehovah's Witnesses, Catholic Poles, Gypsies, and political prisoners. Many scholars do not include these groups in the Holocaust, limiting its definition to the genocide of the Jews, or what the Nazis called the Final Solution. Taking into account all the victims of Nazi persecution, however, the death toll rises considerably: estimates generally place the total number of victims at 9 million to 11 million.

In the Republic of Bosnia-Herzegovina, conflict between the three main ethnic groups—the Serbs, Croats, and Muslims—resulted in genocide committed by the Serbs against the Muslims in Bosnia. Bosnia is one of several small countries that emerged from the break-up of Yugoslavia, a multicultural country created after World War I by the victorious Western Allies. Yugoslavia was composed of ethnic and religious groups that had been historical rivals, even bitter enemies, including the Serbs (Orthodox Christians), Croats (Catholics), and ethnic Albanians (Muslims). The **Srebrenica Genocide** took place in Bosnia in 1995. In the region of Srebrenica, Bosnian-Serb forces killed 8,000 Muslim men and boys in the largest mass murder in Europe since World War II.

Rwanda is one of the smallest countries in Central Africa, with just 7 million people, and comprises two main ethnic groups: the Hutu and the Tutsi. Although the Hutu account for 90 percent of the population, in the past the Tutsi minority was considered the aristocracy of Rwanda and dominated Hutu peasants for decades, especially while Rwanda was under Belgian colonial rule. Following independence from Belgium in 1962, the Hutu majority seized power and reversed the roles, oppressing the Tutsi through systematic discrimination and acts of violence. As a result, more than 200,000 Tutsi fled to neighboring countries and formed a rebel guerrilla army, the Rwandan Patriotic Front. Beginning on April 6, 1994, and for the next 100 days, about 800,000 Tutsi were killed by Hutu militia using clubs and machetes, with as many as 10,000 killed each day.

The current crisis in the African region of **Darfur** began in 2003. After decades of neglect, drought, oppression, and small-scale conflicts in Darfur, two rebel groups, the Sudan Liberation Army/Movement (SLA/M) and the Justice and Equality Movement (JEM), mounted a challenge to Sudan's president, Omar al-Bashir. These groups represent agrarian farmers who are mostly non-Arab black African Muslims from numerous tribes. President al-Bashir's response was brutal. In seeking to defeat the rebel movements, the government of Sudan increased arms and support to local tribal and other militias, which have come to be known as the Janjaweed. Their members are mostly Arab black African Muslims who herd cattle, camels, and other livestock. They have wiped out entire villages, destroyed food and water supplies, and systematically murdered, tortured, and raped hundreds of thousands of Darfurians. At this writing the conflict in Darfur is ongoing.

Analyze major contemporary world issues and trends in terms of their political, social, economic, and geographic characteristics.

Globalization is defined as a national geopolitical policy in which the entire world is regarded as the appropriate sphere for a state's influence. The term is used to describe the changes in societies and in the world economy resulting from dramatic increases in trade and cultural exchange. In economic contexts, *globalization* is often understood to refer almost exclusively to the effects of trade, particularly trade liberalization, or free trade.

A term that seems to be gaining relevance is **cosmopolitan**, which is used to describe something that is made up of diverse peoples, composed of or containing people from different countries and cultures, or having worldwide relevance or scope.

People around the globe are more connected to each other than ever before. Information and money flow more quickly than ever. Goods and services produced in one part of the world are increasingly available in all parts of the world. International travel is more frequent. International communication is commonplace. The world seems to be getting smaller and smaller with the growth of communication spurred by the Internet. This perception is verified when we realize that a person can travel through 12 time zones, halfway around the world, to talk and see friends and relatives using a computerized videophone, without ever leaving home.

The **era of globalization** is fast becoming the preferred term for describing the current times. Just as the Great Depression, the Cold War era, the space age, and the Roaring Twenties are names for particular periods of history, the era of globalization describes the political, economic, and cultural atmosphere of today.

Although some people think of globalization as primarily a synonym for global business, it is much more than that. The same forces that allow businesses to operate as if national borders did not exist also allow social activists, labor organizers, journalists, academics, and many others to work on a global stage. While coming up with the right definition or exact term is difficult, an even greater challenge is deciding whether globalization is good or bad.

FTCE Fact

The era of globalization is the term used for the political, economic, and cultural atmosphere of today.

The power of the **multinational nonstate corporation** can potentially regulate the flow of ideas, people, and capital across state borders more effectively than some national governments. Corporations with worldwide operations can be more powerful than some countries. In response to the power these corporations wield over the lives of millions of workers, a backlash arose in the form of antiglobalization protests that have raged at meetings of the International Monetary Fund and the World Bank, spawning a larger social movement aimed at combating the hegemonic power of capital divorced from the accountability of state sanction or law. Nike, IBM, Coca-Cola, Pepsi, and Starbucks are corporations in this category.

On the positive side, a global emphasis, or **globalism**, has brought advanced medicine and major philanthropic work to many parts of the world. A project like *One Laptop per Child*, which strives to educate underprivileged children around the world through the Internet, also shows the promise of **globalism**.

Identify major world religions and ideologies and their impact on world events.

As mentioned earlier, one of the major themes of world history is war; another is **religion**. From the earliest known evidence of human religion by *Homo sapiens neanderthalensis* around 100,000 years ago to the present day, religion has been an influential aspect of human life.

Today humans from every possible background, location, and social class face numerous challenges and problems. Every day people must confront issues of health, safety, and mortality. It is because of these daily challenges that religion continues to exist. Religion is the universal tool for explaining things we do not understand in the context of the known physical world.

Although there are countless religions, each different from the other, they all serve the same purpose. Each answers questions that all humans seem to be programmed to ask: Why are we here? What happens when I die? How shall I live my life?

Religions found in the United States and the portion of the population practicing each are as follows: Protestant, 52 percent; Roman Catholic, 24 percent; Mormon, 2 percent; Jewish, 1 percent; Muslim, 1 percent; and none, 10 percent. Data on the world's religions are shown in the following table.

Religion	Date Founded	Sacred Texts	Membership	
			Number	Percentage of World
Christianity	30 C.E.	Bible	2.03 billion	32% (dropping)
Islam	622 C.E.	Koran, Hadith	1.22 billion	19% (growing)
Hinduism	1500 B.C.E., with truly ancient roots	Bhagavad-Gita, Upanishads, Rig Veda	828 million	13% (stable)
No religion[1]	—	None	775 million	12% (dropping)
Chinese folk religion	270 B.C.E.	None	390 million	6%
Buddhism	523 B.C.E.	Tripitaka, Sutras	364 million	6% (stable)
Tribal religions, shamanism, animism	Prehistory	Oral tradition	232 million	4%
Atheism	No date	None	150 million	2%
New religions	Various	Various	103 million	2%
Sikhism	1500 C.E.	Guru Granth Sahib	23.8 million	<1%
Judaism	Unknown[2]	Torah, Tanach, Talmud	14.5 million	<1%
Spiritism	Unknown	Unknown	12.6 million	<1%
Baha'i	1863 C.E.	Alkitab Alaqdas	7.4 million	<1%
Confucianism	520 B.C.E.	Lun Yu	6.3 million	<1%
Jainism	570 B.C.E.	Siddhanta, Pakrit	4.3 million	<1%
Zoroastrianism	600 to 6000 B.C.E.	Avesta	2.7 million	<1%
Shinto	500 C.E.	Kojiki, Nohon Shoki	2.7 million	<1%
Taoism	550 B.C.E.	Lao-tzu	2.7 million	<1%
Other	Various	Various	1.1 million	<1%
Wicca[3]	800 B.C.E., 1940 C.E.	None	0.5 million	<1%

Notes:

[1]Persons with no formal, organized religion include agnostics, freethinkers, humanists, and secularists, among others.

[2]There is no consensus on the date of the founding of Judaism. Some claim that Adam and Eve were the first Jews and lived circa 4000 B.C.E.; others suggest that they never existed. Some would place the date at the time of Abraham, circa 1900 B.C.E.; others consider Abraham to be a mythical character. Some date it to the exodus from Egypt circa 1490 B.C.E.; others say that no exodus happened and that the ancient Hebrews were originally a group that gradually separated from the main body of Canaanites and developed a different culture.

[3]Some Wiccans believe that their faith can be traced back to the origins of the Celtic people; others suggest it is a recently created religion. There is no reliable measure of their number.

Source: *www.religioustolerance.org/worldrel.htm*

CHAPTER 6

Knowledge of American History

The following skills are used as a basis to determine your competency for the American history portion of the FTCE Social Science Grades 6–12:

- Analyze the direct relationship of the Age of Exploration on the colonization of the Americas, including its impact on African, Asian, European, and Native American peoples.

- Analyze the cultural, political, and economic developments of the Americas during the colonial era.

- Analyze the causes, events, consequences, and significant individuals of the revolutionary era.

- Evaluate the issues associated with the constitutional era and the early republic.

- Evaluate the impact of westward expansion on the cultural, political, and economic development of the emerging nation.

- Identify the cultural, political, and economic characteristics of the antebellum era.

- Identify causes, events, consequences, and significant individuals of the Civil War and Reconstruction eras.

- Assess the impact of agrarianism, industrialization, urbanization, and the reform movements in the late nineteenth and early twentieth centuries (e.g., temperance, civil rights, populism, progressivism).

- Assess the impact of immigration on cultural, political, and economic development.

- Identify the causes, events, consequences, and significant individuals of the World War I era.

- Identify the cultural, political, and economic developments between World War I and World War II, including the Roaring Twenties, the Harlem Renaissance, the Great Depression, and the New Deal.

- Identify the causes, events, consequences, and significant individuals of the World War II period.

- Identify key causes, events, consequences, and significant individuals related to domestic and foreign affairs during the Cold War era (1945–91).

- Identify causes, events, consequences, and significant individuals associated with movements for equality, civil rights, and civil liberties.

- Identify key individuals, events, and issues related to Florida history.

As a test taker, you may want to develop a study plan for the FTCE. You may want to perfect your strengths, or you might decide to focus on bringing your weaknesses up to an acceptable level. No matter what plan you have, you should keep in mind that the American history portion of the FTCE comprises 30 percent of the total number of questions on the exam.

FTCE Fact

Questions on American History make up 30 percent of the FTCE test.

Analyze the direct relationship of the Age of Exploration on the colonization of the Americas, including its impact on African, Asian, European, and Native American peoples.

In the seventeenth century the nature of colonialism changed. While daring expeditions at sea and discoveries of new lands still defined exploration, European nations had become dependent on the trade and resources of their New World colonies. This prompted governments to encourage settlers to move to colonial territories to establish trading ports and protect land interests. As more unknown lands were discovered, they were quickly claimed by European nations. The great territorial race began with nations clamoring for ownership of the vast land and resources of the New World. By the mid-eighteenth century, nations focused their attention on exploring Africa, the Pacific, and Australia. By the end of the era, European nations fought both each other and existing civilizations in the Far East for shipping and trade strongholds in Asia.

Colonialism and maritime discovery were not the only forces that shaped exploration from 1600 to 1850. Knowledge gained from exploration yielded a new interest in studying the world. The Enlightenment, which brought a resurgence in science, reason, and learning during the late eighteenth century, fostered a climate of scientific curiosity. Not only did people sail the seas to discover and claim new lands, but also they carefully catalogued the various plants, animals, crops, and peoples in the lands they explored. New natural sciences such as biology and geology became popular pastimes. Eventually, the natural sciences gained academic credibility, and by 1830 France, Spain, England, and Holland had national geological and geographical societies.

Analyze the cultural, political, and economic developments of the Americas during the colonial era.

In 1620 English settlers known as the Pilgrims landed at Plymouth, Massachusetts. Although the **Massachusetts Bay Colony** was not the first successful settlement in the New World, it was the first major stronghold in North America. Soon after the English settled in Massachusetts, the Dutch sent settlers to **New Amsterdam** (now New York). Later in the 1600s the French explorer Sieur de **La Salle** claimed the northwestern coast of the Gulf of Mexico for his country, naming the land Louisiana in honor of the French king. In the 1650s the triangular trade route began. Europeans traded slaves for sugar in the West Indies and traded sugar for rum, molasses, and timber in New England. That trade system ensured a steady stream of both raw materials for industry and luxury goods for consumers.

A century later exploration and settlement focused on Asia, the South Pacific, and Australia. In 1776 the British government proposed settlement of New South Wales, the area of Australia explored by **James Cook**. Two years later the first settlers arrived in Australia. They settled around Botany Bay before relocating because of disease and poor soil conditions. Settlement in Australia grew quickly, especially as the French and Dutch claimed ports in the region, and trade in Asia flourished. The entire coastline of Australia was not fully mapped until 1822.

This **mercantile economy**, however, was dependent not only on colonists but also on the procurement of **African slaves**. Exploration and colonialism had a devastating effect on the native populations of Africa and the Americas, especially in terms of the diseases Europeans brought to the populations of other continents. Virgin soil epidemics—deadly outbreaks among populations that previously had no exposure to the diseases—killed millions of people in the New World and Africa. These European diseases changed and adapted to their new climates, sometimes producing more virulent and destructive strains of disease. Thinking that certain environments caused illness, colonists became conscious of where they built their homes and towns, avoiding swamps and beaches. They often avoided fresh air and local fruits and fish, opting instead for dried beef and staples from home. Because most medicines used at that time had natural sources, many people felt deeply connected to their environment.

The English explorer James Cook embarked on perhaps the most ambitious voyage of the era in 1768. Cook's expedition circumnavigated the globe, spending a great deal of time surveying the South Pacific and Indian Oceans. He discovered several island chains and surveyed a large portion of the coast of Australia. He was the first to realize that Australia was a vast continent. In 1778 Cook voyaged to the northern Pacific in search of a passage through North America. He and his crew wintered in California, comprehensively charted the west coast of North America, and sailed as far north as Alaska and the Arctic Circle. Unable to locate an inland passage, Cook and his crew sailed to Hawaii, which he had explored several years earlier. Cook died in the Hawaiian Islands in 1779, but his crew returned home nearly a year later. Cook's long expeditions fundamentally changed the shape of the known world; maps made after his voyages are some of the first to resemble **modern maps**.

Cook possessed a distinct navigational advantage over his predecessors, which greatly expedited his journey and allowed for greater accuracy in mapping. In 1714 the British Parliament offered a prize to anyone who could devise a method for accurately and reliably determining longitude (position on a vertical grid of the earth). For centuries mariners had been able to find their latitude (position on a horizontal grid of the earth), thus aiding the determination of position and distance when traveling north or south and giving a rough position when sailing east or west. However, no means existed for accurately measuring distance and position when sailing west or east, the predominant direction of voyages to the Americas and the Far East. Most scientists thought the best way to solve the longitude problem was through the creation of astronomical charts and complex tables and equations. However, these could only be used in good weather and for a few hours of the day, thus restricting their ultimate usefulness.

In 1735 British inventor **John Harrison** determined that easily calculating longitude is dependent on knowing the exact time. On land the most precise timekeeping devices were clocks. Harrison thus began constructing chronometers, or extremely accurate clocks, for use at sea. He tested several models on various voyages, fine-tuning his models each time to account for the rocking of the ship, vibrations, and other factors that could affect the reliability of the chronometers. After nearly 30 years of work, Harrison perfected his chronometer in 1761. Longitudinal navigation was no longer a mystery. The British Parliament was reluctant to award the promised prize to an amateur scientist, however, and Harrison did not receive it for several years. Realizing the power of Harrison's chronometer, several navigators began to use the timepieces, despite their relatively high cost, before Parliament recognized the magnitude of the discovery.

FTCE Fact

The invention of the chronometer dispelled the mystery of longitude.

Exploration, settlement, and medicine prompted people to look more closely at nature and the environment. In 1798 **Thomas Malthus** published his first essay on population. The work classified peoples by region and racial characteristics and analyzed the relationship between each group and the environment. In the 1820s the first rough theories of evolution appeared. Although no theory proposed a specific scheme for evolving life, the concept of human development began to fascinate a few people interested in the natural sciences.

Along with the questioning of man's antiquity, natural scientists studied the earth itself. In 1930 the Royal Geographical Society was founded in Britain. That same year English geologist **Charles Lyell** published his *Principles of Geology*, a work that served as the standard methodology for the discipline for nearly a century. Natural scientists were fascinated with classifying all aspects of the world around them and probing their interconnectedness. Thirty years later a theory that proposed to explain those very connections would be the center of scientific debate in the nineteenth century. In 1831 the English naturalist **Charles Darwin** embarked on an expedition to the Galapagos Islands, a remote island chain off the coast of present-day Ecuador. His discoveries made aboard the *HMS Beagle* foreshadowed a new age of scientific exploration and the modern era.

European nations came to the Americas to increase their wealth and broaden their influence over world affairs. The Spanish were among the first Europeans to explore the New World and the first to settle in what is now the United States.

By 1650, however, England had established a dominant presence on the Atlantic coast. The first colony was founded at **Jamestown**, Virginia, in 1607. Many of the people who settled in the New World came to escape religious persecution. The Pilgrims, founders of Plymouth, Massachusetts, arrived in 1620. In both Virginia and Massachusetts, the colonists' survival was largely dependent on assistance from Native Americans. New World grains such as corn kept the colonists from starving while, in Virginia, tobacco provided a valuable cash crop. By the early 1700s enslaved Africans made up a growing percentage of the colonial population. By 1770 more than 2 million people lived and worked in Great Britain's 13 North American colonies.

More than 100 years earlier, the **Virginia Company of England** had made a daring proposition: sail to the new, mysterious land, which they called Virginia in honor of Elizabeth I, the Virgin Queen, and begin a settlement. One hundred twenty people made the voyage across the Atlantic. They established Jamestown, Virginia, on May 14, 1607, the first permanent British settlement in North America. Though determined, the settlers had no idea of the severe challenges they faced.

Half of the Jamestown settlers were artisans, craftsmen, soldiers, and laborers, including a tailor, a barber, and two surgeons. The other half comprised "gentlemen," men of wealth who did not have professions and may have underestimated the rough work necessary to survive in the New World. After eight months only 38 of the120 pioneers were still alive. Among the survivors was **Captain John Smith**, an adventurer and explorer. Despite the hardships, his solid leadership kept the colony going those first two years, as new arrivals from England brought the population of Jamestown to 500. After Smith left in 1609, however, more trouble came.

Weather conditions were rough and supplies low. Only 60 of the 500 colonists survived the harsh winter that followed Smith's departure. Jamestown, though it possessed a good harbor, was swampy, infested with mosquitoes, and lacked freshwater sources. The people fought against disease, famine, and the **Algonquian Indians**, whose land the British settlers had claimed. The Algonquian chief, **Powhatan**, at first allowed the visitors to settle, build, and farm in his territory. As more settlers came, however, Powhatan grew tired of the colonists' takeover of his land. Some of the tribe attacked settlers working in the fields.

Nevertheless, the Virginia pioneers had some years of peace and prosperity. Peace came when **Pocahontas**, Powhatan's daughter, married **John Rolfe**, a tobacco farmer from Jamestown. Also, new supplies and leadership eventually arrived from England.

An event of momentous consequence took place in 1619 when a Dutch slave trader exchanged a cargo of captive Africans for food. The Africans became indentured servants, trading labor for shelter and eventual freedom. They were among the first African Americans in the colonies. Racial slavery would not become a common practice until 1680. For all, the struggle for land and survival continued, but Jamestown was just the beginning.

The first year was devastating for the Virginia colonists, with only 32 colonists surviving the winter and only then because Native Americans living in the area came to their aid with food. After a supply ship arrived the next year, they had additional provisions but many more colonists to feed as well. Once again, over the winter most of the colonists died of starvation and from hostile encounters with their Native American neighbors. As the second winter came to a close, ships arrived, and most settlers were ready to leave. But as they were leaving, **Lord Thomas De La Warr** (Delaware is named after him) arrived from England with new supplies and more settlers. He refused to let the survivors return to England. Slowly, as the settlers reached agreements with the local Native American tribes and learned how to grow some of their own crops, the colony began to prosper.

Most of the original Jamestown settlers had come to the New World looking for profit, mainly riches in the form of gold and other precious metals. They had not given enough thought to the perils that they would face in this unknown land. One of the settlers, however, was familiar with hardship and was committed to Jamestown's survival. Captain John Smith had fought in France and Hungary, had been captured, and escaped. Although his personality initially caused some conflicts with the other colonists (he arrived in Jamestown in chains after alienating the leaders of the expedition), he eventually made contact with Chief Powhatan, who provided the colonists with much of their food in that first year. Smith was eventually even appointed leader of the colony.

Pocahontas visited the colonists in the early years, bringing food and other provisions. Several years later, in an attempt to obtain bargaining advantage over Powhatan, the colonists kidnapped Pocahontas and compelled her to stay in Jamestown. John Rolfe, the first colonist to cultivate commercial-quality tobacco and start the colony on its way toward profitability, eventually married her and took her to England. She died the next year as they were preparing to return to Virginia.

Grouped with the **southern colonies**, Virginia started out as a corporate colony (granted by royal charter to a company of investors who have governing rights) but in 1624 became a royal colony (subject to the governing authority of the granting royalty).

In 1607, about the same time as the Jamestown colonization, a group of English colonists attempted to establish a colony in the northern Virginia territory. The colony was located in present-day Maine and was named Popham. It lasted about a year before the discouraged settlers returned to England.

The Pilgrims were the first English colonists to permanently settle in New England in what we call Massachusetts. On September 16, 1620, the ship *Mayflower* set sail from Plymouth, England, on its journey to the New World. There were 102 passengers on the *Mayflower*, including 41 Christian Puritan Separatists, known collectively as the Leiden group. After spending many years in Holland, having been exiled from the English Church, the Puritans were seeking a new life of religious freedom in America. All 102 of the passengers were referred to as the Pilgrims after they arrived. The group had obtained a patent from the London Virginia Company that indentured them into service for the company for seven years after they arrived and settled. To prepare for their life in America, they had sought advice from people who had already visited the New World. Among their advisors was Captain John Smith, who earlier had helped found Jamestown for the Virginia Company.

FTCE Fact

The Mayflower Compact was based on the belief that government is a form of covenant and must originate with the consent of the governed.

It took 66 days to reach New England, and the journey was very hard for the group of people who for the most part had never been on the sea. When they arrived they anchored off the tip of present-day Cape Cod. Before they even set foot on shore they wrote, and all the men signed, an agreement called the **Mayflower Compact**. The compact set the rules to guide the Pilgrims through the early hard times of establishing a new community. Signed on November 21, 1620, the compact served as the official constitution of the Plymouth Colony for many years.

In making the compact the Pilgrims drew on two strong traditions. One was the notion of a social contract, which dated back to biblical times and would receive fuller expression in the works of Thomas Hobbes and John Locke later in the century. The other was the belief in covenants. Puritans believed that covenants existed not only between God and people but also among people. The Pilgrims had used covenants in establishing their congregations in the Old World. The Mayflower Compact is such a covenant in that the settlers agreed to form a government and be bound by its rules.

The compact is often described as America's first constitution, but it is not a constitution in the sense of being a fundamental framework of government. Its importance lies in the belief that government is a form of covenant and that for government to be legitimate, it must derive from the consent of the governed. The settlers recognized that individually they might not agree with all the actions of the government they were creating; but they, and succeeding generations, understood that government could be legitimate only if it originated with the consent of those it claimed to govern.

For nearly a month the Pilgrims explored, by foot and in boats, the area around Cape Cod, using the maps they had obtained in England. During their explorations they had a few minor encounters with the local natives. Finally, on December 21 they decided to settle in a location near a harbor they named Plymouth. Nearly half of the colonists and crew died from illnesses that first winter as they struggled to build their town. The following spring they were visited by a local Wampanoag native named Samoset who, surprisingly, spoke some broken English. Eventually, he introduced the settlers to another native named Squanto, who had lived in the area before the Pilgrims arrived. Squanto had been kidnapped by English explorers and taken to Europe. While he was in Europe the rest of his people died from diseases brought by European explorers. Squanto spoke English very well, and he stayed with the Pilgrims and taught them many valuable skills that enabled them to survive in their new country. He also played a large role in bringing the Pilgrims and the local native population together, leading eventually to a long but restless peace.

About eight years after the Pilgrims arrived in Plymouth, more Puritans came to Massachusetts and settled in Salem. **John Winthrop**, carrying the Massachusetts Bay Charter, arrived in 1630 and founded Boston. Maine was annexed to Massachusetts in 1652, and later the Plymouth Colony was too.

The relationship between the native tribes and the colonists in New England was always strained but generally did not result in much bloodshed. In 1637 colonists, with the cooperation of several local tribes, mounted a devastating attack on the **Pequot** tribe. In 1675 the long accord that had existed between the New England colonists and the local native tribes dissolved in the bloody conflict known as **King Philip's War** (after the leader of the Wampanoag tribe, whom the colonists called Philip but whose native name was Metacom).

In 1623 two groups of English settlers, sent by **Captain John Mason**, arrived in what is now called New Hampshire (after John Mason's home, the county of Hampshire, England) and established a fishing village near the mouth of the Piscataqua River. New Hampshire would remain an English colony throughout the colonial period, even though at various times it came under Massachusetts jurisdiction.

In 1638 **John Wheelwright**, banished from Boston for defending his sister-in-law, **Anne Hutchinson**, founded a settlement called **Exeter** in New Hampshire. In 1639 the settlers signed the **Exeter Compact**, patterned after the Mayflower Compact.

In addition to their holdings in **New York**, the Dutch had settled in **New Netherlands** by 1623. In 1664, after obtaining control of Dutch holdings lying between Virginia and New England, the Duke of York made a proprietary grant to **Sir George Carteret** and **Lord Berkeley** of New Netherlands, which lay between the Hudson and Delaware rivers. These men intended to profit from real estate sales. The new grant was named **New Jersey** for Carteret, who was governor of the Isle of Jersey.

Although the **Dutch West India Company** explored and began to settle the New York area as early as 1614, significant occupation of the area did not occur until 1624, when Dutch settlers arrived at Governors Island and then spread to other areas in the region. In 1626 Peter Minuit arrived at Manhattan Island and, with other Dutch settlers, bought the island from the local Indians for $24 worth of goods. The settlement and fort on the island became known as New Amsterdam and would eventually be called New York City. New Amsterdam was granted self-government and was incorporated by the Dutch in 1653.

In 1664, after King Charles II decided to reclaim the territory between Virginia and New England, **Peter Stuyvesant** surrendered to English forces, and New Amsterdam was given to the King's brother, the Duke of York. The area was renamed New York.

In 1632, Charles I granted a **Maryland Charter to Lord Baltimore** (George Calvert, Baron of Baltimore). Lord Baltimore wanted very much to see the colony become a reality, and his son Cecil saw to it that the new colony was settled. In 1633 the first group of settlers set sail for Maryland to establish a colony led by Leonard Calvert, Cecil Calvert's younger brother.

While scattered Europeans began to settle the area of present-day Rhode Island as early as 1620, the first permanent settlement was not established until 1636. In 1635 **Roger Williams** was driven from Salem, Massachusetts for espousing religious and political freedom. After spending the winter with the local Native Americans, he bought land from the Narragansett Indians and settled in what is now called Providence. The new colony became a haven for those seeking religious freedom.

In 1638 Anne Hutchinson, an intellectual who believed that God revealed himself to individuals without the aid of clergy, was tried and banned from Massachusetts. John Winthrop was leery of Hutchinson's views and cautioned that women could do irreparable damage to their brains by pondering deep theological matters—a view not uncommon for the day. Tried in court for her nonconformist beliefs and banished from Massachusetts, Anne Hutchinson joined other dissenters in Portsmouth, Rhode Island.

The colony of **Rhode Island** was established in 1663, receiving the Royal Charter of Rhode Island and Providence Plantations. Among other unique guarantees, the charter established complete religious freedom in Rhode Island, which was unusual at the time, and later formed the basis for similar provisions in the U.S. Constitution.

Although Rhode Island was one of the first colonies to embrace autonomy from the British and espouse revolutionary ideals, it was the last of the 13 colonies to ratify the federal Constitution and did not become a state until 1790.

Dutch traders had established a permanent settlement near Hartford as early as 1633. Soon English settlers began to arrive in the area from Massachusetts. In 1636, after being driven from Massachusetts, clergyman **Thomas Hooker** and his followers arrived in Hartford and declared freedom from all save, (except), Divine Authority. In 1639 the **Fundamental Orders** were enacted to govern the colony. In 1662 **Connecticut** finally obtained a royal charter under John Winthrop Jr.

South Carolina's outer banks were the scene of the first British colonizing efforts in North America. Both attempts in the late 1500s to form a colony on Roanoke Island did not succeed.

Virginia colonists began to settle the **North Carolina** region in 1653 to provide a buffer for the southern frontier. In 1691 Albermarle, the northern Carolina region, was officially recognized by the English crown. This is the first time the "North Carolina" designation was used.

South Carolina was the site of the first European settlement in North America. In 1526 San Miguel de Gualdape was established by settlers from Hispaniola in an area of the Carolina region that would eventually become Georgia. The party returned to Hispaniola after suffering many deaths from fever the first year.

In 1663 King Charles II created the colony of Carolina (named for King Charles II) by granting to loyal supporters the territory of what is now roughly North Carolina, South Carolina, and Georgia. This colonial charter was challenged by many Virginians who had settled in Albermarle Sound and resented their inclusion in the Carolina charter. Charleston (originally Charles Town, after the king) was founded in 1670 by a group of 200 colonists from English Barbados. The leader of the colonists was **Sir John Yeamans**, a powerful plantation owner on Barbados.

As early as 1647, settlement occurred on what is now **Pennsylvania** soil by Swedish, Dutch, and English settlers in the Delaware River region. In 1681, however, Pennsylvania's colonial status was sealed when the land roughly comprising the present state of Pennsylvania was granted to **William Penn**, a member of the Society of Friends (Quakers), to offset a debt owed to Penn's father. In 1682 the city plan for Philadelphia was laid out and the **Frame of Government** for Pennsylvania was put into effect. In 1683 the first German settlers arrived in Pennsylvania and formed Germantown near Philadelphia.

In 1763 Charles Mason and Jeremiah Dixon, two young British astronomers, were commissioned to establish a borderline between Maryland and Pennsylvania. They worked for more than four years to settle a century-old boundary dispute between the Calverts of Maryland and the Penns of Pennsylvania. This was done by establishing the Mason-Dixon Line.

There were a few Spanish settlements along the coast north of Florida in the sixteenth and early seventeenth centuries, but what is now **Georgia** was originally just the southern portion of the Carolina grant. Hoping to provide a second chance for adventurous members of the English underclass, King George II granted Georgia to **James Edward Oglethorpe**, an English general, in 1732. In addition to its lofty social goals, the new colony was intended to provide protection for its northern colonial partners. Before Oglethorpe and his party settled the area in 1733, Fort King George was the only English occupation in the area. The fort, which was established in 1721, was the southernmost post in the colonies and was situated to provide a buffer against Spanish and French intrusion from the south.

In 1738 General Oglethorpe brought a large military contingent to Georgia, and the following year his troops provided a strong showing against the Spanish in King George's War. General Oglethorpe led his men into Saint Augustine, and although they were not able to obtain a victory there, when the Spanish sailed into Georgia seeking retaliation two years later, he and his soldiers were able to drive the Spanish back to Florida for what turned out to be the last time.

Analyze the causes, events, consequences, and significant individuals of the revolutionary era.

Although it would be hard to point to any one event that singularly led to the American Revolution, war was inevitable given the juxtaposition of the American view that they were entitled to the full democratic rights of Englishmen and the British view that the American colonies were just territories to be used and exploited in whatever way best suited the Crown. The revolutionary era started with the French and Indian War and ended with the Declaration of Independence in 1776.

In the **French and Indian War** (also known as the **Seven Years' War**), the British fought against the French, Austrians, and Spanish. The war raged across the globe. In America it started inauspiciously. **George Washington** was forced to surrender Fort Necessity in the Ohio Valley in 1754. In the following year the British general Edward Braddock attempted to attack the French-held Fort Duquesne. British troops were ambushed by the French and the Indians, and Braddock was mortally wounded. It fell on George Washington to extricate both British and colonial forces from the wilderness.

In 1758 **William Pitt** came out of retirement and took over the British war effort. He directed additional military actions in the North American war theater. He also gave the colonists much greater independence in pursuing the war effort, thus increasing the enthusiasm among colonists toward the war.

In 1764 the British for the first time imposed a series of taxes designed specifically to raise revenue from the colonies. The tax, named the **American Revenue Act**, became popularly known as the **Sugar Act**. One of its major components was the raising of tariff on sugar. The act was combined with a greater attempt to enforce the existing tariffs.

The British, led by **Prime Minister George Greenville**, believed that the colonists should share the burden of sustaining British troops in the colonies. Greenville's first action was to order the navy to enforce the Navigation Acts. He then secured from the British Parliament passage of the Sugar Act. Colonial protests forced the British to scale back the tariff on sugar. The subsequently enacted **Quartering Act** forced colonists to provide housing and food for British troops.

In 1765 the **Stamp Tax** was enacted. It imposed a tax on all legal documents (marriage licenses, newspapers, and 47 other types of documents). The colonists responded with vocal protests. The tax not only hurt their pocketbooks but also was highly visible (i.e., the taxed documents were needed for everyday transactions). In addition, to enforce the tax, the British announced that colonial protesters were to be tried in the hated admiralty courts. Nevertheless, protesters increased in number and began developing new slogans, including "**No taxation without representation**."

FTCE Fact

The Stamp Act imposed a tax on all legal documents.

One result of the protests was the meeting of the Stamp Act Congress in New York, to which many of the colonies sent representatives. Participants at the congress generally agreed to boycott all British imports until the Stamp Tax was repealed. Another reaction to the Stamp Act was the creation of the secret organization known as the **Sons of Liberty**. Led by prominent citizens, the group resorted to coercion to force stamp agents to resign their posts.

In the summer of 1766, **King George III** of England replaced **Prime Minister Rockingham** with **William Pitt**. Pitt was popular in the colonies. He opposed the Stamp Act and believed that colonists were entitled to all the rights of English citizens.

But Pitt suddenly became sick, and **Charles Townshend**, the chancellor of the exchequer, effectively took over the reins of the government. Unlike Pitt, Townshend was not concerned with the subtleties of the rights of American colonists. Townshend wanted to strengthen the power of the British Parliament, which would simultaneously strengthen the power of royal officials. He convinced the Parliament to pass a series of laws imposing new taxes on the colonists. The laws included special taxes on lead, paint, paper, glass, and tea imported by colonists. In addition, the New York legislature was suspended until it agreed to quarter British soldiers. Called the **Townshend Acts**, the laws also ensured that colonial officials, including governors and judges, would receive their salaries directly from the Crown.

The most tangible colonial protest to the Townshend Acts was the revival of an agreement not to import British goods, especially luxury products. The nonimportation agreement slowly grew to include merchants in all the colonies, with the exception of New Hampshire. Within a year importation of British goods dropped almost in half.

In response to colonial protest and increasing attacks on colonial officials by the Sons of Liberty, Lord Hillsborough, the secretary of state for the colonies, dispatched 4,000 troops to restore order in Boston. The daily contact between British soldiers and colonists served to worsen relations.

An armed clash between the British and the colonists was almost inevitable from the moment British troops were introduced in Boston. Brawls were frequent between the British and colonists who were constantly insulting the troops.

On March 5, 1770, a crowd of 60 townspeople surrounded British sentries guarding the customs house. They began pelting snowballs at the guards. Suddenly a shot rang out, followed by several others. Ultimately, 11 colonists were hit. Five died, including **Crispus Attucks**, a former slave.

The British Parliament repealed the duties on all imported goods but tea. Falling colonial imports and rising opposition convinced the British government that its policies were not working. Led by Prime Minister Lord North, Parliament maintained the taxes on tea to underscore the supremacy of Great Britain.

Protests in the colonies against the Stamp Act had barely died down when Parliament passed the Tea Act. The new act granted a monopoly on tea trade in the Americas to the

East India Tea Company. The governor of Massachusetts, Thomas Hutchinson, insisted that tea be unloaded in Boston, despite a boycott organized by the Sons of Liberty.

On the evening of December 16, thousands of Bostonians and farmers from the surrounding countryside packed into the Old South Meeting House to hear **Samuel Adams** speak. Adams denounced the governor for denying clearance for vessels wishing to leave with tea still on board. After the speech the crowd headed for the waterfront. From the crowd 50 individuals emerged dressed as Indians. They boarded three vessels docked in the harbor and threw 90,000 pounds of tea overboard.

The British were shocked by the destruction of the tea in Boston Harbor and other colonial protests. Parliament gave its speedy assent to a series of acts that became known as the **Coercive Acts**, or the **Intolerable Acts**. One result of the acts was the closing of the Port of Boston until the East India Company received compensation for the tea dumped into the harbor. The royal governor took control over the Massachusetts government and declared it would appoint all officials. Sheriffs would become royal appointees, as would juries. In addition, the British took the right to quarter soldiers anywhere in the colonies.

Evaluate the issues associated with the constitutional era and the early republic.

The **First Continental Congress** met in Philadelphia from September 5 to October 26, 1774. Representatives from each colony except Georgia met in Philadelphia. The royal governor in Georgia succeeded in blocking delegates from being sent to the congress.

The representatives gathered to plan their response to the Intolerable Acts. They met to discuss their relationship with Britain and how to assert their rights with the British government. They wanted to appear as united colonies in their reply to Britain.

The purpose of the first congress was not to seek independence from Britain. The congress had three objectives: to compose a statement of colonial rights, to identify the British Parliament's violation of those rights, and to provide a plan that would convince Britain to restore those rights. The members agreed to boycott British goods and passed resolutions asserting colonial rights. They also agreed to meet again in May 1775 if the British did not change their policies.

In retaliation, King George III and the prime minister, Lord North, decided to punish and weaken the colonies by blocking their access to the North Atlantic fishing area.

The first battles of the American Revolution were fought near the Massachusetts townships of **Lexington** and **Concord**. Soon after, on May 10, 1776, the **Second Continental Congress** convened for the first time in Philadelphia, Pennsylvania, at the State House (now called Independence Hall).

The second congress had a few delegates that had not been at the first. Among the 65 delegates were **Thomas Jefferson**, **Benjamin Franklin**, and the congress' new president, **John Hancock**. Thomas Jefferson was a plantation owner and a lawyer who was well known as a writer. Benjamin Franklin wanted independence, but many delegates disagreed. Even after the battles of Lexington and Concord, they were not ready to break away from Great Britain.

The delegates of the Second Continental Congress reached many important decisions, including completely breaking away from Great Britain. On May 15, 1776, they decided to officially put the colonies in a state of defense. The day that the Second Continental Congress met, **Ethan Allen** and **Benedict Arnold** had captured Fort Ticonderoga on Lake Champlain in New York.

Another decision made at the second congress was to better organize the militia of the colonies. They formed an army known as the American Continental Army. On June 14, 1776, the congress officially appointed George Washington as commander in chief of the army. He was elected unanimously. George Washington knew that the army would face great difficulty. He later wrote that Americans were "not then organized as a nation, or known as a people upon the earth. We had no preparation. Money, the nerve of war, was wanting." Great Britain was the most powerful nation on the earth. It was a frightening thought that the Continental Army might need to fight Great Britain.

FTCE Fact

The Second Continental Congress was one of the most important government meetings in the history of the United States.

The second congress also discussed whether to print paper money. That proposal passed, and the printing of paper money started later in the year. The Second Continental Congress was one of the most important government meetings in the history of the United States. It decided some of the most important ideas that the colonists fought for in the Revolutionary War, because members of the second congress wrote and signed the Declaration of Independence. John Hancock's signature was the first and biggest on the Declaration of Independence.

The **Articles of Confederation** was the first governing document of the United States of America. Written in the summer of 1777, the articles were adopted by the Second Continental Congress on November 15, 1777, in York, Pennsylvania, after a year of debate, and gained final ratification on March 1, 1781. At that point the Continental Congress became the Congress of the Confederation. The articles set the rules for operations of the confederation, a loose association of the states. The confederation was capable of making war, negotiating diplomatic agreements, and resolving issues regarding the western territories; it could print money and borrow inside and outside the confederation.

Compared with its successor, the U.S. Constitution, the Articles of Confederation provided stronger protection of individual liberty. Thus, from the libertarian point of view, they were better than the Constitution, but from the state point of view, they were weaker. One major issue was that the articles did not establish a taxing authority for the central government; the federal government had to request funds from the states. A second concern was the provision mandating one vote for every state in the Congress of the Confederation. The larger states were expected to contribute more but had only one vote, although they could remedy this by dividing into smaller states. The articles created a mutual defense confederation designed to manage the American Revolutionary War.

When the war ended in 1783, special interests conspired to create a new "merchant state," much like the British government against which the colonists had rebelled. In particular, holders of war script and land speculators wanted a central government to pay off script at face value and to legalize western land holdings with disputed claims. Many of the participants in the closed Constitutional Convention were script and/or land speculators. Also, manufacturers wanted a high tariff as a barrier to foreign goods, but competition among states made this impossible without a central government. The articles were replaced by the more centralist and authoritarian Constitution on June 21, 1788.

In May 1787, 55 men from 12 states met in Philadelphia to revise the Articles of Confederation. At the outset, however, Governor Edmund Randolph of Virginia presented a plan prepared by James Madison for the design of an entirely new national government. The proposed plan would lead to a four-month process of argument, debate, compromise, and the development of the Constitution of the United States. On September 17, 1787, the final draft of the Constitution was read to the 42 delegates still at the convention. Of the 42 men present, 39 affixed their signatures to the document and notified the Congress of the Confederation that their work was finished. The congress, in turn, submitted the document to the states for ratification, where more argument, debate, and compromise would take place. The state of Delaware was the first to ratify the Constitution. Just nine months after the state ratification process had begun, New Hampshire became the ninth state to ratify, putting the Constitution into effect.

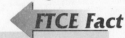

FTCE Fact

The Constitution of the United States took effect in 1788 when it was ratified by New Hampshire.

In the two centuries since its ratification, many changes have been made to the Constitution. However, the basic premises on which the Constitution was framed—the protection of individual rights and liberties, limited government with separation of powers and checks and balances, the federal system, and judicial review—remain at the heart of the "living" document.

The *Federalist Papers* serve as a primary source for interpreting the Constitution. The collection of essays outlines the philosophy and motivation of the proposed system of government. The authors of the *Federalist Papers* wanted to influence the vote in favor of ratification and to shape future interpretations of the Constitution. Each of the 85 essays that make up the *Federalist Papers* was signed "Publius." Although historians still argue about the actual authors of some essays, the general consensus is that 52 were written by Alexander Hamilton, 28 by James Madison, and 5 by John Jay. The *Federalist Papers* is still an excellent reference for anyone wanting to understand the U.S. Constitution.

Evaluate the impact of westward expansion on the cultural, political, and economic development of the emerging nation.

Manifest Destiny was the doctrine used to rationalize U.S. territorial expansion in the 1840s and 1850s. It asserted that expansion of the United States throughout the American continents was both justified and inevitable. The phrase was coined by the U.S. journalist John L. O'Sullivan and was initially used in regard to Mexican and Indian land in Texas and the Southwest. The concept was invoked later in a dispute with Great Britain over Oregon and in relation to territory controlled by the United States as a result of the Spanish-American War.

After an extensive survey of the land west of the Appalachian Mountains, the so-called Northwest Territory, Congress enacted the Northwest Ordinance of 1787, the single most important piece of legislation in the confederation period. The ordinance provided the means by which new states would be created out of the western lands and then admitted into the Union. Governors and judges appointed by Congress would rule a territory until it contained 5,000 free male inhabitants of voting age; then the inhabitants would elect a territorial legislature, which would send a nonvoting delegate to Congress. When the population reached 60,000, the legislature would submit a state constitution to Congress and, on its approval, the state would enter the Union.

The importance of the statute, aside from providing for orderly westward settlement, is that it clarified that the new states would be equal to the old; there would be no inferior or superior states in the Union. Moreover, in the ordinance, Congress assured the settlers of the territories that they would be equal citizens of the United States and would enjoy all the rights fought for in the Revolution. Unlike the Articles of Confederation, the ordinance provided a bill of rights that included many of the basic liberties the colonists had considered essential, such as trial by jury, habeas corpus, and religious freedom. Of note, however, was the important role that property still played in government, a holdover from British theory that only people with a tangible stake in society should partake in its governance. The Northwest Ordinance would, with minor adjustments, remain the guiding policy for the admission of all future states into the Union.

By a treaty signed on April 30, 1803, the United States purchased from France the Louisiana Territory, more than 800,000 square miles of land extending from the Mississippi River to the Rocky Mountains. The price was about $15 million; $11.25 million was to be paid directly, with the balance to be covered by the assumption by the United States of French debts to American citizens.

In 1762 France had ceded Louisiana to Spain, but by the secret Treaty of San Ildefonso (1800) the French regained the area. Napoleon Bonaparte (the future Emperor Napoleon I) envisioned a great French empire in the New World, and he hoped to use the Mississippi Valley as a food and trade center to supply the island of Hispaniola, which was to be the heart of that empire. First, however, he had to restore French control of Hispaniola, where Haitian slaves under Toussaint Louverture had seized power. In 1802 a large army sent by Napoleon under his brother-in-law, Charles Le Clerc, arrived on the island to suppress the Haitian rebellion. Despite some military success, the French lost thousands of soldiers, mainly to yellow fever, and Napoleon soon realized that Hispaniola must be abandoned. Without that island he had little use for Louisiana. Facing renewed war with Great Britain, he could not spare troops to defend the territory; moreover, he needed funds to support his military ventures in Europe. Accordingly, in April 1803 he offered to sell Louisiana to the United States.

Concerned about French intentions, President Thomas Jefferson had already sent James Monroe and Robert R. Livingston to Paris to negotiate the purchase of a tract of land on the lower Mississippi, or at least a guarantee of free navigation on the river. Surprised and delighted by the French offer of the whole territory, the Americans immediately negotiated the treaty with the French.

At one stroke the United States would double its size, an enormous tract of land would be open to settlement, and the free navigation of the Mississippi would be assured. Although the Constitution did not specifically empower the federal government to acquire new territory by treaty, Jefferson concluded that the practical benefits to the nation far outweighed any possible violation of the Constitution. The Senate concurred with this decision and voted ratification on October 20, 1803. The Spanish, who had never given up physical possession of Louisiana to the French, did so in a ceremony at New Orleans in November that year. In a second ceremony on December 20, 1803, the French turned Louisiana over to the United States.

FTCE Fact

The Louisiana Purchase doubled the size of the United States.

The Spanish settled what is today Mexico. As the American colonists had done against Great Britain nearly 50 years earlier, the Mexicans fought for and won independence from Spain in 1821. Within about a decade, conflict erupted between the two newly formed countries as a direct result of different national policies. The United States had a policy of westward expansion, Manifest Destiny, while Mexico had a policy of self-protection. The Americans believed that the United States had the right to expand westward to the Pacific Ocean, while the newer nation of Mexico was primarily concerned with protecting itself from outside powers. Therefore, one of the strongest examples of Manifest Destiny is the Mexican-American War. From the beginning the United States considered the war an opportunity for land expansion, and Mexico feared those expansionist goals.

To protect its northern borders, Mexico needed to populate the area. The Mexican government continued the policy started by Spain of allowing Americans to settle Texas.

The Americans had to follow Mexican law, religion, and customs. The settlement of Texas played into the United States' expansionist plans.

Eventually, Mexico closed Texas to prevent more Americans from entering. This angered the Americans wanting to enter as well as Americans already living in Texas. Texas revolted against Mexico in 1833. After gaining independence from Mexico, Texas wanted to join the Union immediately, but the U.S. Congress voted against it. Congress was worried that annexation of Texas would anger Mexico, which had never officially recognized Texas as independent, and lead to war. In addition, if Texas were to become a state, it would be a slave state. At the time the United States had an even balance between slave and free states. Texas entering the Union would disrupt the balance, giving slave states an advantage in both the House and Senate. Because the United States was not ready to annex Texas, Texas declared itself a sovereign country. In 1837 President Andrew Jackson formally recognized Texas as a country.

However, most Texans wanted to be part of the United States and be able to enjoy the protections that the federal government provided states. President John Tyler could not get the two-thirds majority needed to admit Texas. Instead, he changed the law to require only a simple majority. It was not until 1845 and two presidents later that Texas was annexed into the United States. Mexico protested the admission of Texas into the United States, a protest that the United States saw as an excuse to send troops into Texas.

The Mexican-American War lasted two years and ended with the signing of the Treaty of Guadalupe on February 2, 1848. The United States had succeeded in winning the war and, with the Treaty of Guadalupe, succeeded in fulfilling its Manifest Destiny. The treaty itself represented U.S. expansionist goals. Bankrupt from the war, Mexico agreed to $15 million as payment for the vast land. In addition, the United States agreed to forgive all Mexican debts.

A few years later it was discovered that the boundary information in the Treaty of Guadalupe was inaccurate. Diplomatic tension followed. In 1853 the United States negotiated with Mexico to resolve the boundary dispute that resulted at the termination of the Mexican War and to purchase the land in question. In what became known as the Gadsden Purchase, the United States paid $10 million for a strip of territory south of the Gila River in what is now southwestern New Mexico and southern Arizona.

Identify the cultural, political, and economic characteristics of the antebellum era.

Antebellum is a Latin word meaning "before war." In United States history and historiography, the term *antebellum* is often used to refer to the period of increasing sectionalism leading to the American Civil War, instead of the term *pre–Civil War*. In that context the antebellum period is often thought to have begun with the Kansas-Nebraska Act of 1854, although sometimes it is defined as extending as far back as 1812. The period after the Civil War is called the postbellum or Reconstruction era.

In the decades before the Civil War, diverging economies contributed to growing sectional differences between the North and South. Between 1790 and 1860, commercial agriculture replaced subsistence agriculture in the North, and household production was replaced by factory production. Massive foreign immigration from Ireland and Germany greatly increased the populations of cities. In the South, slavery impeded the development of industry and cities and discouraged technological innovation.

During the 1850s the nation's political system became incapable of resolving sectional disputes between the North and South. The acquisition of vast new territories during the 1840s reignited the issue of whether slavery would be allowed to expand into the western territories.

The Compromise of 1850 was an attempt to solve this problem by admitting California as a free state but permitting slavery in the rest of the Southwest. But the compromise included a fugitive slave law opposed by many Northerners. The **Kansas-Nebraska Act** proposed to solve the problem of the status of territories by allowing the settlers to decide whether or not to have slavery, in the name of popular sovereignty. But that led to violent conflict in Kansas and the rise of the Republican Party.

The ***Dred Scott* decision** eliminated possible compromise solutions to the sectional conflict, and John Brown's raid on Harpers Ferry convinced many Southerners that a majority of Northerners wanted to free the slaves and incite a race war.

Free blacks in the antebellum period were outspoken about the injustice of slavery. Their ability to express themselves, however, was determined by whether they lived in the North or the South. Free southern blacks continued to live under the shadow of slavery, unable to travel or assemble as freely as those in the North. It was also more difficult for free blacks in the South to organize and sustain churches, schools, and fraternal orders like the Masons.

Although their lives were circumscribed by numerous discriminatory laws even in the colonial period, freed African Americans, especially in the North, were active participants in American society. Black men enlisted as soldiers and fought in the American Revolution and the War of 1812. Some owned land, homes, and businesses and paid taxes. During brief periods in some northern cities, black property owners voted. A small number of free blacks owned slaves. Although the slaves that most free blacks purchased were relatives whom they later manumitted (released from slavery), a few owned slave-worked plantations in Louisiana, Virginia, and South Carolina.

Free African American Christians established their own churches, which became hubs of the economic, social, and intellectual lives of blacks in many areas of the fledgling nation. Blacks were also outspoken in print. *Freedom's Journal*, the first black-owned newspaper, began operation in 1827. It and other early writings by blacks fueled the attack against slavery and racist conceptions of the intellectual inferiority of African Americans.

African Americans also engaged in achieving freedom for others, which was a complex and dangerous undertaking. Enslaved blacks and their white sympathizers planned secret flight strategies and escape routes for runaways to make their way to freedom. Although it was neither subterranean nor a mechanized means of travel, the network of routes and hiding places was known as the underground railroad. Some free blacks were active "conductors" on the underground railroad, while others simply harbored runaways in their homes. Free people of color such as Richard Allen, Frederick Douglass, Sojourner Truth, David Walker, and Prince Hall earned national reputations by writing, speaking, organizing, and agitating on behalf of their enslaved compatriots.

Thousands of freed blacks, with the aid of interested whites, returned to Africa with the aid of the American Colonization Society and colonized what eventually became Liberia. While some African Americans chose this option, most considered themselves Americans and focused their efforts on achieving equality within the United States.

Agrarians such as Thomas Jefferson believed that agriculture was the most beneficial and productive of all human activities. Men like him feared the nation becoming dominated by industrial workers and city dwellers. Farmers and farms held center stage in the antebellum world, because by as late as 1850 they accounted for 85 percent of the population. Early and heavy immigration by whites into New England, New York, New Jersey, and Pennsylvania created conditions that led to rapid population growth and family farming. The South had slave labor and landed aristocracy; the rest of the nation lacked both.

Over the decades, differences between the northern and western states and the southern states increased. Perhaps the most distinctive difference was slavery. Certainly it was the most contentious. By 1850 nearly 37 percent of Southerners were slaves, and in South Carolina slaves were the majority. Conflict between the slavery-based agricultural system of the South and the family farm–based system of the North and West led to both intellectual and political conflict.

People from New England, Pennsylvania, and New York were the chief settlers of the Midwest. Southerners chiefly settled in Kentucky, Tennessee, Alabama, Mississippi, Louisiana, Arkansas, and Texas. Although not dominant, a number of Southerners settled in Southern Indiana, Ohio, and Illinois. New Englanders and immigrants from Europe were heavily represented in the Great Lakes states. By 1860 the population of the new northern states beyond the Appalachian Mountains exceeded that of new southern states beyond the Appalachians. Although most immigrants sought farmland, many who moved to the Far West were miners seeking gold in California and Colorado.

Improvements in transportation, such as the Erie Canal and rail lines, enabled farmers by 1860 to buy more than twice as many manufactured products with a given output as they could have in 1820.

In 1815, when New York's population surpassed that of the previously largest state, Virginia, tobacco's prospects were declining because American tobacco had lost a large part of its market to Turkey. Early immigrants to a new area typically improved the land and then sold it and moved farther West. As the soil became exhausted, the latecomers moved west to lands opened by pioneers. "Old stock" Americans (descendants of early settlers) made up the majority of the pioneer farmers moving westward from the older states, taking with them their tools, equipment, and livestock. Penniless immigrants from Europe settled in eastern cities and became wageworkers.

Setbacks in tobacco cultivation were the result of much of the suitable land wearing out, the slave trade closing, and cotton cultivation increasing and causing slave prices to rise. It became more profitable for many Virginians to sell their slaves to cotton planters in the lower South than to employ them in Virginia to raise tobacco. Although slaves were removed from the tobacco fields and used in cultivating cotton instead, they were not removed from plantations cultivating sugar, an important crop along the Gulf Coast.

Before 1790 wool dominated the textile industry. Once a cheap method for removing seeds was developed, however, cotton quickly replaced wool. As a result, cotton cultivation swept away cattle, indigo, and pine trees through much of the Piedmont South. The cotton gin made producing cotton cheap enough that the average person could afford cotton clothing. Moreover, the new technology transferred the center of cotton growing from the coast, where long-staple cotton was grown, to the interior of the South, where short-staple cotton, from which seeds are harder to remove, was grown. By 1840 the center of cotton cultivation had shifted to the west, and Mississippi alone produced more than Georgia and South Carolina combined. Planting much of the cotton in Alabama, Mississippi, and Louisiana were men who had moved there after wearing out the land they had earlier farmed in the older cotton states.

FTCE Fact

Eli Whitney's cotton gin changed the focus of crop cultivation in the South.

Cotton was an almost perfect crop for the lower South. It was easy to grow, and its demands were met by the region's climate and soil. In the region between the cotton South and the wheat North, the main crop was corn. Cattle, hemp, and tobacco were produced in the vicinity of Lexington, Kentucky; Nashville and Knoxville, Tennessee; and what is now Charleston, West Virginia. Corn was also a widely planted crop in these hilly regions.

Northern farmers did not need as much labor as did southern farmers because the crops grown in the North, grains, were not as labor intensive as cotton, rice, sugar, and tobacco. Also, mechanical methods of harvesting grains were developed early because they were simpler to build than the machines needed to harvest southern crops. Although the South has often been branded as backward because of its less-developed transportation system, less urbanization, and less industrialization, the per capita income of its free citizens in the antebellum period seems to have grown just about as fast as it did in the rest of the country. The antebellum South was successfully feeding its people and exporting very large amounts of its agricultural output.

The cash crops of the North—wheat, corn, oats, hogs, and cattle—were also subsistence crops. This was not true of cotton, the South's chief cash crop. Therefore, unlike the southern farmer, the northern farmer participating in the market economy (cash cropping) only had to extend the same activities he would pursue anyway to feed his family. The cotton farmer, on the other hand, distributed his resources between growing cotton for cash and growing corn, hogs, cattle, and other foods to be used for subsistence. The typical slave-state farm in 1860 had a value of $7,101. In the free states the average farm was worth $3,311. Slave owners constituted the wealthiest class in the nation. The average slave owner was more than five times as wealthy as the average Northerner and more than 10 times as wealthy as the average Southerner without slaves.

Improved transportation and the resulting competition from western farmers caused farmers in the Northeast to reduce their production of grain and shift to dairy farming and truck gardening, both of which provided them with products to sell to city dwellers that would not face competition from western farmers. Therefore, thanks to improvements in transportation and communications, the antebellum period saw national markets developing for western farmers and eastern manufacturers, thereby stimulating both.

From 1783 to 1815 the nation's financial system was only a bit more complicated than during colonial times. Capital was primarily invested in local business ventures. Only a few corporations existed, and they were in endeavors such as canals and banks. The interruption of foreign credit flows during the Revolution forced American merchants to create their own financial institutions. Banking was the chief political issue at both the state and national level until the 1840s, when the slavery issue began to heat up.

From the start, banking in the United States was conducted on the basis of fractional reserves. In the antebellum period bank reserves consisted of gold and silver. Fractional reserve banking allows banks to create money. They do so by making loans. For example, if you deposit $100 in gold in a bank in exchange for a $100 demand deposit, $100 less money is in circulation in the form of coins but $100 more in checkbook money; therefore, the amount of money in circulation has not changed. Because your bank has to keep on hand only a fraction of the $100 in reserves you have provided—say, $10—it loans the other $90 to someone. Now the amount of money in circulation has increased by $90.

During the antebellum period the federal government minted gold and silver coins, and commercial banks provided paper money. Banks issued bank notes in exchange for gold and silver or customers' promissory notes. The amount of domestically produced gold expanded substantially in the antebellum period. It first grew significantly when gold was discovered in Georgia. Gold output expanded even more when gold was discovered in California and then in Colorado. Another source of gold was foreign trade.

The nation's first commercial bank, the Bank of North America, was founded in Philadelphia in 1781. It did not take long for commercial banks to come to dominate the banking business. While today they only issue checkbook money, in the antebellum period they issued all our currency (bank notes and paper money). Unlike previous American banks, called private banks, the Bank of North America was incorporated.

By 1790 commercial banks had been established in Philadelphia, New York, Boston, and Baltimore. By 1800 at least one chartered bank could be found in every state but Vermont, Georgia, North Carolina, and New Jersey. In the nation's early years, commercial banks accounted for the majority of its financial intermediaries.

The first banks were established to underwrite the trading activities of merchants. In the colonial and early national periods, mercantile activity was almost the only economic activity going on in America besides agriculture. The loans these banks made were short term because that was what merchants needed. However, by the 1840s the growing demand for long-term financing by transportation companies, manufacturers, and southern planters led to more banks making long-term loans. Difficulties they encountered during the depressed early 1840s caused some states to forbid banks from making many long-term loans.

The cornerstone of nineteenth-century banking was what is called either the real-bills doctrine or the commercial loan doctrine. The theory behind the doctrine was that if a bank only made productive, short-term, self-liquidating loans, bank notes would expand and contract in step with trade; thus, there would be no inflation or deflation. Although the doctrine was widely accepted, banks often did not follow it. A short-term, self-liquidating loan is expected to be quickly repayable through the proceeds of the sale of what was acquired with the borrowed money. Loans to finance retail inventories are an example.

The belief behind the commercial loan doctrine is that by lending only to finance the production or sale of already-produced goods, the price level could rise only briefly, because additional goods would soon be on the market to absorb the money created by the making of the loan. After the goods were sold, the money supply would shrink because the loan would then be repaid. That theory would not have worked even if all banks had followed it, because businesses that wanted, for instance, to get the money to build a new store would simply tell its bank that it was borrowing the money for the inventory of an existing store. If the bank did not make the loan, the business would buy the inventories anyway with cash on hand. If the loan was made, there would be no more goods on the market than there otherwise would have been, but the money supply would be greater.

A characteristic of American banking that set it apart from banking in the rest of the world, and one that has had a significant impact on the timing and direction of economic development in this country, is that states have often limited the areas in which banks can operate. As a result, although a state might have many banks relative to its population, most of those banks could be monopolies or near monopolies.

Another distinguishing characteristic of the monetary system was the fact that it was a bimetallic standard; that is, the federal government minted two types of specie (coins), gold and silver. The problem with the bimetallic standard was that periodically one or the other type of specie would stop circulating because the metals' relative market prices varied from the ratio of the price in silver the mint paid for gold to the price in gold it paid for silver. Sometimes people could profit by taking gold to a government mint and exchanging it for silver; other times the reverse was true. The government, of course, could only mint what was being brought to it, so that was what was available to circulate.

The mechanics of bank lending in the antebellum period differed significantly from that of today, but the economic effects of their operations were the same. Back then, in exchange for their promissory notes or mortgages, borrowers received bank notes (paper money). Today a borrower gets a deposit on which checks can be written. Like paper money, checks are part of the money supply. Checks did not come into wide use until the late nineteenth century.

Most bank notes circulated at a discount (below face value). That is, although a merchant would, for instance, accept a $10 gold piece for some merchandise, he would charge more than $10 if offered bank notes. The more doubtful a merchant was that a bank would redeem its notes, either because the merchant was familiar with the bank's bad record or knew little about it, the greater the discount. Bank notes from a distant bank would carry the highest discount because of the lack of knowledge about the bank and the cost of presenting those notes to it for redemption. Counterfeiting was a significant problem because nobody could be familiar with the appearance of the many different banks' notes in circulation and because making good counterfeit money was easy.

Many people distrusted banks, believing them to be engines of inflation that profited a few and harmed everybody else. In some states the hostility to banks was so intense that the institutions were banned. Antibank sentiment was most common in the West and least common in the Northeast. Other states sought to take control of banking by creating a state banking monopoly or near monopoly. According to their critics, banks increased the incidence of usury, diverted funds from agriculture, and drove specie out of circulation and out of the country.

After the 1830s so many people were so suspicious of banks that seven states outlawed them. Only private banks that did not issue bank notes operated in those states. Some commercial banks were established in other states (including Georgia) with the intention of circulating most of their notes in the seven states. These banks were called wildcat banks, supposedly because they were located in the backwoods where wildcats roamed. People who received notes from wildcat banks were not expected to show up asking that they be redeemed.

During the antebellum period state regulation of banking gradually increased. States set ceilings on the ratio of the bank notes (paper money) a bank issued to its specie (coin) reserves and on the ratio of its deposits and bank notes to the capital invested by its owners. That capital was supposed to be provided in the form of specie. Banks that issued bank notes had to be incorporated; there was no federal regulation. Although the requirement was that banks redeem their bank notes in specie on demand, this was frequently not enforced during money panics—liquidity crises resulting from the public withdrawing gold from banks.

Some states, including New York, established deposit insurance funds that in the long run were not very successful. In the late 1830s, as the nation fell into a depression, a few states tried to remove politics from the process of obtaining a bank charter by passing free-banking laws. If a bank met certain requirements, a state official had to issue it a charter. New York and Georgia were the first to pass free-banking laws, and many free banks were established in the former. Previously, a bank could get a charter only from the state legislature, a process that might require paying the state a subsidy, making it a loan, or bribing legislators.

Assuming a monetary system is well run, trade carried out by the use of money is far more efficient than trade conducted by barter. To prevent a price level decline, the money supply must rise as trade increases because the possible increase in the velocity of money is limited. The equation of exchange explains this:

Money supply × Velocity of money

= Average price per transaction × Number of transactions

Producers suffer when the price level declines because they have to buy inputs at a higher price level than they can sell outputs. Creditors gain, however, because the dollars they receive from debtors have a greater purchasing power than those they loaned. But bad-debt losses rise as a result of producers' profits declining or turning negative.

Inflation is another cause of problems. Inflation discourages saving and investment. Before the Civil War the only time inflation produced serious problems was during the Revolutionary War.

The Bank of the United States was the first federally chartered bank. It was chartered in 1791. Both the federal government and private investors owned stock in the federally chartered bank. The government financed its investment in the bank with a loan from the bank. Today that bank is called the First Bank of the United States to distinguish it from a second bank with the name Bank of the United States that was chartered later in the antebellum period.

The First Bank of the United States tried to control other banks and was the federal government's fiscal agent; that is, the government deposited its funds in the bank, and the bank disbursed funds for the government. It was the nation's most important bank because it was the largest. Regular commercial banking was the source of most of its income. (This is not true of the current central bank, the Federal Reserve System.) The First Bank of the United States made itself a force for bank stability by systematically presenting other banks' notes to them for specie redemption.

Many Southerners did not believe that the First Bank of the United States would benefit them. Therefore, it got its charter because it had a great deal of support in the North. Rural interests on the frontier that needed easy credit, farm debtors, and some businesses desiring easy credit also opposed the First Bank. Opposition arose primarily from the First Bank refusing to accept the bank notes of banks that would not redeem their notes in specie, thus making it difficult for many banks to expand their lending. The

First Bank lost its federal charter, but it continued to operate under a Pennsylvania state charter.

Some banks, like the Suffolk Bank in New England, tried to prevent other banks from issuing bank notes in the same way as the federally chartered banks did, demanding that they redeem their bank notes in gold. (If the ratio of a bank's notes constantly rose relative to its stock of gold, it would eventually be forced out of business because it could not meet redemption demands; thus, taking away some of a bank's holdings of gold would reduce the amount of bank notes it could safely issue.) Preventing inflation was not the Suffolk Bank's only motive. It also saw an opportunity to increase its profits, because banks created bank notes in making loans, and the fewer loans other banks made, the more the Suffolk Bank could make. The Suffolk Bank's success meant that New England bank notes circulated at par throughout New England. This was the only region that was successful in controlling the quantity of its bank notes.

After the First Bank of the United States lost its federal charter, the number of state-chartered banks rose rapidly. By 1816 there were 246 banks. The U.S. Treasury did not attempt to restrain the banks' note issuances, and the number of bank notes in circulation tripled between 1811 and 1816. Demand deposits (checking accounts) also rose. Between 1830 and 1837 the number of state-chartered banks doubled, and their note issue nearly tripled. The business boom those banks financed drove cotton prices from 9 cents to 18 cents per pound.

President Thomas Jefferson tried to prevent war with England by encouraging passage of the Embargo Act (1807), which banned trade with the warring countries of England and France. The act led to the collapse of U.S. foreign trade and was repealed in 1809. The negative impact of the loss of foreign trade was concentrated in New England and port cities. The impact on manufacturing and the subsequent War of 1812 was positive.

FTCE Fact

Fiat money is money simply because the government says that it is.

Financing the War of 1812 was difficult. The federal government did not tax income back then because the levying of taxes directly on individuals was unconstitutional. Therefore, the government had to resort to issuing fiat money—money that is money because the government says it is, not because it is redeemable in gold or silver.

During the War of 1812, the federal government was so financially strapped that the state department could not even afford to pay its stationery bill. It was only the willingness of Secretary of State James Madison to pledge his personal fortune as security that enabled General Andrew Jackson to obtain the funds he needed to move his troops to New Orleans, where U.S. troops had their greatest victory on land of the War of 1812. (Unfortunately, unknown to General Jackson, U.S. diplomats in Europe had already signed a peace treaty.)

The British attack on Washington led to the closure of all the banks in Washington and Baltimore, and the banks in Philadelphia and New York closed shortly thereafter. Only New England banks were able to maintain specie convertibility. Under these circumstance, some opponents of the First Bank of the United States changed their minds. Moreover, people who loaned the United States money to finance the war were very much interested in another Bank of the United States being established, because they thought it would protect their interests.

Most congressmen from the South and West supported chartering a second Bank of the United States, but because of the many large commercial banks in the North, the proposition met with opposition there. However, a second federally chartered bank was established that operated much like the first. State-chartered banks were promised that no sudden resumption of specie redemption would occur—even though that was the objective of those favoring the bank's charter.

What we today call the Second Bank of the United States dealt only in bills of exchange, gold and silver, and the sale of goods pledged as security that were obtained as a result of loan defaults. It issued bank notes and dealt in foreign exchange (foreign currencies). A bill of exchange is an unconditional order in writing drawn on one party by a second party commanding payment to the second or a third party. The firm that the bill of exchange is drawn on has bought on credit from the firm that draws it. Usually, a bill of exchange arises in foreign trade. It is negotiable, so the party drawing it can get cash by selling it before it comes due. It will sell at a discount—that is, less than its value at maturity. A bank bill of exchange is one drawn by an exporter on the importer's bank, which has given its permission for this to be done. A person can pay a creditor by turning over to it a bill of exchange. Southerners who exported cotton to Europe used bills of exchange to pay off Northerners from whom they had purchased manufactured goods.

The Second Bank of the United States was denounced as an antidemocratic monopoly. President Andrew Jackson was suspicious of banks and believed the Second Bank was unconstitutional and too closely associated with a monied oligarchy and foreigners. He vetoed its rechartering, although it continued to operate under a state charter until it failed in 1841 during the depression that began in 1837. After its demise Jackson began putting the federal government's funds in some state-chartered banks, six of which were closely associated with some of his advisers. As a result, they were referred to as his pet banks.

After 1840 New York City became the nation's reserve city. That is, banks elsewhere deposited their surplus gold there. These banks could then offer note redemption in New York, which was the nation's major port and the source of many commercial transactions. New York banks used much of this gold to make call loans—loans that became due whenever the lending bank decided to demand they be repaid. Call loans were usually made to people buying stocks. Because stocks are such risky investments, banks would not lend for their purchase except through call loans.

During the antebellum period some states and cities issued fiat money that was called skin plasters. The name referred to the money not being worth much because it was issued in sufficient amounts to cause it to depreciate rapidly. People were often induced to accept the fiat money because the issuing government would accept it in payment of taxes.

Many historians believe that in the 1800s banks aggravated and accentuated the ups and downs of the business cycle by offering credit (loans) liberally during the upswing of the cycle, when their specie reserves were high, and drastically reducing the amount of credit during the downswing. Changes in the levels of banks' reserves in the antebellum period were closely correlated to fluctuations in exports and imports. All else being equal, banks' specie reserves would rise when exports (mostly agricultural commodities, primarily cotton) and/or their prices rose and would decline when the reverse took place. Rising imports and/or their prices would diminish banks' reserves, and vice versa.

Some have blamed the Second Bank of the United States for not preventing inflation in 1817 and 1818. Then, they complain, it caused a contraction from 1818 to 1820 by refusing to accept the notes of state banks that would not redeem them and reducing its lending. Only a Supreme Court decision prevented some states from shutting down the Second Bank's offices in their states.

Identify causes, events, consequences, and significant individuals of the Civil War and Reconstruction eras.

The American Civil War (1861–65) was one of the most violent times in the history of the United States. More than 600,000 men died, more than in all wars and conflicts the United States has fought since that time.

During the Revolutionary War and the early years under the Constitution, differences between the North and South were dwarfed by their common interest in establishing a new nation. But sectionalism steadily grew stronger. During the nineteenth century the South remained almost completely agricultural, with an economy and a social order largely founded on slavery and the plantation system. These mutually dependent institutions produced the staple crops, especially cotton, from which the South derived its wealth. The North had its own great agricultural resources, was always more advanced commercially, and was also expanding industrially.

Hostility between the two sections grew perceptibly after 1820, the year Congress enacted the Missouri Compromise in the hope of reaching a permanent solution to the primary hostility-arousing issue: whether to extend or prohibit slavery in the federal territories of the West. Difficulties over the tariff of 1824 (which led John C. Calhoun and South Carolina to nullification and to an extreme states' rights stand) and troubles over internal improvements were also involved, but the territorial issue nearly always loomed largest. In the North moral indignation increased with the rise of the abolitionists in the 1830s. The concept of nullification, as stated by John C. Calhoun, held that any state could unilaterally, or in cooperation with other states, refuse to comply with any federal law that a convention selected by the people of the state ruled was unconstitutional. Because slavery was not adaptable to much of the territorial lands that eventually would be admitted as free states, the South became more anxious about maintaining its position as an equal in the Union. Southerners thus strongly supported the annexation of Texas (certain to be a slave state) and the Mexican War and even agitated for the annexation of Cuba.

The Compromise of 1850 marked the end of the period that might be called the era of compromise. The deaths in 1852 of Henry Clay and Daniel Webster left no leader of national stature but only sectional spokesmen, such as W. H. Seward, Charles Sumner, and Salmon P. Chase in the North and Jefferson Davis and Robert Toombs in the South. With the Kansas-Nebraska Act (1854) and the consequent struggle over "bleeding" Kansas, the factions first resorted to shooting. The South was ever alert to protect its "peculiar institution," even though many Southerners recognized slavery as an anachronism in a supposedly enlightened age. Passions aroused by arguments over the fugitive slave laws (which culminated in the *Dred Scott* case) and over slavery in general were further excited by the activities of the northern abolitionist John Brown and by the vigorous proslavery utterances of William L. Yancey, one of the leading southern fire-eaters. The **fire-eaters** were a group of proslavery extremists from the South who urged the southern states to break from the Union and form the new nation called the Confederate States of America.

The "wedges of separation" caused by slavery split large Protestant sects into northern and southern branches and dissolved the Whig Party. Most southern Whigs joined the Democratic Party, one of the few remaining, if shaky, nationwide institutions. The new Republican Party, heir to the Free-Soil Party and to the Liberty Party, was a strictly northern phenomenon. The crucial point was reached in the presidential election of 1860, in which the Republican candidate, Abraham Lincoln, defeated three opponents: Stephen A. Douglas (northern Democrat), John C. Breckinridge (southern Democrat), and John Bell (Constitutional Union Party).

Lincoln's victory was the signal for the secession of South Carolina (December 20, 1860), and that state was followed out of the Union by six other states: Mississippi, Florida, Alabama, Georgia, Louisiana, and Texas. Immediately the question of federal property in those states became important, especially the forts in the harbor of Charleston, South Carolina. The outgoing president, James Buchanan, a northern Democrat, vacillated between yielding to the southern proslavery wing of his party and sincerely attempting to avert war. The question of the forts was still unsettled when Lincoln was inaugurated, and several efforts to reunite the sections, notably the Crittenden Compromise offered by Senator J. J. Crittenden, had proved futile. Lincoln resolved to hold Sumter. The new Confederate government under President Jefferson Davis was equally determined to oust the Federals.

FTCE Fact

The Civil War began on April 12, 1861, when the Confederates fired on Fort Sumter in the harbor at Charleston, S.C.

On April 12, 1861, the Confederate commander P. G. T. Beauregard, acting on instructions, ordered the firing on Fort Sumter. The Civil War had officially begun. Lincoln immediately called for troops to be used against the seven seceding states, which were soon joined by Arkansas, North Carolina, Virginia, and Tennessee, completing the 11-state Confederacy. In the first important military campaign of the war, untrained

Union troops under Irvin McDowell, advancing on the Confederate capital of Richmond, Virginia, were routed by equally inexperienced Confederate soldiers led by Beauregard and Joseph E. Johnston in the first battle of Bull Run on July 21, 1861. That fiasco led Lincoln to bring up George B. McClellan, fresh from his successes in West Virginia.

After the retirement of Winfield Scott in November 1861, McClellan was for a few months the chief northern commander. The able organizer of the Army of the Potomac, he nevertheless failed in the peninsular campaign in which Robert E. Lee succeeded the wounded Johnston as commander of the Confederate Army of Northern Virginia. Lee planned the diversion in the Shenandoah Valley, which, brilliantly executed by Thomas J. (Stonewall) Jackson, worked perfectly. Next to Lee himself, Jackson, with his famous "foot cavalry," was the South's greatest general.

Lee then went on to save Richmond in the Seven Days Battles and was victorious in the second battle of Bull Run, thoroughly trouncing John Pope. However, Lee failed in his first invasion of enemy territory. In September, McClellan, whom Lincoln had restored to command of the defenses of Washington, checked Lee in Maryland. When McClellan failed to attack the Confederates as they retreated, Lincoln removed him again, this time permanently.

Two subsequent Union advances on Richmond, the first led by Ambrose E. Burnside and the second by Joseph Hooker, ended in resounding defeats. Although Lee lost Jackson at Chancellorsville, the victory prompted him to try another invasion of the North. With his lieutenants Richard S. Ewell, James Longstreet, A. P. Hill, and J. E. B. (Jeb) Stuart, he moved through the Shenandoah Valley into southern Pennsylvania. There the Army of the Potomac, under still another new chief, George G. Meade, rallied to stop Lee again in the greatest battle of the war.

With the vastly superior sea power built up by Secretary of the Navy Gideon Welles, the Union established a blockade of the southern coast, which, though by no means completely effective, limited the South's foreign trade to the uncertain prospects of blockade running. In cooperation with the army, the Union navy also attacked along the coasts. The forts guarding New Orleans, the largest Confederate port, fell to a fleet under David G. Farragut, and the city was occupied by troops commanded by Benjamin F. Butler. The introduction of the ironclad warships the *Monitor* and the *Merrimack* had revolutionized naval warfare, to the ultimate advantage of the industrial North. On the other hand, Confederate cruisers, built or bought in England and captained by men such as Raphael Semmes, destroyed or chased from the seas much of the U.S. merchant marine.

Britain never formally recognized the Confederacy (neither did France) and maintained peaceful relations with the Union. The important element in winning popular support for the Union in England and France was the Emancipation Proclamation, which Lincoln issued in September 1862, after the battle at Antietam, the first conflict fought on northern soil.

For a time the proclamation appeased the anti-Lincoln Radical Republicans in Congress, among them Benjamin F. Wade, Zachariah Chandler, Thaddeus Stevens, and Henry W. Davis, with whom Secretary of the Treasury Salmon P. Chase and Secretary of War Edwin M. Stanton were allied. Not all Unionists were abolitionists, however, and the Emancipation Proclamation was not applied to the border states of Delaware, Maryland, Kentucky, and Missouri or any southern state under Union control. For Lincoln and kindred moderates, such as Postmaster General Montgomery Blair, the restoration of the Union, not the abolition of slavery, remained the principal objective of the war.

The Union victories at Gettysburg and Vicksburg in July 1863 marked a definite turning point in the war. Both sides now had seasoned, equally valiant soldiers, and in Lee and Ulysses S. Grant, each had a superior general. But the North, with its larger population and comparatively enormous industry, enjoyed a tremendous material advantage. Both sides also resorted to conscription, even though it met some resistance.

On the political front a movement within the Republican Party to shelve Lincoln had collapsed as the tide turned in the Union's favor. With Andrew Johnson, Lincoln's own choice for vice president over the incumbent Hannibal Hamlin, the president was renominated in June 1864. Lincoln was easily reelected.

After the fall of Atlanta, which had contributed to Lincoln's victory, Sherman's troops made their destructive march through Georgia. Hood had failed to draw Sherman back by invading Union-held Tennessee, and after the battle of Franklin, Hood's army was almost completely annihilated by Thomas at Nashville. Sherman presented Lincoln with the Christmas gift of Savannah, Georgia, and then moved north through the Carolinas. Farragut's victory at Mobile Bay had effectively closed that port, and on January 15, 1865, Wilmington, North Carolina, was also cut off.

Following Sheridan's victory at Five Forks, the Petersburg lines were breached and the Confederates evacuated Richmond. With his retreat blocked by Sheridan, Lee, wisely giving up the futile contest, surrendered to Grant at the Appomattox Courthouse on April 9, 1865. The surviving Confederate troops also yielded when they heard of Lee's capitulation, thus ending the conflict that resulted in more than 600,000 casualties.

FTCE Fact

More than 600,000 men died during the American Civil War—more deaths than from any other war.

The long war was over, but for the victors the peace was marred by the assassination of Abraham Lincoln, the greatest figure of the war. The former Confederate states, after enduring the unsuccessful attempts of Reconstruction to impose a new society on the South, were readmitted to the Union, which had been saved and in which slavery was now abolished. The Civil War brought death to more Americans than did any other war, including World War II. Photographs by Mathew Brady and others reveal some of the horror behind the statistics. The war cost untold billions and nourished rather than canceled hatred and intolerance, which persisted for decades. Many of the patterns now taken for granted in American national life, especially a strong central government, were established as a result of the war. Virtually every battlefield, with its graves, is either a national or a state park. Monuments commemorating Civil War figures and events are conspicuous in almost all sizable northern towns and are even more numerous in the Upper South.

After the North defeated the South in the Civil War, politicians faced the task of putting the divided country back together. There was great debate about how severely the former Confederate states should be punished for leaving the Union. With the assassination of President Lincoln in 1865, it was up to President Andrew Johnson to try to reunite former enemies. The Reconstruction Acts of 1867 laid out the process for readmitting southern states into the Union. In 1865 the Thirteenth Amendment outlawed slavery. The Fourteenth Amendment (1868) provided former slaves with national citizenship, and the Fifteenth Amendment (1870) granted black men the right to vote. However, these were only the first steps toward reconstructing the fragmented nation.

The year 1865 represented the last days of the Confederacy. The larger and better-equipped Union forces had successfully enforced a blockade on Confederate states by land and sea. Federal troops had either occupied or destroyed all the major industrial areas, which caused starvation and riots against the Confederate government.

On March 20, 1865, the southern government resorted to arming the slaves in a last ditch effort to equalize the manpower disadvantage.

There were two major issues to be resolved once the Confederacy had been defeated:

- Were the rebel states still part of the United States?

- Was the president or the Congress responsible for Reconstruction?

Lincoln had always claimed that the 11 Confederate states had never left the Union. In 1862 he had appointed provisional governors in Louisiana, North Carolina, and Tennessee. As early as December 8, 1863, he had already announced a plan of Reconstruction that included amnesty to all Southerners who would take an oath of loyalty and recognition of the governments of states in which 10 percent of the prewar electorate took the oath and renounced slavery.

Louisiana and Arkansas took the required steps in 1864, but Congress refused to let their representatives sit in the House. President Johnson adopted Lincoln's plan and recognized the loyal governments in Arkansas, Louisiana, Tennessee, and Virginia, which Lincoln had set up. By December 1865 every Confederate state except Texas had taken the steps. Texas conformed on April 6, 1866, and on December 6 that year President Johnson announced to Congress that the Union was restored.

Congress, however, refused to endorse what Johnson had done. A joint committee of six senators and nine representatives was formed instead to oversee the management of the former Confederacy. The committee considered the confederate states to be "conquered provinces," and they were effectively put under the trusteeship of Congress.

On December 18, 1865, the Thirteenth Amendment abolishing slavery was ratified by 27 states and formally proclaimed. The federal government established the Freedmen's Bureau on February 19, 1866, to protect freed slaves from the harsh Black Codes being enacted in some states. The codes effectively tied the freed slaves to the land on which they lived and worked.

Later that year, on April 9, Congress passed a Civil Rights Act that bestowed citizenship on African Americans. The act granted the same civil rights to all persons born in America (except Indians). Johnson vetoed the bill because he said that it infringed on the rights of states that were not represented in the House. The act was passed over Johnson's veto, but the Supreme Court ruled that the act was unconstitutional.

The congressional joint committee then formulated the Fourteenth Amendment to the Constitution to get around the apparent unconstitutionality of the Civil Rights Act. The amendment passed Congress on June 13, 1866, and was submitted to the states for ratification. The Fourteenth Amendment defined American citizenship and included African Americans. It provided federal protection to freed slaves whose rights could not be limited by state governments. Ratification was denied by most of the southern states but was made a requirement for readmission into the Union. Tennessee accepted the amendment, but the other southern states awaited the upcoming congressional elections and possibly a more sympathetic Congress.

Johnson's party captured a two-thirds majority in both houses, giving the Radical Republican Party control over Reconstruction. Although they were members of Johnson's party, the Radicals were much more antagonistic toward the South than he was. On March 2, 1867, Congress passed the First Reconstruction Act over Johnson's veto. Martial law was declared over the former Confederate states, which were divided into five regions.

The new requirements for states to be readmitted to the Union were ratification of the Fourteenth Amendment and universal suffrage guaranteeing that African Americans would be given the right and opportunity to vote. In the Omnibus Act of 1868, seven states met the requirements and were readmitted to the Union: Arkansas, Alabama, Florida, Georgia, Louisiana, North Carolina, and South Carolina. Georgia soon returned to military rule when all the African American representatives were dismissed from the state legislature. It was allowed to return to self-rule only when the state ratified the Fifteenth Amendment, guaranteeing equality for the freed slaves, and allowed African Americans to return to the House.

Despite being vetoed by Congress, Johnson faithfully executed their decisions. He appointed military commanders who led 20,000 troops (including African American militia) into the South. Governments that he had previously set up were displaced, and 703,000 African Americans and 627,000 whites were registered as voters. In Alabama, Florida, Louisiana, Mississippi, and South Carolina, black voters were in the majority. In other states a black-white coalition formed under the Radical Republican banner. Southern whites allied with the Radicals were called scalawags. Northerners who went south to assist in Reconstruction were called carpetbaggers.

Meanwhile, Radicals in Congress were consistently overriding Johnson's vetoes and placed some important limitations on his executive power. Johnson was prevented from naming judges to the Supreme Court and was deprived of being the commander in chief of the armed forces. The Covode Resolution of February 24, 1868, passed in the House by a vote of 126 to 47 and called for the impeachment of the president. The charges included allegedly violating the Tenure of Office Act and the Command of the Army Act and bringing disgrace on the U.S. Congress. The impeachment vote, however, did not receive the required two-thirds majority.

> **FTCE Fact**
>
> In 1868 Congress called for the impeachment of then-President Andrew Johnson. It fell one vote short of the required 2/3 majority.

The Supreme Court played a major role in determining the legality and constitutionality of many of the laws passed during Reconstruction. The Court decided that it was unconstitutional to set up martial law where civil courts were in operation. In *Texas vs. White*, decided in 1869, the Court upheld Lincoln's position that the Union was indivisible and indissoluble. The Court also decided that the loyalty oaths were wrong and invalidated them.

At the conclusion of the Civil War, the United States remained bitterly divided. Reconstruction and its failure left southern whites in a position of firm control over blacks, denying them their civil rights and keeping them in economic, social, and political second-class status.

Assess the impact of agrarianism, industrialization, urbanization, and the reform movements in the late nineteenth and early twentieth centuries (e.g., temperance, civil rights, populism, progressivism).

An unprecedented wave of immigration, 37 million people between 1840 and 1920, served to provide cheap labor for American industry and to create diverse communities in previously undeveloped areas, such as California. The expansion of industry and population had a substantial cost as well. Native American tribes were generally forced onto small reservations so that white farmers and ranchers could take their lands. Abusive industrial practices led to the rise of the labor movement in the United States, which was sometimes violent.

The United States began its rise to international power in this period with substantial population and industrial growth domestically, along with numerous imperialist ventures abroad. By the late nineteenth century, the United States had become a leading global industrial power, building on new technologies (such as the telegraph and the Bessemer process), an expanding railroad network, and abundant natural resources to usher in the second Industrial Revolution.

During this period the United States helped liberate Cuba from Spanish rule and annexed Hawaii and Puerto Rico. At the end of the Spanish-American War, it acquired the Philippines and, after suppressing an independence movement, began modernizing the islands, especially in terms of public health measures to stop epidemics that killed hundreds of thousands. Deciding not to permanently keep the Philippines, it promised independence in 1946.

The United States' late entry into World War I on the side of the Allied Powers shifted the balance of the war and made the United States a major military, as well as financial, power.

Writers, publishers, and editors were effective in advancing the causes of labor, women's suffrage, temperance, socialism, and minorities through newspapers and magazines during the late nineteenth and early twentieth centuries, at different levels. Journalists had great influence on the people of America, and the things that were written in their newspapers quite often aroused contention on certain issues. That contentiousness often went on to inspire changes in the way people were living. Newspapers and magazines offered people an outlet for expressing their views, helped others to become educated on topics, and let still others have their voices heard.

Until the middle of the nineteenth century, the center of the city was the most fashionable place to live. Merchants, lawyers, and manufacturers built substantial townhouses on the main thoroughfares within walking distance of the docks, warehouses, offices, courts, and shops where they worked. Poorer people lived in back alleys and courtyards of the central city. Markets, shops, taverns, and concert halls provided services and entertainment. The middle classes lived a little farther from the center, and other poor people lived in the suburbs, farther from the economic and governmental centers and away from urban amenities such as police patrols, water pumps, and garbage collection. Cities were densely populated because people had to live within walking distance of work and shops. Streets were narrow, just wide enough to accommodate pedestrians and wagons.

Following are some noted individuals of this era:

- **Carl Sandburg** (1878–1967) changed the course of American poetry. His influence has not always been acknowledged, but his characteristic unrhymed lines of varying length, his evocations of American urban and rural life, his compassion for the working class, and his love of nature have all left their mark.

- **William Haywood** (1869–1928), known as "Big Bill," was a radical militant labor leader who founded the Industrial Workers of the World (IWW). At the age of 15 he began working as a miner. He led the Western Federation of Miners from 1900 to 1905 and in 1905 helped found the IWW, which aimed to organize all workers into "one big union." In 1906 Haywood and others were tried for the murder of a former governor of Idaho, but the noted trial lawyer Clarence Darrow won their acquittal. In 1918, the last year of World War I, Haywood and 165 other IWW leaders were convicted of sedition for opposing the U.S. war effort. Haywood jumped bail in 1921 and went to the Soviet Union, where he remained until his death.

- **Theodore Dreiser** (1871–1945) was the leading American exponent of literary naturalism and is best known as the author of *An American Tragedy* and *Sister Carrie*. The limitations of Dreiser's awkward style are offset by the raw energy of his narratives and by his gift for depicting the lives of common people.

- **Ida Tarbell** (1857–1944) was a Pennsylvania journalist, editor, and biographer who became famous as a muckraker through her well-documented articles on political and corporate corruption in the *McClure's* and *American* magazines. Her two-volume *History of the Standard Oil Company* (1904) led to federal action against the giant corporation. She also wrote a biography of Abraham Lincoln (1900) and an autobiography, *All in a Day's Work* (1939).

The Industrial Revolution of the nineteenth and twentieth centuries transformed urban life and gave people higher expectations for improving their standard of living. The increased number of jobs, along with technological innovations in transportation and housing construction, encouraged migration to cities. Development of railroads, streetcars, and trolleys in the nineteenth century enabled city boundaries to expand. People no longer had to live within walking distance of their jobs. With more choices about where to live, people tended to seek out neighbors of similar social status, if they could afford to do so. The wealthy no longer had to live in the center of the city, so they formed exclusive enclaves far from warehouses, factories, and docks. Office buildings, retail shops, and light manufacturing characterized the central business districts. Heavier industry clustered along the rivers and rail lines that brought in raw materials and shipped out finished products. Railroads also allowed goods to be brought into downtown commercial districts. By the second half of the nineteenth century, specialized spaces—retail districts, office blocks, manufacturing districts, and residential areas—characterized urban life.

Wealthy families like the Carnegies, Mellons, Rockefellers, and Morgans created separate neighborhoods for themselves by building mansions on large plots of land at the edges of the cities or in the countryside. Housing developments of similar-looking single- or multiple-family dwellings, built by speculators, sprouted on the edges of cities. These often catered to a new middle class of white-collar employees in business and industry. The houses faced broader streets and increasingly had plots of grass in front and sometimes in the rear. New apartments were spacious and often had balconies, porches, or other amenities. By 1900 more than a third of urban dwellers owned their own homes, one of the highest rates in the world at the time. This "progress" led the era of 1890 to 1917 to be labeled the Progressive Era.

As the middle classes left the bustle and smoke of cities, poorer people—newcomers from the countryside and immigrants primarily from Europe—moved into the old housing stock. Landlords took advantage of the demand for housing by subdividing city houses into apartments and by building tenements, low-rent apartment buildings that were often poorly maintained and unsanitary. Immigrants gravitated to the cheap housing and to the promise of work in or near the centers of cities or around factories. Now the rich lived in the suburbs and the poor near the city centers.

In the 50 years from 1870 to 1920, the number of Americans in cities grew from 10 million to 54 million. Into the twentieth century cities grew in population and expanded geographically by absorbing nearby communities. In 1898 New York City acquired Brooklyn, Queens, and the Bronx as boroughs, political divisions that are like counties. Chicago grew from about 300,000 inhabitants in 1870 to more than 1 million in 1890. Three-quarters of the city's residents were born outside the United States, and while some found work and a comfortable existence, many suffered severe poverty. That poverty, however, was largely invisible to the rich living on the outskirts of the city, since the poor were concentrated in distant neighborhoods.

The growth of cities outpaced the ability of local governments to extend clean water, garbage collection, and sewage systems into poorer areas, so conditions in cities deteriorated. In the late nineteenth century cities were large, crowded, and impersonal places devoted to making money. Not surprisingly, corruption was rampant in city government and city services, in the construction industry, and among landlords and employers. High rents, low wages, and poor services produced misery in the midst of unprecedented economic growth.

The progressive movement of the late nineteenth and early twentieth centuries succeeded in reducing some of the corruption and in establishing housing codes, public health measures, and civil service examinations in city governments. Progressive regulatory approaches to the problems of cities expanded during the New Deal in the 1930s.

Upward mobility, homeownership, educational opportunities, and cheap goods softened many of the disadvantages of nineteenth-century urban life. Beautification programs, electrification, and construction of libraries, parks, playgrounds, and swimming pools gradually improved the quality of urban life in the twentieth century, although poor areas received fewer benefits. Poverty, particularly among new arrivals, and low wages remained problems in the cities throughout the nineteenth and twentieth centuries. Labor unions helped raise wages and benefits for many workers, particularly the most skilled, from 1900 to 1950.

Although murder was rare in the nation in the late nineteenth century, rates rose in cities. Robbery and theft were commonplace, and prostitution flourished more openly than before. Cheap newspapers exaggerated increases in crime with sensational stories. Professional police forces were created in the late nineteenth century to keep order and to protect property. Prohibition, which existed from 1920 to 1933, had the unintended effect of increasing organized crime in America, because manufacturing, importing, and selling illegal alcohol provided a financial windfall for gangs of criminals in the cities. The money was used to expand the influence of organized crime into gambling, prostitution, narcotics, and some legitimate businesses.

Elizabeth Cady Stanton has been called the founder and philosopher of the women's rights movement. For many years she was its chief writer and speaker, she helped define many goals. She was born in 1815 in Upstate New York. Her father, Judge Daniel Cady, was a distinguished lawyer and a member of the New York legislature. She was the fourth of five daughters in the family, born after the death of the only son. Her father encouraged her studies and independent thought. She achieved a much higher level of education than most women at that time. Her father showed her how laws could be changed, although he was reluctant to see her involved in such "unfeminine" activities.

She was very suspect of organized religion and the preachers of the day who used the Bible to keep "women in their place." In 1839 she met Harry Stanton, who was active in the antislavery movement. After a brief courtship he proposed and she accepted. Everyone was against the marriage, especially her father, who opposed abolitionism and doubted Stanton could support his daughter. Under parental pressure Elizabeth broke off the engagement, but a year later she felt she needed to run her own life. She and Stanton married with the understanding that it was a marriage of equals; the word *obey* was removed from the ceremony, and she also kept her maiden name, becoming Elizabeth Cady Stanton. In the course of their life together they had several children.

Susan B. Anthony, born in 1820, had more opportunities than most women because she was a member of the Society of Friends (Quakers), a group with a strong tradition of equality for women. Her father supported his daughters' aspirations and tried to give them the best education possible. He encouraged them to be self-reliant and self-supporting. Susan went to school and then worked as a teacher. She was considered quite honest, and in her youth her tendency toward intolerance and severity in her moral judgments were tempered by her sense of humor and sympathy for people. She chose never to marry but dedicated her life to the movement for reform.

Stanton and Anthony would become the leaders of the women's suffrage movement.

This was also an era of regulation of big business. With the support of President Benjamin Harrison, Congress passed the Sherman Antitrust Act in 1890. John Sherman, a lawyer and senator from Ohio, was the author of the legislation that attempted to curb the growth of monopolies. The act declared illegal any business combination that sought to restrain trade or commerce. Penalties for violation of the act included a $5,000 fine and/or a year's imprisonment. The act was unable to achieve its original objectives for two main reasons: the vague wording of the legislation and the absence of a strong, independent commission for its enforcement.

In 1894 the attorney general, Richard Olney, used the Sherman Antitrust Act against the American Railway Union during the Pullman strike. As a result, Eugene Debs, the president of the union, was imprisoned for contempt of court.

In 1914 Henry De Lamar Clayton, a lawyer from Alabama, drafted what became known as the Clayton Antitrust Act. The act strengthened the power of government in dealing with monopolies. It forbade agreements between companies to fix or control prices for the purpose of lessening competition. It also prohibited individuals from serving as directors of competing corporations.

Assess the impact of immigration on cultural, political, and economic development.

In the late 1800s people in many parts of the world decided to leave their homes and immigrate to the United States. Fleeing crop failure, land and job shortages, rising taxes, and famine, many came to the United States because it was perceived as the land of economic opportunity. Others came seeking personal freedom or relief from political and religious persecution. With hope for a brighter future, nearly 12 million immigrants arrived in the United States between 1870 and 1900. During the 1870s and 1880s most people were from Germany, Ireland, and England—the principal sources of immigration before the Civil War. That would change drastically in the next three decades.

Immigrants entered the United States through several ports. Those from Europe generally came through East Coast facilities, while those from Asia generally entered through West Coast centers. More than 70 percent of all immigrants, however, entered through New York City, which came to be known as the Golden Door. Throughout the late 1800s, most immigrants arriving in New York entered at the Castle Garden depot near the tip of Manhattan. In 1892 the federal government opened a new immigrant-processing center on Ellis Island in New York Harbor.

Although immigrants often settled near ports of entry, a large number found their way inland. Many states, especially those with sparse populations, actively sought to attract immigrants by offering jobs or land for farming. Many immigrants wanted to move to communities established by previous settlers from their homelands.

Once settled, immigrants looked for work. There were never enough jobs, and employers often took advantage of the immigrants. Men were generally paid less than other workers, and women less than men. Social tensions were also part of the immigrant experience. Often stereotyped and discriminated against, many immigrants suffered verbal and physical abuse because they were "different." While large-scale immigration created many social tensions, it also produced a new vitality in the cities and states in which the immigrants settled. The newcomers helped transform American society and culture, demonstrating that diversity, as well as unity, is a source of national strength.

A relatively large number of Chinese immigrated to the United States between 1849, when the California gold rush started, and 1882, when federal law stopped their immigration. The Naturalization Act of 1870 restricted U.S. citizenship to only "white persons and persons of African descent," meaning that all Chinese were placed into a category that made them ineligible for citizenship from that time until 1952 when racial restrictions on citizenship were nullified.

Although most immigrants came to settle in the United States permanently, many worked for a time and returned home with whatever savings they had set aside from their work. Many Chinese immigrants, for example, were single men who worked for a while and returned home. At first they were attracted to North America by the gold rush in California. Many prospected for gold on their own or labored for other miners. Soon many opened their own businesses such as restaurants, laundries, and other personal service concerns. After the gold rush Chinese immigrants worked as agricultural laborers, on railroad construction crews throughout the West, and in low-paying industrial jobs. At the beginning of the twentieth century, the Italians were the main group entering the United States. Most Italians found unskilled work in America's cities. There were large colonies in New York, Philadelphia, Chicago, Baltimore, and Detroit. From 1900 to 1910 more than 2 million immigrants arrived. Willing to work long hours for low wages, the Italians began to rival the Irish for much of the unskilled work available in industrial areas. That sometimes led to hostilities breaking out between the two groups of workers. The Italians were also recruited into the garment industry. By the outbreak of the First World War, they had replaced the Jews as the main group in the sweat trade.

In 1919 Woodrow Wilson appointed A. Mitchell Palmer as his attorney general. Worried by the revolution that had taken place in Russia in 1917, Palmer became convinced that communist agents were planning to overthrow the American government. Palmer recruited John Edgar Hoover as his special assistant, and together they used the

Espionage Act (1917) and the Sedition Act (1918) to launch a campaign against radicals and left-wing organizations.

Palmer claimed that communist agents from Russia were planning to overthrow the American government. On November 7, 1919, the second anniversary of the Russian Revolution, more than 10,000 suspected Communists and anarchists were arrested in what became known as the Palmer raids. Palmer and Hoover found no evidence of a proposed revolution, but a large number of these suspects were held without trial for a long time.

Persecution of Jews by the Nazis in Germany in the 1930s increased the desire to immigrate to the United States. Arrivals included Albert Einstein, Alfred Adler, Edward Teller, Karen Horney, Erich Fromm, Kurt Weill, and Hanns Eisler.

With the onset of hard economic times in the 1870s, other immigrants and European Americans began to compete for the jobs traditionally reserved for the Chinese. With economic competition came dislike and even racial suspicion and hatred. Such feelings were accompanied by anti-Chinese riots and pressure, especially in California, for the exclusion of Chinese immigrants from the United States. The result of this pressure was the Chinese Exclusion Act, passed by Congress in 1882. It was the first piece of legislation to restrict free entry into the country for a specific ethnic group. The Chinese were prohibited from immigrating to the United States, a racial policy of exclusion that lasted until 1943 when the act was repealed. Chinese laborers already in the country were allowed to leave and then reenter provided they showed that they had a certificate of eligibility. Those who were not eligible were deported.

The act was amended on July 5, 1884, extending the prohibition against Chinese immigrants for another 10 years and denied access to all Chinese except government officials. Chinese immigrants were denied entry to the United States for the next 20 years.

The first general federal immigration law was a further reaction against the new immigrant groups: southern and eastern Europeans (Italians, Slavs, Poles, and Russians) pouring into the United States for the first time. The federal law was a compromise with state and local authorities attempting to deal with the great influx of immigrants. Port-of-entry states faced economic hardships when indigent and sick immigrants landed at their doors requiring medical care and housing. States greatly resented having to fully fund services for immigrants. Eastern state governments wanted the federal government to provide economic support to ease the financial burdens of immigration.

The federal government responded by passing the **Immigration Act of 1882**. The law imposed the first 50-cent head tax on all immigrants entering the United States. The collected funds were used to pay inspectors responsible for determining who would and would not be allowed to enter the United States. The law excluded specific immigrant groups with the potential of becoming dependents of state government, such as convicts, lunatics, and persons unable to provide for themselves. The Immigration Act of 1882 ended the period of federal inaction toward immigration and took control over the issue.

Identify the causes, events, consequences, and significant individuals of the World War I era.

The causes of **World War I** are not clear cut. Historians agree that the war had been building up for some time before 1914. The following are some aspects of the political environment that made war likely:

- **Alliance systems:** From the end of the Franco-Prussian War, a system of secret alliances developed in Europe and eventually split the continent into two hostile sides. Because so many powers were involved in mutual defense agreements, when the war began it involved nearly every country of Europe. Some powers were forced by these alliances to support policies they did not condone. Additionally, the secret alliances fostered an environment of suspicion and the belief that more secret agreements existed than was the case.

- **Imperialism:** The competition for colonies was another source of international antagonism. The great powers divided Africa among them, established spheres of influence in China, and sought protectorates elsewhere. Eventually, the rush to appropriate new territories was bound to spark disagreements over boundaries of control.

- **Militarism:** All the countries within the hostile camps were building large armies and navies during the prewar years. As a by-product, a class of professional and powerful military officers developed and tended to dominate the civil authorities. In addition, before the conflict happened, the militaries of each country had drawn up complete plans for mobilization. These plans only awaited the go-ahead signal. The existence of secret battle plans stimulated espionage, which in turn aroused greater hatred and fear.

- **Nationalism:** Strong feelings of nationalism fed the fires of hatred in prewar Europe. It turned the French against the Germans and turned the Russians against the Austrians. Nationalistic speeches and writings (especially in countries like Germany) hastened the war by painting it as the best test for proof of national superiority.

The spark that ignited the flame and transformed Europe's underlying problems into a frenzy of hostilities happened in the Balkans. On June 28, 1914, Archduke Francis Ferdinand, heir to the throne of Austria-Hungary, was assassinated while visiting Sarajevo. At first it appeared to be another Balkan crisis that might pass without a major disturbance, but a month later Austria severed relations with Serbia, a move that preceded war by only a few days.

Germany supported Austria's actions, while Russia stepped forward to defend its small Balkan ally. Despite frantic efforts by would-be peacemakers to localize the war, it spread rapidly, involving next France and Belgium and soon Great Britain. As the world looked on, Europe erupted into war almost overnight.

American relations with European nations were at the time generally friendly, especially with Great Britain. President Woodrow Wilson called on his countrymen to take no sides and to be impartial. But neutrality for America was not possible. Wilson decided to ask Congress to recognize that a state of war existed between the United States and Germany on April 6, 1917. The resolution passed both houses and the President signed it, thus ending the neutrality.

New weapons revolutionized combat in World War I. Combat, previously seen as a rapid, noble, and relatively ephemeral activity, adopted a new model: trench warfare. The new style of warfare was brought about principally by new technology that arose from the furnaces and factories of industrial Europe.

The following are the principal types of weaponry used in World War I:

- **Machine guns:** These weapons were first used in the American Civil War to devastating effect. But by World War I their effectiveness had reached frightening new levels, able to fire up to 600 bullets a minute (the equivalent of 250 men with rifles).

- **Artillery:** As an upgraded version of the cannon, artillery enabled troops to combine the force of many cannons into one. For four years the British had been using artillery to fire a total of 170 million shells during that time. For years German scientists had been developing the biggest artillery ever known. Called Big Bertha, it was so powerful it could fire at the heart of Paris from a distance of 75 miles. The shells were upgraded as well. High-explosive shells had thin casings filled with tiny lead pellets. Using these shells, artillery fire killed hundreds and thousands of men.

- **Gas grenades:** Invented by the Germans, gas grenades were highly toxic, very effective weapons. The three types of gas primarily used in the grenades were chlorine gas, phosgene gas, and mustard gas. When people breathed the gas from an exploded grenade, their lungs would burn, and ultimately they would die in agony. Gas masks were issued to every soldier, but they were not effective, and many people died.

- **Transportation:** The need to transport troops to the battlefields and other places prompted massive increases in transportation systems. British forces used everything from trains to lorries and even taxis.

- **Communication:** In 1914 both radios and telephones were the main modes of communication. These were very vital for the troops in trenches.

- **Tanks:** Tanks at first were giant blocks of metal that could carry one or two soldiers and traveled at about 3 miles per hour. But scientists and manufacturers kept making new and improved tanks, and by 1918 the Anglo-American Mark 8 could carry up to eight men and fire 208 shells and 13,000 bullets.

- **Aircraft:** The ability to use planes in warfare was one of the greatest advances in the technology of war. The types of aircraft used ranged from small scout planes to huge blimp bombers called Zeppelins.

- **Naval units:** The British specialized in battleships, and the Germans specialized in submarines.

Technology during World War I reflected a trend toward industrialism and mass production that began 50 years earlier during the American Civil War and continued through many smaller conflicts in which new weapons were tested. August 1914 marked the end of a relatively peaceful century in Europe characterized by unprecedented invention and new science. The nineteenth-century vision of a peaceful future fed by ever-increasing prosperity through technology was largely shattered by the war, and it became apparent that whatever gains in prosperity and comfort that technology brought to civilian life would always be under the shadow of the horrors technology brought warfare.

The earlier years of World War I can be characterized as a clash of twentieth-century technology with nineteenth-century tactics. That dichotomy resulted in ineffectual battles with huge numbers of casualties on both sides. Not until the final year of the war did the major armies take effective steps in revolutionizing command and control methods and tactics to adapt to the modern battlefield. Tactical reorganizations (such as shifting the focus of command from companies of 100 or more men to squads of about 10 men) went hand in hand with armored cars, the first submachine guns, and automatic rifles that could be carried and used by one soldier.

With the end of World War I, the decade of the 1920s was a period of tremendous change in the United States. Here are some facts:

- The U.S. population was 106,521,537.

- About 2,132,000 Americans were unemployed, putting the unemployment rate at 5.2 percent.

- The average life expectancy was 53.6 years for males and 54.6 years for females.

- Roughly 343,000 men were in the military (down from 1,172,601 in 1919).

- The average annual salary was $1,236; a teacher's salary was about $970 a year.

- The Dow Jones reached a high of 100 and a low of 67.

- The illiteracy rate reached a new low of 6 percent of the population.

- Gangland crime included murder, swindles, and racketeering.

- It took 13 days to reach California from New York. There were 387,000 miles of paved road.

President Wilson presented **14 points** in a speech delivered to a joint session of Congress in 1918. In his speech Wilson intended to set out a blueprint for lasting peace in

Europe after World War I. The idealism displayed in the speech gave Wilson a position of moral leadership among the Allies and encouraged the Central Powers to surrender.

The speech was delivered more than 10 months before the Armistice with Germany ended World War I, but the 14 points became the basis for the terms of the German surrender, as negotiated at the Paris Peace Conference in 1919 and documented in the Treaty of Versailles. However, only four of the points were adopted completely in the postwar reconstruction of Europe, and the U.S. Senate refused to ratify the Treaty of Versailles.

The end of World War I saw the United States retreat into isolation. In addition to the Senate's refusal to ratify the peace treaty, the U.S. did not join the League of Nations, the international organization that was the less-successful interwar predecessor of the United Nations. The U.S. raised tariffs early in the 1920s (although not to levels that appreciably discouraged imports). Perhaps most importantly, the 1920s saw the end of free immigration into the United States. Migration from Asia had been restricted for several generations, and migration from Africa had never been an issue. But until the mid-1920s migration from Europe had been unrestricted.

More than 1.2 million immigrants had come to the United States in 1914. Once the immigration restrictions of the 1920s took effect, the overall total was fixed at only about 160,000 immigrants a year. Moreover, different nations had different quotas. The quotas for immigrants from northern and western Europe were more than ample for the demand. The quotas for immigrants from southern and eastern Europe were very small.

The United States tried to pretend that the rest of the world did not really exist, and as people turned inward, they found that they had plenty to do. In the 1920s the United States became a modern middle-class economy of radios, consumer appliances, automobiles, and suburbs. Nearly 30 million motor vehicles were on the road in 1929, one for every five residents of the country. Mass production made the postwar United States the richest society the world had ever seen.

Mass production, as it was developed in the United States in the early years of the twentieth century, carried the American economic system on to its logical next step. Henry Ford planned large-scale production of his Model N in 1905 to reduce the need for expensive skilled labor as much as possible.

Ford minimized his costs by building a capital-intensive plant that excelled only at building automobiles, nothing else. The increase in capital intensity increased the potential risk. The productivity and profitability of the Ford plant depended on a high rate of production. Anything that threatened the pace of production—a union strike or anarchist sabotage—threatened to be very expensive. Ford could employ unskilled workers in jobs that had previously required highly skilled craftsmen, but only if he kept his workforce happy.

Moreover, in "moving the work to the men" by means of the assembly line, Ford engineers found a method to speed up slow workers and slow down fast workers. The factory as machine would monitor the progress of its human elements and immediately signal where a unit was not accomplishing its job satisfactorily by the buildup of work at that station. The task of management was made much simpler because the assembly line forced the pace of workers and made it obvious where bottlenecks occurred. Fixed overhead costs were spread over larger volumes of production, making lower prices possible.

The same set of forces can be seen at work in other industries as well. For example, Theodore N. Vail, president of American Telephone and Telegraph, argued that the telephone business exhibited enormous economies of scale. The realization of these economies of scale required the highest output and the lowest practical prices to make sure that the output could be sold. Vail distinguished two competitive strategies for producing net revenue: by a large percentage of profit on a small business or a small percentage of profit on a large business. In America the second strategy worked best.

The strategy of investing heavily in fixed capital, producing the maximum output at low prices, and using the productive expertise to forge technological leadership and low-cost positions became characteristic of American industry throughout the twentieth century. It was made possible because half of North America was the single economic unit of the United States. With no obstacles to shipping commodities beyond state lines, the possibilities of benefiting from a low-price, high-volume strategy were much greater than in Europe, especially in the interwar years of active trade restrictions.

The flip side of mass production was mass consumption: the creation of America as a middle-class society comprising a growing number of people living in suburban areas and using automobiles to commute and shop. The speed with which the products of mass production diffused through America was astonishing. Not only automobiles but also washing machines, refrigerators, electric irons, electric and gas stoves—a whole host of inventions and technologies—greatly transformed the economy of the typical American household.

Thomas Edison invented the incandescent lightbulb in 1879. By 1882 New York City had its first central generating station. By 1910 the alternating-current electric motor had become a low-cost provider of mechanical power that could be made small enough to run a fan or large enough to power a locomotive. Eight percent of American households were wired for electricity in 1907; 35 percent were wired by 1920; and 80 percent were wired by the beginning of World War II. Thus, the 1920s was the decade of consumer appliances. By the start of World War II, 79 percent of households had electric irons and 50 percent had washing machines, refrigerators, and vacuum cleaners.

An important novelty lay in the rapid spread of a new form of purchase: installment credit. The major consumer appliances had long lifetimes and relatively high prices. Businesses found that their potential markets were much larger if they were willing to loan a large portion of the purchase price to the consumer for one to five years.

Identify the cultural, political, and economic developments between World War I and World War II, including the Roaring Twenties, the Harlem Renaissance, the Great Depression, and the New Deal.

Following World War I (called "the war to end all wars"), talented young authors, some expatriates in France, wrote about their feelings of disillusionment and alienation. A sense of rebellion developed, and in defiance of the Victorian idea of decency they considered hypocritical, authors began to write frankly about sexuality. Three important groups emerged during this period.

First, the **Algonquin Round Table** was an informal group of American literary men and women who met each weekday for lunch at a large round table in the Algonquin Hotel in New York City during the 1920s and 1930s. Many of the best-known writers, journalists, and artists in New York City were in the group. Among them were Dorothy Parker, Alexander Woollcott (who famously stated, "All the things I really like are immoral, illegal, or fattening"), Heywood Broun, Robert Benchley, Robert Sherwood, George S. Kaufman, Franklin P. Adams, Marc Connelly, Harold Ross, Harpo Marx, and Russel Crouse.

Second, the **Harlem Renaissance** is considered the first important movement of black artists and writers in the United States. Centered in the Harlem neighborhood of New York City, the movement dispersed to other urban areas during the 1920s and promoted the publication of more black writers than ever before. This group included Zora Neale Hurston, W. E. B. DuBois, Langston Hughes, Jean Toomer, and Alain Locke.

Third, the **Lost Generation** was a group of self-exiled expatriates who lived and wrote in Paris between the wars. These writers, looking for freedom of thought and action, changed the face of modern writing. Realistic and rebellious, they wrote what they wanted and fought censorship for profanity and sexuality. They incorporated Freudian ideas into their characters and styles. This group included Ernest Hemingway, Gertrude Stein, John Dos Passos, Henry Miller, and F. Scott Fitzgerald.

The powerful economic might of America from 1920 to October 1929 is frequently overlooked or simply submerged by the more exciting topics of Prohibition and the gangsters, the Jazz Age, and the Ku Klux Klan. The Eighteenth Amendment had banned the manufacture, sale, and transport of alcohol in America. But it was clear to some that millions neither wanted this law nor would respect it. The huge demand for the illegal commodity was filled by the gangsters who dominated most major cities but most famously Chicago, with Al Capone.

Capone was dubbed "Public Enemy Number 1." He had moved to Chicago in 1920 and worked for Johnny Torrio, the city's leading figure in the underworld. Capone was given the tasks of intimidating his boss's rivals within the city, forcing them to hand over their territories to Torrio, and convincing speakeasy operators to buy illegal alcohol from Torrio.

Capone was very good at what he did. In 1925 Torrio was nearly killed by a rival gang, and he decided to get out of the criminal world while he was still alive. Torrio handed over his "business" to Capone. Within two years Capone was earning $60 million a year from alcohol sales alone. Other rackets earned him another $45 million a year.

For all his power, Capone still had enemies from other surviving gangs in the city. He drove everywhere in an armor-plated limousine, and wherever he was, so were his armed bodyguards. Violence was a daily occurrence in Chicago; 227 gangsters were killed in the space of four years, and on Saint Valentine's Day in 1929 seven members of the O'Banion gang were shot dead by gangsters dressed as police officers.

In 1931, the law finally caught up with Capone. He was convicted of tax evasion and sentenced to 11 years in jail. In prison his health declined, and when he was released he retired to his Florida mansion, no longer the feared man he had been from 1925 to 1931.

The Great Depression was the worst economic disaster in U.S. history, and it spread to virtually the entire industrialized world. The Depression began in late 1929 and lasted for about a decade. Although many factors played a role in bringing about the Depression, the main cause was the combination of the greatly unequal distribution of wealth throughout the 1920s and the extensive stock market speculation that took place during the latter part of that same decade. The imbalance of wealth existed on many levels. Money was distributed disparately between the rich and the middle class, between U.S. industry and agriculture, and between the United States and Europe. The result was an unstable economy. Excessive speculation in the late 1920s kept the stock market artificially high but eventually led to large market crashes.

Herbert Hoover was president when the Great Depression began. The economy continued to drop almost every month. Franklin D. Roosevelt was elected president in 1932. His **New Deal** reforms gave the government more power and helped ease the Depression. As nations increased their production of war materials at the start of World War II, the Great Depression ended. The increased production provided jobs and put large amounts of money back into circulation.

Franklin D. Roosevelt was governor of New York when the stock market crashed in October 1929, creating the worst economic depression in American history. Roosevelt made strenuous attempts to help people without work. He set up the New York State Emergency Relief Commission and appointed the respected Harry Hopkins to run the agency. Another popular figure with a good record for helping the disadvantaged, Frances Perkins, was recruited to the team as state industrial commissioner. With the help of Hopkins and Perkins, Roosevelt introduced state assistance for the unemployed and those too old to work.

Roosevelt was seen as a great success as governor of New York and was the obvious choice as the Democratic presidential candidate in 1932. Although Roosevelt was vague about what he would do about the Depression, he easily beat his unpopular Republican rival, Herbert Hoover. In a measure that garnered substantial popular support, Roosevelt, in his first days of office, moved to put to rest one of the most divisive cultural issues of the 1920s. He supported and signed a bill to legalize the manufacture and sale of beer, an interim measure pending the repeal of Prohibition, for which a constitutional amendment (the Twenty-first) was already in process. The amendment was ratified in 1933.

Roosevelt's first act as president was to deal with the country's banking crisis. Since the beginning of the Depression, a fifth of all banks had been forced to close. As a consequence, approximately 15 percent of people's life savings had been lost. By the beginning of 1933, the American people were starting to lose faith in the banking system, and a significant proportion were withdrawing their money and keeping it at home. The day after taking office as president, Roosevelt ordered all banks to close. He then asked Congress to pass legislation guaranteeing that savers would not lose their money if another financial crisis occurred.

On January 1, 1934, the U.S. government created the Federal Deposit Insurance Corporation (FDIC). With the public still reeling from the financial chaos of the Great Depression, the federally backed corporation provided the stability and reassurance needed to restore people's faith in banks. The FDIC receives no taxpayer funding. Instead, the FDIC charges deposit insurance premiums that are paid by members. Savings and certificates of deposit, when combined, are generally insured up to $100,000 per depositor in each financial institution insured by the FDIC. Deposits held in different ownership categories, such as single or joint accounts, may be insured separately.

On March 9, 1933, Franklin D. Roosevelt called a special session of Congress. He told the members that unemployment could only be solved "by direct recruiting by the Government itself." For the next three months Roosevelt proposed, and Congress passed, a series of important bills that attempted to deal with the problem of unemployment. The special session of Congress became known as the Hundred Days and provided the basis for Roosevelt's New Deal.

The government created a series of agencies to put citizens to work and to get America producing again:

- Works Progress Administration (WPA)

- Civilian Conservation Corps

- National Youth Administration

- Farm Security Administration

- National Recovery Administration

- Public Works Administration

Projects administered by the WPA included the following:

- Federal Writers' Project (1935–39)

- Federal Theatre Project (1935–39)

- Federal Art Project (1935–43)

As well as trying to reduce unemployment, Roosevelt also attempted to reduce the misery for people unable to work. One of the agencies Roosevelt formed was the Federal Emergency Relief Administration, which provided federal money to help those in desperate need.

Other legislation passed by Roosevelt included the following:

- Agricultural Adjustment Act (1933)

- National Housing Act (1934)

- Federal Securities Act (1934)

- Social Security Act (1935)

During the 1936 presidential election, Roosevelt was attacked for not keeping his promise to balance the budget. The National Labor Relations Act was unpopular with businessmen who felt that it favored the trade unions. Some went as far as accusing Roosevelt of being a Communist. However, the New Deal was extremely popular with the electorate, and Roosevelt easily defeated the Republican Party candidate, Alfred M. Landon, by 27,751,612 votes to 16,681,913.

Identify the causes, events, consequences, and significant individuals of the World War II period.

World War II began in September 1939 when Britain and France declared war on Germany following Germany's invasion of Poland. Although the outbreak of war was triggered by Germany's invasion of Poland, the causes of the war are more complex.

In 1919 David Lloyd George of England, Vittorio Orlando of Italy, Georges Clemenceau of France, and Woodrow Wilson of the United States met to discuss how Germany was to be made to pay for the damage resulting from World War I. Wilson wanted a treaty based on a 14-point plan he proposed as a way to bring peace to Europe. Clemenceau wanted revenge and assurance that Germany would never start another war. Lloyd George personally agreed with Wilson but knew that the British public agreed with Clemenceau. He tried to find a compromise between the American and French proposals.

Germany had been expecting a treaty based on Wilson's 14 points and were not happy with the terms of the Treaty of Versailles. However, they had no choice but to sign the document. The main terms of the treaty were as follows:

- **War guilt clause:** Germany should accept the blame for starting World War I.

- **Reparations:** Germany had to pay $13 billion for the damage caused by the war.

- **Disarmament:** Germany was only allowed to have a small army and six naval ships. No tanks, no air force, and no submarines were allowed. The Rhineland area was to be demilitarized.

- **Territorial clauses:** Land was taken from Germany and given to other countries. Union with Austria was forbidden.

The German people were very unhappy with the treaty and thought it was too harsh. Germany could not afford to pay the money, and during the 1920s the people in Germany were very poor. There were not many jobs, and prices for food and basic goods were high. The **Weimar Republic** is the nickname historians have given to the German state during the period from 1919 to 1933 in honor of the city of Weimar. In that city a national assembly convened to write and adopt a new constitution (which became effective on August 11, 1919) for the German Reich following the nation's defeat in World War I. That first attempt to establish a liberal democracy in Germany happened during a time of civil conflict and failed with the ascent of Adolf Hitler and the Nazi Party. People were dissatisfied with the government and voted into power Adolf Hitler, a man who promised to rip up the Treaty of Versailles.

Adolf Hitler became the chancellor of Germany in January 1933. Almost immediately he began secretly building up Germany's army and weapons. In 1934 he increased the size of the army, began building warships, and created a German air force. Compulsory military service was also introduced.

Britain isolated itself at that time. Although Britain and France were aware of Hitler's actions, they were also concerned about the rise of communism and believed that a stronger Germany might help to prevent the spread of communism to the West.

During the 1930s many politicians in both Britain and France came to see that the terms of the Treaty of Versailles had placed restrictions on Germany that were unfair. Hitler's actions were seen as understandable and justifiable. When Germany began rearming in 1934, many politicians felt that Germany had a right to protect itself. It was also argued that a stronger Germany would prevent the spread of Communism westward.

In 1936 Hitler argued that because France had signed a new treaty with Russia, Germany was under threat from both countries and it was essential to German security that troops be stationed in the Rhineland. France was not strong enough to fight Germany without British help, and Britain was not prepared to go to war at that point. Further, many believed that because the Rhineland was a part of Germany, it was reasonable for German troops to be stationed there.

In 1936 Hitler ordered German troops to enter the Rhineland. At this point the German army was not very strong and could have been easily defeated. Yet neither France nor Britain was prepared to start another war.

Hitler also made two important alliances in 1936. The first was called the Rome-Berlin Axis Pact, which allied Hitler's Germany with Mussolini's Italy. The second, called the Anti-Comitern Pact, allied Germany with Japan.

Hitler's next step was to begin taking back the land that Germany had lost as a result of the Treaty of Versailles. In March 1938 German troops marched into Austria. The Austrian leader was forced to hold a vote asking the people whether they wanted to be part of Germany. The results of the vote were fixed and showed that 99 percent of Austrian people wanted Anschluss (union with Germany). The Austrian leader asked Britain, France, and Italy for aid. Hitler promised that Anschluss was the end of his expansionist aims, and not wanting to risk war, the other countries did nothing. Hitler did not keep his word and six months later demanded that the Sudetenland region of Czechoslovakia be handed over to Germany.

In May 1937 Neville Chamberlain became prime minister of Britain. He believed that the Treaty of Versailles had treated Germany badly and that a number of issues associated with the Treaty needed to be put right. He felt that giving in to Hitler's demands would prevent another war. This policy, adopted by Chamberlain's government, became known as the **Policy of Appeasement**.

The most notable example of appeasement was the **Munich Agreement of September 1938**. The leaders of Germany, Britain, France, and Italy signed the agreement, which stated that Germany would regain the Sudetenland but make no further territorial claims. The Czech government was not invited to the conference and protested the loss of the Sudetenland. They felt betrayed by both Britain and France with whom it had made alliances. Stalin was angry at not being invited either. However, the Munich Agreement was generally viewed as a triumph and an excellent example of securing peace through negotiation rather than war. The phrase **"peace for our time"** was spoken on September 30, 1938, by Chamberlain in his speech concerning the Munich Agreement; it is primarily remembered for its irony.

Hitler was not a man of his word and in March 1939 invaded the rest of Czechoslovakia. Despite calls for help from the Czech government, neither Britain nor France was prepared to take military action against Hitler. However, some action was now necessary, and believing that Poland would be Hitler's next target, both Britain and France promised they would take military action against Hitler if he invaded Poland. Chamberlain believed that faced with the prospect of war against Britain and France, Hitler would stop his aggression. Chamberlain was wrong. German troops invaded Poland on September 1, 1939.

The League of Nations was an international organization set up in 1919 to help keep world peace. It was intended that all countries would be members of the league and that disputes arising between countries would be settled by negotiation rather than by force. If negotiations failed, the league's member countries would stop trading with the aggressive country, and if that failed, member countries would use their armies to fight. The United States did not join the League. In theory the League of Nations was a good idea and did have some early successes, but ultimately it was a failure. The whole world was hit by the Great Depression. Trade was reduced, businesses lost income, prices fell, and unemployment rose.

In 1931 Japan was hit badly by the Depression. People lost faith in the government and turned to the army to find a solution. The army invaded Manchuria in China, an area rich in minerals and resources. China appealed to the League of Nations for help. The Japanese government was told to order the army to leave Manchuria immediately. However, the army took no notice of the government and continued its conquest of Manchuria. The league then called for countries to stop trading with Japan, but because of the Depression, many countries did not want to risk losing trade and did not agree to the request. The league then made a further call for Japan to withdraw from Manchuria, but Japan's response was to leave the League of Nations.

In October 1935 Italy invaded Abyssinia. The Abyssinians did not have the strength to withstand an attack by Italy and appealed to the League of Nations for help. The league condemned the attack and called on member states to impose trade restrictions on Italy. However, the trade restrictions were not carried out because they would have little effect. Italy would be able to trade with nations that were not members of the league, particularly America. Further, Britain and France did not want to risk Italy attacking them.

To stop Italy's aggression, the leaders of Britain and France held a meeting and decided that Italy could have two areas of land in Abyssinia provided no further attacks on the African country occurred. Although Mussolini accepted the plan, the public outcry in Britain led to the plan being dropped.

The following are the main reasons for the failure of the League of Nations:

- **Not all countries joined the league.** Although the idea for the League of Nations had come from Woodrow Wilson, an election before the signing of the treaty brought in a new Republican administration that refused to join. As punishment for having started World War I, Germany was not allowed to join, and Russia was excluded because of a growing fear of Communism. Other countries initially decided not to join, and some joined but later left.

- **The league had no power.** The main weapon of the league was to ask member countries to stop trading with an aggressive country. However, this did not work because the aggressive county could still trade with nonmember countries. When the world was hit by the Great Depression in the late 1920s, countries were reluctant to lose trading partners to nonmember countries.

- **The league had no army.** Soldiers were to be supplied by member countries. However, countries were reluctant to get involved and risk provoking an aggressive country into taking direct action against them. Therefore they failed to provide troops.

- **The league was unable to respond quickly.** The Council of the League of Nations only met four times a year, and all nations had to agree to decisions. When countries called for the league to intervene, the league had to set up an emergency meeting, hold discussions, and gain the agreement of all members. This process meant that the league could not act quickly to stop an act of aggression.

HIROHITO

The man known as Tenno to his subjects and Hirohito to the rest of the world ranks as one of the most enigmatic figures of the twentieth century. The ambiguity surrounding his role in leading Japan to war makes simple judgments of him all but impossible. The cultural barriers may be even more formidable than the factual ones: to many of his subjects, the "emperor of heaven" was not really a man at all but the living embodiment of the Japanese people. From every perspective, however, his life offers a powerful lens through which to view Japan's tumultuous history in the twentieth century.

Installed as crown prince at the age of 15, Hirohito assumed the throne in 1926 with the death of his father, Emperor Yoshihito. Because his father had been a weak and sickly man, Hirohito ruled more in the shadow of his grandfather, Emperor Meiji, who presided over Japan's opening up to the West in the late nineteenth century. Even before he assumed the throne, Hirohito reflected the same fascination with the West, particularly after a six-month tour of Europe in 1921, when he picked up a lifelong taste for Western food and clothes.

He presided over one of the largest and most costly military ventures in human history. In the decades after the war, the accepted version of events held that Hirohito was essentially a pawn of the militarists who gained control of the government shortly after he took the throne. General Douglas MacArthur, convinced he needed the emperor to run a smooth occupation, played no small part in establishing that perspective of the Japanese ruler. With Hirohito's quiet manner, love of haiku and marine biology, the image of the peace-loving man who was powerless to stop his country's murderous expansion took hold. But in the decade since his death, a more open inquiry into what happened has convinced many historians that this version, while partially true, is far from accurate. Hirohito's ability to thwart the militarists was certainly limited—he was more a symbol of the state than an actual ruler—but he was not nearly as blameless as his defenders would have it.

On August 15, 1945, the Japanese people heard the voice of their emperor for the first time, and while he avoided using the word *surrender*, his meaning was clear. Japan had lost 2.3 million soldiers and 800,000 civilians in the war. In the difficult days ahead, the emperor did provide a much-needed measure of national unity. Hirohito did his part to remake Japan along an American model, backing the new constitution, renouncing his divinity, and trying gamely to play the part of Japan's first democrat. By the time the emperor's 62-year reign came to an end, Japan had risen like a phoenix out of the postwar rubble to become one of the world's richest countries. It was in demonstrating this remarkable capacity for change that Hirohito truly became the living symbol of his people.

The December 1941 Japanese raid on Pearl Harbor in Hawaii was one of the great defining moments in history. A single carefully planned and well-executed stroke removed the U.S. navy's battleship force as a possible threat to the Japanese Empire's southward expansion. America, unprepared and now considerably weakened, was abruptly brought into World War II as a full combatant.

Eighteen months earlier, President Franklin D. Roosevelt had transferred the U.S. fleet to Pearl Harbor as a presumed deterrent to Japanese aggression. The Japanese military, deeply engaged in the seemingly endless war it had started against China in mid-1937, badly needed oil and other raw materials. Commercial access to those supplies was gradually curtailed as the conquests continued. In July 1941 the Western powers effectively halted trade with Japan. From then on, as the desperate Japanese schemed to seize the oil and mineral-rich East Indies and Southeast Asia, a Pacific war was virtually inevitable.

By late November 1941, with peace negotiations clearly approaching an end, informed U.S. officials fully expected a Japanese attack on the Indies, Malaya, and probably the Philippines. Completely unanticipated was the prospect that Japan would attack to the east as well.

The U.S. fleet's Pearl Harbor base was reachable by an aircraft carrier force, and the Japanese navy secretly sent one across the Pacific with greater aerial striking power than had ever been seen on the world's oceans. Its planes hit just before 8 A.M. on December 7, 1941. Within a short time, five of eight battleships at Pearl Harbor were sunk or sinking, and the rest were damaged. Several other ships and most combat planes based in Hawaii were also knocked out, and more than 2,400 Americans were dead. Soon after, Japanese planes eliminated much of the American air force in the Philippines, and a Japanese army was ashore in Malaya.

Japan's successes, achieved without prior diplomatic formalities, shocked and enraged the previously divided American people into a level of purposeful unity rarely seen before. The anger at the "sneak attack" on Pearl Harbor fueled a determination to fight. Once the battle of Midway in early June 1942 had eliminated much of Japan's striking power, that same anger stoked a relentless war to reverse Japan's conquests and remove it, and its German and Italian allies, as future threats to world peace.

The key leaders of World War II on the Allied side were President Franklin D. Roosevelt, President Harry S. Truman, Prime Minister Winston S. Churchill, Soviet leader Joseph Stalin, French leader Charles de Gaulle, French leader Henri Giraud, and General Chiang Kai-shek of China.

The **Tehran Conference** was the meeting of Joseph Stalin, Franklin D. Roosevelt, and Winston Churchill between November 28 and December 1, 1943, in Tehran, Iran. It was the first World War II conference among the Big Three (the Soviet Union, the United States, and the United Kingdom) that Stalin attended. It succeeded the Cairo Conference and was followed by the Yalta and Potsdam conferences. The chief discussion centered on the opening of a second front in Western Europe. At the same time a separate protocol pledged the three countries to recognize Iran's independence. Most importantly, the conference was organized to plan the final strategy for the war against Nazi Germany and its allies.

The four-power occupation of Germany was finalized at the **Yalta Conference**. Germany was to be divided between Great Britain, the United States, the Soviet Union, and France. A provisional government of Poland was agreed on. But the conference ended with some issues unresolved. Churchill did not trust Stalin, but Roosevelt did. The Yalta Conference may have been the forerunner to the Cold War.

World War II came to an official end in May 1945, but Roosevelt had died the month before. Vice President Harry Truman became president and carried on the policies of Churchill and Roosevelt. He attended the **Potsdam Conference** along with Stalin and Churchill. The unconditional surrender of the Axis Powers had been made a reality at Potsdam. But while Churchill was at the conference, his first term as prime minister came to an end. The Conservative Party lost the majority in the House of Commons. The Churchill and Roosevelt era had come to an end, but their policies for peace in the free world continued.

Identify key causes, events, consequences, and significant individuals related to domestic and foreign affairs during the Cold War era (1945–91).

The Western democracies and the Soviet Union discussed the progress of World War II and the nature of the postwar settlement at conferences in Tehran (1943), Yalta (February 1945), and Potsdam (July–August 1945). After the war, disputes between the Soviet Union and the Western democracies, particularly over the Soviet takeover of eastern European states, led Winston Churchill to warn in 1946 that an **"iron curtain"** was descending through the middle of Europe. For his part Joseph Stalin deepened the estrangement between the United States and the Soviet Union when he asserted in 1946 that World War II was an unavoidable and inevitable consequence of "capitalist imperialism" and implied that such a war might recur.

The **Cold War** was a period of East–West competition, tension, and conflict short of full-scale war but characterized by mutual perceptions of hostile intention between military and political alliances, or blocs. There were real wars, sometimes called proxy wars because they were fought by Soviet allies rather than the Soviet Union itself, along with competition for influence in developing countries (primarily Africa and South America) and a major nuclear arms race between the superpowers (the United States and the Soviet Union).

After Stalin's death East–West relations went through phases of alternating relaxation and confrontation, including a cooperative phase during the 1960s and another, termed **détente**, during the 1970s. A final phase during the late 1980s and early 1990s was hailed by President Mikhail Gorbachev—and even more so by the president of the new post-communist Russian republic, Boris Yeltsin, and by U.S. President George H.W. Bush—as beginning a partnership between the two nations that could address many global problems.

As part of the Cold War, Nikita Khrushchev conceived the idea of placing intermediate-range nuclear missiles in Cuba as a means of countering an emerging lead of the United States in developing and deploying strategic missiles. He also presented the scheme as a means of protecting Cuba from another U.S.-sponsored invasion, such as the failed attempt at the Bay of Pigs in April, 1961. This brought on what is known as the **Cuban Missile Crisis**.

After obtaining Fidel Castro's approval, the Soviet Union worked quickly and secretly to build missile installations in Cuba. On October 16, 1962, President John Kennedy was shown reconnaissance photographs of Soviet missile installations under construction in Cuba. On October 22, after seven days of guarded and intense debate in the U.S. administration and denials by Soviet diplomats that installations for offensive missiles were being built in Cuba, President Kennedy made a televised address announcing the discovery of the installations and proclaiming that any nuclear missile attack from Cuba would be regarded as an attack by the Soviet Union and would be responded to accordingly. He also imposed a naval quarantine on Cuba to prevent further Soviet shipments of offensive military weapons from arriving there.

During the crisis the two sides exchanged many letters and other communications. Khrushchev sent letters to Kennedy indicating the deterrent nature of the missiles in Cuba and the peaceful intentions of the Soviet Union. In one long, rambling letter to Kennedy, Khrushchev seemingly proposing that the missile installations would be dismantled and personnel removed in exchange for United States assurances that it or its proxies would not invade Cuba. A second letter suggested that missile installations in Cuba would be dismantled if the United States dismantled its missile installations in Turkey. The Kennedy administration decided to ignore the second letter and to accept the offer outlined in the previous letter. Khrushchev then announced that he would dismantle the installations and return them to the Soviet Union, expressing his trust that the United States would not invade Cuba. Further negotiations were held to implement the October 28 agreement, including a U.S. demand that the Soviets remove light bombers from Cuba, and to specify the exact form and conditions of U.S. assurances not to invade Cuba.

The **Vietnam War** was a military struggle fought from 1959 to 1975, with the North Vietnamese and the National Liberation Front (NLF) in conflict with U.S. forces and the South Vietnamese army. From 1946 until 1954, the Vietnamese had struggled for their independence from France during the First Indochina War. At the end of that war the country was temporarily divided into North and South Vietnam. North Vietnam came under the control of the Vietnamese Communists who had opposed France and aimed for a unified Vietnam under communist rule. South Vietnam was controlled by Vietnamese who had collaborated with the French.

In 1965 the United States sent in troops to prevent the South Vietnamese government from collapsing. Ultimately, however, the United States failed to achieve its goal, and in 1975 Vietnam was reunified under communist control. In 1976 the country officially became the Socialist Republic of Vietnam. During the conflict about 3 million to 4 million

Vietnamese on both sides were killed; in addition, another 1.5 million to 2 million Lao and Cambodians were drawn into the war. More than 58,000 Americans lost their lives.

Identify causes, events, consequences, and significant individuals associated with movements for equality, civil rights, and civil liberties.

American society has undergone important changes during the last 50 years. Three of the primary factors leading to social and cultural change were the expanded role of women in the workplace; the influence of new immigrant groups, particularly Asians and Latin Americans; and the technology revolution.

One result of the modern campaign for women's rights is an increasingly large percentage of women in America's labor force. For example, in 1960 women made up only 32 percent of the U.S. workforce; by 1994 the proportion had increased to 46 percent. In 1960 only 35 percent of American women were working outside the home; by 1990 that proportion had risen to nearly 60 percent, and there were millions of working mothers. By the end of the 1970s, many American women were working in nontraditional jobs. Two outstanding examples of this were Sandra Day O'Connor and Sally Ride. In 1981 President Ronald Reagan appointed Sandra Day O'Connor the first woman to the Supreme Court. Two years later Sally Ride, who was the first female astronaut in the United States, became the first American woman in space. Women in the workplace have faced discrimination because of their sex. Because the Civil Rights Act of 1964 prohibited sex discrimination by employers, American women could seek relief from job discrimination in federal court. The federal courts have consistently protected employment opportunities for American women by citing not only the Civil Rights Act but also the equal protection clause of the Fourteenth Amendment.

The twentieth-century struggle to expand civil rights for African Americans involved the National Association for the Advancement of Colored People (NAACP), the Congress of Racial Equality, the Urban League, the Southern Christian Leadership Conference, and other organizations. The civil rights movement, led especially by Martin Luther King Jr. in the late 1950s and 1960s, and the executive leadership provided by President Lyndon B. Johnson, encouraged the passage of the most comprehensive civil rights legislation to date, the **Civil Rights Act of 1964**. As first proposed by President Kennedy in June 1963, the act prohibited discrimination for reason of color, race, religion, or national origin in places of public accommodation covered by interstate commerce—for example, restaurants, hotels, motels, and theaters. By the time it had passed both houses of Congress, the act included Title IV, encouraging the desegregation of public schools, and Title VII, forbidding discrimination in employment based on race, color, religion, national origin, or sex (including same-sex discrimination).

In 1965 passage of the **Voting Rights Act** placed federal observers at polls to ensure equal voting rights. The **Civil Rights Act of 1968** dealt with housing and real estate discrimination. In addition to congressional action on civil rights, other branches of the government took steps to promote equality. The most notable of these were the Supreme Court decisions in 1954 and 1955 declaring racial segregation in public schools unconstitutional and the court's rulings in 1955 banning segregation in publicly financed parks, playgrounds, and golf courses.

In 1972 the Senate passed the Equal Rights Amendment (ERA), intended to prohibit all discrimination based on sex, but after failing to win ratification in a sufficient number of states, the ERA was abandoned. Since the 1970s several gay rights groups have worked, mainly on the local and state levels, for legislation preventing discrimination in housing and employment. In another extension of civil rights protection, the Americans with Disabilities Act (1990) barred discrimination against disabled persons in employment and provided for improved access to public facilities.

MARTIN LUTHER KING JR.

Among the people with key roles in the civil rights movement was **Martin Luther King Jr.** Intelligent, dedicated, charismatic, and religious, King had what it took to inspire the conscience of the American public. He appealed to the moral sense of Americans, and after years of leading civil rights activists in nonviolent protest and direct action, his leadership helped to desegregate the South.

Martin Luther King Jr. was born in Atlanta, Georgia, to Alberta Williams King and Reverend Martin Luther King Sr. In Atlanta King excelled in school, easily skipping the ninth and twelfth grades. When he was fifteen, he received a unique opportunity. Under a special program created for high school students, King was admitted to Morehouse College. He began college in the fall of 1944.

Despite his achievements in high school, King found that college was more challenging. He was only able to read at an eighth-grade level. Despite this hindrance, King still managed to finish college in 1948 with a bachelor's degree in sociology. Although he had previously considered pursuing a career in the law or medicine, he decided after graduation to enter the ministry.

In the fall of 1948, he began attending Crozer Theological Seminary in Chester, Pennsylvania. At Crozer he approached his studies with a seriousness he had not shown before. He studied the works of theologians like Reinhold Niebuhr and took a particular interest in Mahatma Gandhi's philosophy of nonviolent resistance. However, King was heavily influenced by Niebuhr's idea of man's sinfulness. He believed that this sinfulness prevented nonviolent resistance from being effective. King, therefore, would never come to accept nonviolent resistance until it was put into action years later during the Montgomery bus boycott.

As opposed to King's mediocre work at Morehouse, at Crozer his professors were impressed with his intellectual ability. At the suggestion of a professor, King decided to pursue a doctorate degree. He received his bachelor's degree in Divinity in 1951, and enrolled at Boston University to study systematic theology that fall. While in Boston he met Coretta Scott, and they married in 1953. During their marriage they had four children. He received his Ph.D. in 1955.

In 1954 King became the pastor of Dexter Avenue Baptist Church in Montgomery, Alabama. Shortly thereafter, on December 1, 1955, Rosa Parks was arrested after she refused to give up her seat to a white rider on a Montgomery city bus. Based on Parks's decision to contest the arrest, the Montgomery Improvement Association was founded to organize the boycott of city buses. The members of the association elected King as president.

Nonviolent resistance slowly began to emerge as the defining force in the protest. During the boycott, King received numerous threats, and his home was bombed. King and his family were not harmed, but the incident cemented his belief in the effectiveness of nonviolent resistance. After more than a year, the boycott ended when the Supreme Court affirmed the district court's order to desegregate the city's buses.

After successfully navigating the bus boycott, King emerged as a national figure. King and other ministers founded the Southern Christian Leadership Conference (SCLC), which served to organize civil rights events throughout the South.

In 1959 King furthered his knowledge of Gandhi's nonviolent philosophy when he visited India. On his return King moved to Atlanta, Georgia, to minister with his father at Ebenezer Baptist Church. While a co-pastor, King also stayed involved with the SCLC.

In October 1960 King participated in a student sit-in and was arrested and sentenced to prison. His sentence received nationwide media attention. After President Dwight Eisenhower decided not to intervene, presidential candidate John F. Kennedy got involved, and King was released.

King continued to participate in nonviolent protests. King, A. Philip Randolph, Bayard Rustin, and other civil rights leaders organized the March on Washington for Jobs and Freedom. It took place on August 28, 1963, at the Lincoln Memorial. At the march King gave his famous "I Have a Dream" speech. More than 250,000 people gathered at the memorial to hear the speech, which was broadcast over radio and television.

In 1963 *Time* magazine named King "Man of the Year," and he received the Nobel Peace Prize in 1964. This was also an important year for the civil rights movement. As the movement had garnered widespread support, the Civil Rights Act of 1964 was passed.

After 1965 some African Americans became impatient with King's method of nonviolent resistance. During the 1965 march for voting rights conducted in Selma, Alabama, opposition became more prevalent when the marchers, who were led by King, marched across the Edmund Pettus Bridge but stopped when confronted by a barricade of state troopers. King and the marchers kneeled, prayed, and then turned around.

Radical African Americans believed that King should have handled the Selma situation differently. As the black power movement became stronger and Malcolm X's message of black nationalism became more accepted by northern urban blacks, King increasingly became a controversial figure.

Despite the growing dissatisfaction with King's tactics, he expanded his focus to include opposition to the Vietnam War. However, King's disagreement with the war led to strained relations with the President Johnson's administration.

King also began focusing on the poor of all races. In the spring of 1968, in the midst of planning the Poor People's March on Washington, King left for Memphis, Tennessee, to lead a strike of city sanitation workers. It was there that he delivered his last speech, "I've Been to the Mountaintop." The next day, on April 4, 1968, while standing on the balcony of his motel, he was shot. He was 39 years old. A few months later, on June 8, 1968, James Earl Ray was arrested in London, England. Ray pled guilty to murder (to avoid the death penalty) and was sentenced to 99 years in prison.

ROSA PARKS

On December 1, 1955, 43-year-old **Rosa Parks**, known as the **Mother of the Civil Rights Movement**, boarded a Montgomery, Alabama, city bus after finishing work as a tailor's assistant at the Montgomery Fair department store. As all black patrons were required to do, she paid her fare at the front of the bus and then reboarded in the rear. She sat in a vacant seat in the back next to a man and across the aisle from two women.

After a few stops the seats in the front of the bus became full and a white man who had boarded, stood in the aisle. The bus driver asked Parks, the man next to her, and the two women to let the white man have their seats. As the others moved, Parks remained in her seat. The bus driver again asked her to move, but she refused. The driver called the police, and she was arrested.

The arrest of Parks sparked the bus boycott in Montgomery. Community leaders spread the word that a one-day bus boycott was scheduled for December

5. On that cold and cloudy morning, onlookers watched as the buses drove by with few black passengers onboard. The boycott lasted for 381 days and was a success. On December 20, 1956, buses were desegregated.

Parks was born on February 4, 1913, in Tuskegee, Alabama, to James and Leona McCauley. At the age of two, Parks, her brother, and her mother moved to Pine Level, Alabama, to live with her grandparents. She later attended the Montgomery Industrial School for Girls, which was funded by liberal northern women and went on to study at the Alabama State Teachers College.

After graduation she moved with her husband, Raymond Parks, to Montgomery. Parks and her husband joined the local chapter of the NAACP. She acted as the secretary from 1943 to 1956. She also worked to help improve conditions for African Americans. She worked on cases involving such issues as flogging, peonage, rape, and murder.

Because of her stand against bus segregation, Parks lost her seamstress job. In 1957 she and her husband moved to Detroit, where she served on the staff of Representative John Conyers from 1965 to 1988.

In 1979 Parks won the Spingarn Medal for her civil rights work. Additionally, in her honor the Southern Christian Leadership Council established the annual Rosa Parks Freedom Award. In 1987 she founded the Rosa and Raymond Parks Institute for Self-Development to help young people. She received the Presidential Medal of Freedom in 1996 and the Congressional Gold Medal in 1999. Parks died of natural causes at her home in Detroit on October 24, 2005.

MALCOLM X

Malcolm X was initially known for his controversial stance on racial separatism, but after a pilgrimage to Mecca, while he still advocated black nationalism, he also accepted a more orthodox Islamist view of the "true brotherhood" of man. He came to believe that there was a potential for cross-racial alliance.

Named Malcolm Little by his parents, Malcolm X was born on May 19, 1925, in Omaha, Nebraska. Malcolm's father, Earl Little, was an outspoken supporter of the black nationalist Marcus Garvey. As a result he received numerous death threats and was forced to move his family several times. While the family was in Lansing, Michigan, their home was burned down. Two years later Malcolm's father was murdered. Malcolm's mother had an emotional breakdown and was unable to care for Malcolm and his siblings. The children were split up and sent to foster homes.

Malcolm dropped out of high school and at first worked odd jobs in Boston, Massachusetts. But he soon moved to Harlem in New York City, where he became involved in criminal activity. Malcolm moved back to Boston, where he was convicted of burglary in 1946.

While Malcolm was in prison, he converted to the Muslim religious sect the Nation of Islam. On his release in 1952, he changed his last name to X because he considered the name Little to have been a slave name. The Nation of Islam's leader, Elijah Muhammad, made Malcolm a minister and sent him around the country on speaking engagements. Malcolm spoke about black pride and separatism, encouraging African Americans to reject the civil rights movement's focus on integration and equality.

Malcolm was a charismatic speaker and soon was able to use newspapers, television, and radio to spread the Nation of Islam's message. Membership to the Nation of Islam increased dramatically because of Malcolm's speeches. However, while many blacks were embracing his message, civil rights leaders rejected him. Malcolm also became a concern of the government. The Federal Bureau of Investigation began surveillance of him and infiltrated the Nation of Islam.

While Malcolm had garnered increasing attention, his relationship with Elijah Muhammad became strained in 1963. Malcolm learned that contrary to Muhammad's teaching of celibacy until marriage, Muhammad was having sexual relations with six women. Malcolm felt that Muhammad was committing fraud and refused to keep it a secret.

When President John F. Kennedy was assassinated on November 22, 1963, Malcolm publicly described it as "the chickens coming home to roost." Because of this comment, Muhammad silenced him for 90 days.

In March 1964 Malcolm left the Nation of Islam and founded the Muslim Mosque, Inc. A month later he took a pilgrimage to Mecca, Saudi Arabia. It was there that his view of separatism changed. He discovered that white and black Muslims could coexist. While he still advocated black nationalism, he also accepted a more orthodox Islamic view of the "true brotherhood of man" and believed that there was a potential for a cross-racial alliance.

When he returned to the United States, Malcolm stopped advocating separatism and instead relayed the message of integration and world brotherhood. However, he discovered that the Nation of Islam wanted to assassinate him. On February 14, 1965, his home was firebombed, but no one was hurt.

A few days later on February 21, 1965, while Malcolm was on stage at Manhattan's Audubon Ballroom, three gunmen shot him to death. The gunmen were arrested and convicted. It was later discovered that they were members of the Nation of Islam. Malcolm was buried on February 27, 1965, in Hartsdale, New York.

JAMES MEREDITH

Although **James Meredith** was not the first African American to apply and be denied admission to the University of Mississippi, his fate would be much different from that of the four before him. With the assistance of the NAACP, Meredith would eventually be admitted to the University of Mississippi and become its first black student.

Meredith applied for admission to the University of Mississippi on January 31, 1961. At the time of his application, he was a student at Jackson State College, an all-black school. On February 4, 1961, Meredith received a telegram denying his admission. On February 7 Meredith sent a letter to the Department of Justice requesting assistance. In the meantime Meredith wrote the university numerous times requesting that his application be considered for the summer session.

Finally, on May 31, 1961, the NAACP Legal Defense and Educational Fund filed suit in the U.S. District Court. The suit alleged that Meredith was refused admission to the university based solely on his race. After numerous legal battles and appeals, the Supreme Court handed down its decision on September 10, 1962, upholding Meredith's right to admission at the University of Mississippi.

Enforcing the Supreme Court's ruling was not easy. Mississippi's governor, Ross Barnett, vowed publicly to block the admission of Meredith to the state university. Barnett was appointed registrar of the university and used his position to prohibit Meredith's admission. In addition, the Mississippi legislature passed a law that prohibited any person who was convicted of a state crime from admission to a state school. This law was clearly targeted at Meredith, who had been convicted of false voter registration.

In spite of the efforts to block Meredith's registration, on September 30 a deal to allow Meredith to register was made between Attorney General Robert Kennedy and Barnett. Meredith was secretly escorted onto campus. Deputy federal marshals, U.S. border patrolmen, and federal prison guards were stationed on and around the campus to protect Meredith. A mob of more than 2,000 protesters converged on the campus. Those standing guard were assaulted throughout the night with guns, bricks, Molotov cocktails, and bottles. Tear gas was used to control the crowd. Federal troops arrived, and the mob retreated. In the end two people were dead, 160 were injured, and 28 marshals had been shot.

On the morning of October 1, 1962, James Meredith registered at Ole Mississippi. Meredith would go on to finish his education at the university and graduate in 1964. In 1966 he published the book *Three Years in Mississippi*, in which he recounted his experiences at the university.

JAMES FARMER

U.S. civil rights leader **James Farmer** led the Congress of Racial Equality (CORE) and introduced the nonviolent sit-ins and Freedom Rides that became symbols of the civil rights movement of the early 1960s. His efforts, along with those of others, led to the passage of the Civil Rights Act of 1964 and the Voting Rights Act of 1965.

James Leonard Farmer was born on January 12, 1920, in Marshall, Texas. He grew up in Holly Springs, Mississippi, where his minister father taught theology at all-black Rust College. Farmer studied at Wiley College in Texas and Howard University in Washington, D.C. Influenced by the nonviolent methods of Indian leader Mahatma Gandhi, he helped found CORE in 1942. After the South disregarded the Supreme Court decision that segregated seating on interstate buses was unconstitutional, CORE protested in May 1961 with the first Freedom Ride in which blacks and whites rode together. Subsequent Freedom Rides became symbols of the civil rights movement of the early 1960s.

Farmer served as national director of CORE from 1961 to 1966, after which he ran for Congress; served as an assistant secretary of the Department of Health, Education, and Welfare; wrote books on labor and race relations; and taught at several colleges. In 1998 he was awarded the Presidential Medal of Freedom by President Bill Clinton. Farmer died on July 9, 1999, in Fredericksburg, Virginia.

EMMETT TILL

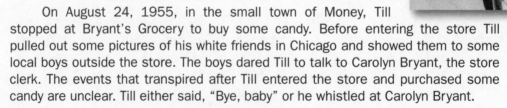

Fourteen-year-old **Emmett Till** was excited about his trip from his home in Chicago's south side to the Mississippi Delta to visit relatives. Before his departure, his mother, Mamie Till Bradley, a teacher, had done her best to advise him about how to behave when interacting with white people. Till's mother understood that in Mississippi race relations were different from those in Chicago. In Mississippi more than 500 blacks had been lynched since 1882, and racially motivated murders were not unfamiliar, especially in the Delta where Till was going.

On August 24, 1955, in the small town of Money, Till stopped at Bryant's Grocery to buy some candy. Before entering the store Till pulled out some pictures of his white friends in Chicago and showed them to some local boys outside the store. The boys dared Till to talk to Carolyn Bryant, the store clerk. The events that transpired after Till entered the store and purchased some candy are unclear. Till either said, "Bye, baby" or he whistled at Carolyn Bryant.

Till did not understand the magnitude of his act. He continued to think nothing of the event as three days passed without incident. However, on the fourth day, early Sunday morning, Roy Bryant, Carolyn's husband, and J. W. Milam,

Roy's half-brother, knocked on the door of the home where Till was staying. With a pistol and flashlight in hand, they asked for Till. The men woke Till, told him to get dressed, and took him out of the house. Several hours later Mamie Till was notified of her son's kidnapping. A search of the area was conducted, and Mamie Till notified Chicago newspapers of her son's disappearance. Bryant and Milam were arrested for kidnapping.

Three days later Till's body was discovered in the Tallahatchie River. It was weighted down by a 75-pound cotton gin fan tied around Till's neck with barbed wire. His face was so mutilated that the body could be identified only by the ring that Till had been wearing. The trial of Bryant and Milam ultimately brought a verdict of not guilty. The case led northern blacks to realize that they could be victimized by southern violence against blacks and brought national attention to civil rights issues.

THURGOOD MARSHALL

Thurgood Marshall is best known for serving as the first black Supreme Court Justice, but before his career on the bench, he successfully argued civil rights cases on behalf of the NAACP.

Marshall was born on July 2, 1908, in Baltimore, Maryland. He received his bachelor's degree in 1930 from Lincoln University, where he graduated cum laude. He went on to attend law school at Howard University. In 1933 he graduated magna cum laude. In 1936 Marshall began working for the NAACP and later became the director of NAACP's Legal Defense and Education Fund. In his legal career Marshall argued 32 cases before the U.S. Supreme Court and won 29 of them. One of those cases, *Brown v. Board of Education* (1954), made segregation in public schools unconstitutional.

In 1961 Marshall's success as an attorney gained national recognition when President John F. Kennedy nominated him to the U.S. Court of Appeals for the Second Circuit. Marshall's nomination was met with opposition, but months later he was finally confirmed by the Senate. In July 1965 President Lyndon Johnson appointed Marshall as the U.S. solicitor general. Two years later President Johnson nominated him to the U.S. Supreme Court.

As a Supreme Court Justice, Marshall was a strong advocate for civil rights and was steadfast in his goal to end discrimination. He retired from the court in 1991 and died on January 24, 1993.

The 1954 United States Supreme Court decision in **Oliver L. Brown et al. v. the Board of Education of Topeka, Kansas, et al.** is among the most significant judicial turning points in the development of our country. Originally led by Charles H. Houston and later Thurgood Marshall and a formidable legal team, the case dismantled the legal basis for racial segregation in schools and other public facilities. By declaring that the discriminatory nature of racial segregation violates the Fourteenth Amendment, which guarantees all citizens equal protection under the law, *Brown v. Board of Education* laid the foundation for shaping future national and international policies regarding human rights. The case was not simply about children and education. The laws and policies struck down by this court decision were products of the human tendencies to prejudge, discriminate against, and stereotype other people by their ethnic, religious, physical, or cultural characteristics. Ending this behavior as a legal practice caused far-reaching social and ideological implications that continue to be felt throughout our country. The *Brown* decision inspired and galvanized human rights struggles across the country and around the world.

What this legal challenge represents is at the core of U.S. history and the freedoms we enjoy. The *Brown* decision reaffirmed the sovereign power of the people of the United States in the protection of their natural rights from arbitrary limits and restrictions imposed by state and local governments. These rights are recognized in the Declaration of Independence and guaranteed by the U.S. Constitution. Despite its importance, however, the *Brown* case is often misunderstood, and the facts of the case have been overshadowed by myths and mischaracterizations. *Brown v. Board of Education* was not the first challenge to school segregation. In 1849 African Americans filed suit against an educational system that mandated racial segregation in the case of *Roberts v. City of Boston*. Oliver Brown, the namesake of the 1954 decision, was just one of the nearly 200 plaintiffs from five states who were part of the NAACP cases brought before the Supreme Court in 1951. The Kansas case was named for Oliver Brown as a legal strategy to have a man head the plaintiff roster.

The *Brown* decision initiated educational and social reform throughout the United States and was a catalyst in launching the modern civil rights movement. Although bringing about change in the years since the *Brown* case has been difficult, the victory brought this country one step closer to living up to its democratic ideas.

Identify key individuals, events, and issues related to Florida history.

Called the Sunshine State, Florida is known for its balmy, sunny weather and beautiful beaches. Juan Ponce de León, in search of the elusive fountain of youth, was the first European to explore Florida. Saint Augustine, founded by the Spanish in 1565, is the oldest permanent European settlement in the continental United States. Statehood for Florida came in 1845. Florida's state flower is the orange blossom, which is particularly fitting because oranges are a main export of the state. Because of its shape and location—a long peninsula between the Atlantic Ocean and the Gulf of Mexico—Florida attracts millions of visitors each year to its many seaside resort areas, making tourism a major industry. The capital is Tallahassee.

Florida became an organized territory of the United States on March 30, 1822. The Americans merged East Florida and West Florida (although most of West Florida was annexed to the Orleans and Mississippi territories) and established a new capital in Tallahassee, conveniently located halfway between the East Florida capital of Saint Augustine and the West Florida capital of Pensacola. The boundaries of Florida's first two counties, Escambia and Saint Johns, approximately coincided with the boundaries of West and East Florida, respectively.

As settlement increased, pressure grew on the U.S. government to remove the Native Americans from their lands in Florida. To the chagrin of Georgia landowners, the Seminole harbored and integrated runaway blacks, and clashes between whites and Native Americans grew with the influx of new settlers. In 1832 the U.S. government signed the Treaty of Payne's Landing with some of the Seminole chiefs, promising them lands west of the Mississippi River if they agreed to leave Florida voluntarily. Many of the Seminole left at that time, while those remaining prepared to defend their claims to the land. White settlers pressured the government to remove all the indigenous people, by force if necessary, and in 1835 the U.S. Army arrived to enforce the treaty.

The **Second Seminole War** began at the end of 1835, with the Dade Massacre, when Seminole ambushed U.S. troops marching from Fort Brooke (Tampa) to reinforce Fort King (Ocala), killing or mortally wounding all but one of the 108 soldiers. Between 900 and 1,500 Seminole warriors effectively employed guerrilla tactics against U.S. troops for seven years. The war dragged on until 1842. The U.S. government is estimated to have spent between $20 million and $40 million on the war, at the time an astronomical sum. Almost all the Seminole were forcibly exiled to Creek lands west of the Mississippi; about 300 were allowed to remain in the Everglades.

On March 3, 1845, Florida became the twenty-seventh state of the United States of America. Almost half of the state's population comprised black slaves working on plantations.

The Seminole

Two legendary Seminole leaders were the famous warrior **Osceola** (also known as William Powell) and the inspirational medicine man **Abiaka** (also known as Sam Jones). Elegant in dress, handsome of face, passionate in nature and giant of ego, Osceola masterminded successful battles against five baffled U.S. generals, murdered a U.S. Indian agent, took punitive action against any Seminole who cooperated with the white man, and stood as a national manifestation of the Seminole's strong reputation for not surrendering.

Osceola was not a chief, but his skill as an orator and his bravado in conflict earned him great influence over Seminole war actions.

Osceola's capture, under a controversial flag of truce offered by General Thomas Jessup, remains today one of the blackest marks in American military history. A larger-than-life character, Osceola is the subject of numerous myths; his 1838 death in a Charleston, South Carolina, prison was the front-page story in newspapers around the world. At the time of his death, Osceola was the most famous American Indian.

Though his exploits were not as well publicized, Seminole medicine man Abiaka may have been more important to the internal Seminole war machine than Osceola. Abiaka was a powerful spiritual leader who used his "medicine" to stir Seminole warriors into a frenzy. His genius directed Seminole gains in several battles, including the 1837 ambush now known as the battle of Okeechobee.

Many years older than most of the Seminole leadership of that era, wise old Abiaka was a staunch resistor of removal. He kept the resistance fueled before and after Osceola's period of prominence and, when the fighting had concluded, was the only major Seminole leader to remain in Florida. Starved, surrounded, sought with a vengeance, Abiaka would answer no flag of truce, no offer of compromise, no demand of surrender. His final camp was in the Big Cypress Swamp, not far from the Seminole's Big Cypress community of today.

By May 10, 1842, when a frustrated President John Tyler ordered the end of military actions against the Seminole, more than $20 million had been spent, 1,500 American soldiers had died, and still no formal peace treaty had been signed. At that time it was the most costly military campaign in the young country's history. Thirteen years later a U.S. Army survey party seeking the whereabouts of Abiaka and other Seminole groups was attacked by Seminole warriors under the command of the colorful Billy Bowlegs. The nation invested its entire reserve into the apprehension of the ambushers.

The eventual capture and deportation of Bowlegs ended aggressions between the Seminole and the United States. Unlike their dealings with other Indian tribes, however, the U.S. government could not force surrender from the Florida Seminole. Historians estimate there may have been only a few hundred unconquered Seminole men, women, and children left all hiding in the swamps and Everglades of South Florida. No chicanery, no offer of cattle, land, liquor, or God could lure the last few from their perches of ambush deep in the wilderness.

Following Abraham Lincoln's election in 1860, Florida joined other southern states in seceding from the Union. Secession took place January 10, 1861, and after less than a month as an independent republic, Florida became one of the founding members of the Confederate States of America. Because Florida was an important supply route for the Confederate Army, Union forces operated a blockade around the entire state. Union troops occupied major ports such as Cedar Key, Jacksonville, Key West, and Pensacola. Though numerous skirmishes occurred in Florida, including the battle of Natural Bridge and the battle of Gainesville, the only major battle was the battle of Olustee near Lake City.

After meeting the requirements of Reconstruction, including ratifying amendments to the U.S. Constitution, Florida was readmitted to the United States on July 25, 1868.

During the late nineteenth century, Florida started to become a popular tourist destination as railroads expanded into the area. Railroad magnate Henry Plant built a luxury hotel in Tampa, which later became the campus for the University of Tampa. Henry Flagler built the Florida East Coast Railway from Jacksonville to Key West and constructed numerous luxury hotels along the route, including in the cities of Saint Augustine, Ormond Beach, and West Palm Beach.

In February 1888 Florida had a special tourist: President Grover Cleveland, his wife, and some members of his staff. He visited the Subtropical Exposition in Jacksonville where he gave a speech supporting tourism to the state; then he took a train to Saint Augustine, meeting Henry Flagler, and then continued by train to Titusville, where he boarded a steamboat and visited Rock Ledge. On his return trip he visited Sanford and Winter Park.

The 1920s were a prosperous time for much of the nation. Florida's new railroads opened up large areas to development, spurring a Florida land boom. Investors of all kinds, mostly from outside Florida, raced to buy and sell rapidly appreciating land in new communities such as Miami and Palm Beach. Most of the people who bought land in Florida did so without stepping foot in the state, by hiring people to speculate and buy the land for them. By 1925 the market ran out of buyers to pay the high prices, and soon the boom became a bust. The 1926 Miami Hurricane further depressed the real estate market. The Great Depression arrived in 1929, but by that time economic decay already consumed much of Florida.

Florida's first theme parks emerged in the1930s and included Cypress Gardens (1936) near Winter Haven and Marineland (1938) near Saint Augustine. Walt Disney chose central Florida as the site of his planned Walt Disney World Resort in the 1960s and began purchasing land. In 1971 the first component of the resort, the Magic Kingdom, opened and began the dramatic transformation of the Orlando area into a resort destination with a wide variety of theme parks. Besides Disney World, the Orlando area today features the Universal Orlando Resort, Sea World, and Wet 'n Wild.

Starting in the early twentieth century and accelerating as World War II began, the state has proven itself to be a major hub for the U.S. armed forces. Naval Air Station Pensacola was originally established in 1826 and became the first U.S. naval aviation facility in 1917. As the entire nation mobilized for World War II, many bases were established in Florida, including Naval Air Station Jacksonville, Naval Station Mayport, Naval Air Station Cecil Field, and Homestead Air Force Base. Eglin Air Force Base and MacDill Air Force Base (now the home of U.S. Central Command) were also developed during that time. During the Cold War, Florida's coastal access and proximity to Cuba continued the development of those and other military facilities. Since the end of the Cold War, some military facilities in Florida have closed, including major bases at Homestead and Cecil Field, but the military presence is still significant.

Because of Florida's low latitude, it was chosen in 1949 as a test site for the country's nascent missile program. Patrick Air Force Base and the Cape Canaveral launch site began to take shape in the 1950s. By the early 1960s the space race was in full swing and generated a huge boom in the communities around Cape Canaveral. That area is now known as the Space Coast and features the Kennedy Space Center. It is also a major center of the aerospace industry. To date all manned orbital space flights launched by the United States have been launched from Kennedy Space Center.

Florida's population is continually changing. After World War II the state was transformed as air conditioning and the interstate highway system encouraged migration from the north. In 1950 Florida was ranked twentieth among the states in population; by 2003 Florida was ranked fourth. With its low tax rates and warm climate, Florida became the destination for many retirees from the Northeast and Canada. The Cuban Revolution of 1959 led to a large wave of Cuban immigration into southern Florida, which transformed Miami into a major center of commerce, finance, and transportation for all of Latin America. Immigration from Haiti and other Caribbean states continues to the present day.

Knowledge of Social Science and Its Methodology

The following skills are used as a basis to determine your competency for the social science and methodology portion of the FTCE Social Science Grades 6–12:

- Identify the social science disciplines, including anthropology, psychology, and sociology.

- Identify social science concepts (e.g., culture, class, technology, race, gender).

- Analyze the interrelationships between social science disciplines.

- Interpret tabular and graphic representations of information related to the social sciences.

- Identify appropriate strategies, methods, tools, and technology for the teaching of social science.

- Evaluate and interpret examples of primary source documents to show historical perspective.

Identify the social science disciplines, including anthropology, psychology, and sociology.

The social sciences are a group of academic disciplines that study human aspects of the world. They diverge from the arts and humanities in that the social sciences tend to emphasize the use of the scientific method in the study of humanity, including quantitative and qualitative methods. Knowledge of one discipline typically requires knowledge of another. The social sciences are intertwined.

- **Anthropology** has been called "the most scientific of the humanities, and the most humanistic of the sciences." Anthropology is a science of humankind. It studies all facets of society and culture, including tools, techniques, traditions, language, beliefs, kinships, values, social institutions, economic mechanisms, cravings for beauty and art, and struggles for prestige. It describes the impact of humans on other humans. With the exception of the physical anthropology discipline, anthropology focuses on human characteristics generated and propagated by humans themselves.

- **Sociology** is the study of how we become members of groups, how we move among groups, and how being in various groups affects individuals and the groups in which they participate.

- **Political science** is the study of the principles of government, the manner in which government conducts itself, how we identify ourselves as citizens of a particular nation, how we participate in our political structure and how it affects us, and what motivates us to affiliate ourselves with certain points of view or parties.

- **History** is the study of the past and how it affects our views of the present.

- **Psychology** is an academic and applied discipline involving the scientific study of mental processes and behavior.

- **Geography** is the study of the earth and its features, inhabitants, and phenomena.

- **Economics** is the study of the production, distribution, and consumption of goods and services.

- **Civics** is the branch of political science that deals with local government and the duties and rights of citizenship.

Identify social science concepts (e.g., culture, class, technology, race, gender).

Concepts lie at the core of social science theory and methodology. They provide substance to theories, form the basis of measurement, and influence the selection of cases. A wide range of examples from political science and sociology, such as revolution, welfare state, international disputes and war, and democracy, illustrate the theoretical and practical issues of concept construction and use. The consequences of valid concept construction can be explored in both qualitative and quantitative analyses. In education there is no more critical issue than socioeconomic status (SES). The Florida Comprehensive Assessment Test (FCAT) results are often discussed in terms of the SES of the students. Race, poverty, and English as a second language are all elements said to affect academic outcomes; they are seldom isolated but most often mixed in one student or one school.

Analyze the interrelationships between social science disciplines.

No critical economic condition in life escapes political significance. Almost all social science issues span the spectrum of the disciplines. In fact, it may be difficult to find an issue that only affects one social science discipline. For instance, a hurricane is a fact of life in Florida. It has elements of weather and geography but also has economic and political affects, especially if preparation or evacuation is poor. Another example is the beautiful beaches of Florida. A beach is a geographic description, but in Florida all population centers, except Orlando, are on the coast. This can bring developmental issues, including water use and the politics of growth. Environmental issues are another factor.

Interpret tabular and graphic representations of information related to the social sciences.

Maps, charts, and graphs are common illustrations used in the social sciences. Photographs and globes are also useful. In today's age of technology, video on the Internet is commonly used by teachers to set the tone for a topic to be explored. Videos on sites like *http://streaming.discoveryeducation.com/index.cfm* can be extremely helpful.

Identify appropriate strategies, methods, tools, and technology for the teaching of social science.

Engaging students in social science studies requires the use of a wide variety of tools and technology. Interdisciplinary activities are one approach to this challenge. Asking the

English teacher to cooperate with you on a writing project using your content as the topic is a great idea. Active learning is one approach that works. An example is to give students a project that requires their own research that culminates in a PowerPoint presentation by teams or individuals. An advanced technique is to give digital cameras to teams of students and allow them to take pictures of concepts like democracy. The students brainstorm what pictures might be good, go searching, and return to present their photos to the group with a visual presentation. This type of project internalizes learning for students.

The use of technology is still relatively new for most teachers. Almost everyone can use a computer, but to create a curriculum that requires productive student work is more challenging. It is a good idea to require students to use sites like the Library of Congress that have internal search engines. Asking students simply to do Google searches can lead to off-task behavior and other problems. Be sure to explore any site yourself before directing your students to it.

Evaluate and interpret examples of primary source documents to show historical perspective.

Primary source documents allow you to get closer to the subject matter. To get the most information from a document, you must examine who wrote it, why it was written, the intended audience, the author's motives or intentions, when it was written, and what information is being presented. It is critical to teach students about primary and secondary sources that show historical perspective. Do not assume that students who use the Internet can differentiate among various types of information. Before using the large inventory of primary and secondary sources, spend some time with students showing examples of each source.

Primary sources are actual records that have survived from the past, such as diaries, journals, letters, photographs, and articles of clothing. **Secondary sources** are accounts of the past created by people writing about events sometime after they happened.

For example, your history textbook is a secondary source. Someone wrote most of your textbook long after historical events took place. Your textbook may also include some primary sources, such as direct quotes from people living in the past or excerpts from historical documents. Primary sources are original records created at the time historical events occurred or well after events in the form of memoirs and oral histories. Primary sources may include letters, manuscripts, diaries, journals, newspapers, speeches, interviews, memoirs, documents produced by government agencies such as Congress or the office of the president, photographs, audio recordings, moving pictures or video recordings, research data, and objects or artifacts such as works of art or ancient roads, buildings, tools, and weapons. These sources serve as the raw material to interpret the past, and when they are used along with previous interpretations by historians, they provide the resources necessary for historical research.

People living in the past left many clues about their lives. These clues include both primary and secondary sources in the form of books, personal papers, government documents, letters, oral accounts, diaries, maps, photographs, reports, novels and short stories, artifacts, coins, stamps, and many other things. Historians call all these clues the **historical record**.

Because there is no review process or regulation for public documents posted on the Web, students will need to judge for themselves the quality of the material they find. Teach them how to ask questions like the following:

- Who is the author? What expertise does he or she have on this topic? Who sponsors the site? Check the domain name to see if it is a university, business, organization, or an individual.

- Does the information presented seem accurate? Are the facts verifiable?

- What is the stated purpose of the site? Check the "About" link if there is one. What position or opinion is presented, and does it seem biased? What kind of sites does this one link to?

- On what date was the page created? Do you need more current information? Do links on the site still connect to their destination?

The Internet is a tremendous tool for individualizing and differentiating instruction, but it comes with challenges. Structured work with specific sites is the best choice. Never suggest that students use a site that you have not yourself reviewed in detail. It is very dangerous to allow students to use a search engine like Google to find their own information. The risks far outweigh the benefits. Specific sites like the Library of Congress (*www.loc.gov/*) are best.

Practice Test 1

FTCE Social Science

ANSWER SHEET FOR PRACTICE TEST 1

1 _____   2 _____   3 _____   4 _____   5 _____

6 _____   7 _____   8 _____   9 _____   10 _____

11 _____   12 _____   13 _____   14 _____   15 _____

16 _____   17 _____   18 _____   19 _____   20 _____

21 _____   22 _____   23 _____   24 _____   25 _____

26 _____   27 _____   28 _____   29 _____   30 _____

31 _____   32 _____   33 _____   34 _____   35 _____

36 _____   37 _____   38 _____   39 _____   40 _____

41 _____   42 _____   43 _____   44 _____   45 _____

46 _____   47 _____   48 _____   49 _____   50 _____

51 _____   52 _____   53 _____   54 _____   55 _____

56 _____   57 _____   58 _____   59 _____   60 _____

61 _____   62 _____   63 _____   64 _____   65 _____

66 _____   67 _____   68 _____   69 _____   70 _____

71 _____   72 _____   73 _____   74 _____   75 _____

76 _____   77 _____   78 _____   79 _____   80 _____

81 _____   82 _____   83 _____   84 _____   85 _____

86 _____   87 _____   88 _____   89 _____   90 _____

91 _____   92 _____   93 _____   94 _____   95 _____

96 _____   97 _____   98 _____   99 _____   100 _____

101 _____ 102 _____ 103 _____ 104 _____ 105 _____

106 _____ 107 _____ 108 _____ 109 _____ 110 _____

111 _____ 112 _____ 113 _____ 114 _____ 115 _____

116 _____ 117 _____ 118 _____ 119 _____ 120 _____

121 _____ 122 _____ 123 _____ 124 _____ 125 _____

Practice Test 1

The two practice tests included in this guide give you a chance to find out just how much you know and what you need to study. Each test has a blank answer sheet, the test, and an answer key with explanations and cross-references to the relevant chapters. Approach taking the tests in any way you like, but use them as a learning tool.

The questions in Practice Test 1 are relatively basic and follow the order of the review chapters. Practice Test 2 is somewhat harder, with more difficult questions that require higher-order thinking, and the questions are not in order of any specific skill or competency. At times you will be asked more than facts. You will be required in some questions to mix and match information and interpret the data for the correct answer.

If you do not know a particular answer because the facts are too detailed or in a content area in which you are weak, try not to get frustrated. Use your test-taking skills to see if you can eliminate possible answers. If you have to guess an answer, do your best to improve your odds. Sometimes a question will have one or more answer choices that are obviously incorrect. The more answer choices you can eliminate, the better your chances of guessing the correct answer from the remaining choices.

1. Longitude and latitude are an example of which theme of geography?

    A. Location

    B. Place

    C. Region

    D. Movement

2. Which of the following phrases best exemplifies the concept of continentality?

    A. The temperature in Tampa was a scorching 86 degrees yesterday.

    B. Clearwater Beach, which is located on the Gulf of Mexico, has cooler summers than does the inland city of Orlando.

    C. Tampa is hotter than Atlanta because it is closer to the equator.

    D. Summer rains typically flow from west to east.

3. The two components of a climate graph are

    A. the amount of rainfall and temperature of an area.

    B. temperature highs and lows for a specific time of year.

    C. the amount of rain expected in the tourist seasons.

    D. future rainfall and temperature changes caused by global warming.

4. Which of the following are related to the human systems component of geography?

    I.   war

    II. retirees moving from the Midwest to Florida

    III. immigration

    IV. college students coming to Florida on spring break

    V.   Floridians living on the beach

    A. II and IV

    B. III, IV, and V

    C. II, III, IV, and V

    D. I, II, III, IV, and V

5. Which of the following statements is (are) true?

    A. There are at least 6,000 cultures in the world.

    B. Poverty cannot realistically be called a culture.

    C. The earth's surface is 50 percent water.

    D. All the above are true.

Use the following chart to answer questions 6 through 9.

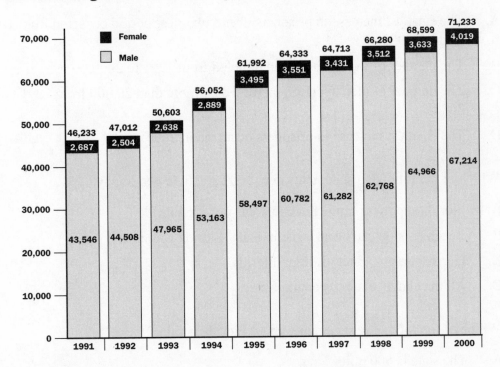

6. The largest increase in female prisoners occurred between

    A. 1999 and 2000.

    B. 1994 and 1995.

    C. 1997 and 1998.

    D. 1990 and 1991.

7. The largest increase in male prisoners occurred between

    A. 1994 and 1995.

    B. 1999 and 2000.

    C. 1992 and 1993.

    D. 1995 and 1996.

8. The largest increase in total prisoners occurred between

 A. 1996 and 1997.

 B. 1991 and 1992.

 C. 1994 and 1995.

 D. 1993 and 1994.

9. Which of the following statements about the chart is false?

 A. The smallest increase in prisoners over a two-year period occurred from 1991 through 1992.

 B. The number of women in prison doubled from 1991 to 2000.

 C. The number of men in prison increased by more than 20,000 from 1991 to 2000.

 D. The smallest increase in prisoners occurred in 2000.

10. Which of the following statements does NOT relate to geography?

 A. Florida supplies orange juice to areas outside Florida.

 B. Beach erosion can be an issue in many Florida counties.

 C. Hurricanes are a fact of life in Florida.

 D. All the above relate to geography.

11. Which of the following statements about Florida is false?

 A. The state is 500 miles long.

 B. It is bordered by Georgia, the Atlantic Ocean, and the Gulf of Mexico.

 C. The geographic center of Florida is near Brooksville in Hernando County.

 D. Almost 12,000 square miles of Florida is covered by water, making it the third wettest state after Alaska and Michigan.

12. Air-conditioning is an example of humans

 A. adapting to the environment.

 B. modifying the environment.

 C. depending on the environment.

 D. protecting the environment.

13. Which of the following statements about regions is false?

    A.   The United States is an example of a formal region.

    B.   A cellular service area is an example of a functional region.

    C.   The Deep South is a functional region defined by the southern culture that depended on slavery in the years before and during the Civil War.

    D.   The Great Lakes is a formal region in the United States.

14. Which of the following geographic terms would NOT be used in references to Florida?

    A.   winds

    B.   floods

    C.   high altitudes

    D.   continentality

Use the following map of Florida to answer questions 15 through 18.

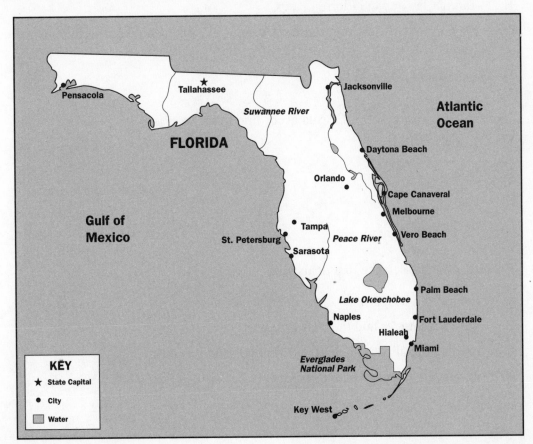

15. The star symbol in the "Key" box indicates

    A.   a major city.

    B.   the state capital.

    C.   a critical tourist area.

    D.   a major university.

16. The northernmost city on the west coast of Florida according to the map is

    A.   Saint Petersburg.

    B.   Naples.

    C.   Pensacola.

    D.   Tallahassee.

17. What bodies of water are noted on the map?

    A.   Lake Okeechobee and the Suwannee River

    B.   Tampa Bay and the Florida Keys

    C.   the Gulf of Mexico, the Atlantic Ocean, Lake Okeechobee, and the Suwannee River

    D.   Everglades National Park

18. The southernmost point of Florida according to the map is

    A.   Key West.

    B.   Miami.

    C.   Naples.

    D.   the Dry Tortugas.

19. Economics is the science that deals with

    A.   money and its uses.

    B.   scarce resources and their allocation.

    C.   production, allocation, and use of goods and services.

    D.   market and planned economies.

20. Economics attempts to answer three basic questions. Which of the following is NOT one of them?

    A.   What goods and services should be produced?

    B.   For whom should goods and services be produced?

    C.   How should goods and services be produced?

    D.   Who should profit from the sales of the goods and services produced?

21. If a teacher decides to relax over the summer and play golf instead of teaching at the juvenile detention facility, which offers instruction year round, the money that teacher does not earn would, by an economist, be called

    A.   25 percent of the teacher's annual salary (because the summer break lasts three months).

    B.   the cost of a vacation.

    C.   the opportunity cost.

    D.   payment for playtime.

22. The essence of a market economy is

    A.   excellent planning.

    B.   freedom.

    C.   capitalism.

    D.   supply and demand.

23. A market economy relies on _____ to allocate resources.

    A.   government

    B.   good planning

    C.   market forces

    D.   small businesses

24. An example of a country with a planned economy is

    A.   Germany.

    B.   France.

    C.   Japan.

    D.   Australia.

25. Resources that are readily abundant are considered

    A.   free goods.

    B.   worthless.

    C.   priceless.

    D.   scarce.

26. Scarce resources include

    A.   oil.

    B.   coal.

    C.   clean water.

    D.   all the above.

27. Scarcity is maintained by

    A.   demand.

    B.   multinational corporations.

    C.   diamond cartels.

    D.   business owners.

28. In economics, the factors of production are

    A.   location, location, location.

    B.   labor, capital, land, and entrepreneurship.

    C.   supply and demand.

    D.   money, motivation, and action.

29. Quotas, license fees, and subsidies are part of

    A.   a market economy.

    B.   a communist society.

    C.   the free enterprise system.

    D.   a planned economy.

30. Macroeconomics is the study of the elements of economics on the

    A.   business level.

    B.   national level.

    C.   family level.

    D.   government level.

31. Microeconomics is the study of the economic behavior of

    A.   firms and families.

    B.   nations.

    C.   individuals.

    D.   governments.

32. Which of the following has the highest barrier to entry?

    A.   the automotive industry

    B.   a sporting goods store

    C.   a farm

    D.   a lemonade stand

33. Which of the following has the lowest barrier to entry?

    A.   the automotive industry

    B.   a sporting goods store

    C.   a farm

    D.   a lemonade stand

34. Perfect competition is

    A.   a theoretical extreme.

    B.   found only in the United States.

    C.   the same as an oligopoly.

    D.   the same as a monopoly.

35. In a monopoly

   A. everyone is happy.

   B. the firm is equal to an industry.

   C. many sellers are protected by government regulation.

   D. no one is happy.

36. An example of monopolistic competition is

   A. the film industry.

   B. agriculture.

   C. public education.

   D. the automotive industry.

37. An oligopoly is

   A. a market form in which a market or industry is dominated by a small number of sellers.

   B. a government with a king or queen.

   C. a market form with a large number of sellers guaranteeing the lowest price.

   D. great for consumers.

38. Which of the following is NOT a characteristic of monopolistically competitive markets?

   A. There are many producers and many consumers in a given market.

   B. There are high barriers to entry and exit.

   C. Firms have a degree of control over price.

   D. Consumers have clearly defined preferences, and sellers attempt to differentiate their products from those of their competitors.

39. Which of the following sectors is NOT part of macroeconomics?

   A. consumers

   B. businesses

   C. government

   D. nonprice competition

40. The Federal Reserve uses three monetary policy tools to influence the availability and cost of money and credit. Which of the following is NOT one of the policies?

    A. open-market operations

    B. discount rate

    C. reserve requirements

    D. establishing tariffs and fees

41. The document(s) embodying the ideals of individual freedom commonly associated with the United States is (are) the

    A. Declaration of Independence.

    B. Constitution.

    C. Articles of Confederation.

    D. both A and B.

42. What are civil rights?

    A. the protections and privileges of personal power given to all citizens by law

    B. human rights

    C. natural rights

    D. both B and C

43. What conflict(s) did the framers of the U.S. Constitution face?

    A. slavery

    B. power of the president

    C. large versus small states

    D. all the above

44. The system of checks and balances was designed to

    A. protect the people from an oppressive form of government.

    B. minimize foreign intervention.

    C. help maintain the financial stability of the new government.

    D. do all the above.

45. Which of the elements below is NOT part of political science?

    A. government structures

    B. political institutions

    C. government policies

    D. All the above are part of political science.

46. Article I of the Constitution creates

    A. a bicameral legislature.

    B. a unicameral legislature.

    C. the presidency.

    D. the judicial branch.

47. The entities in the legislative branch of the U.S. government have many checks on their power. Which of the following statements about those checks is NOT true?

    A. Senate members were originally chosen by the state legislatures.

    B. The House was granted some exclusive powers, like initiating revenue bills and impeaching officials.

    C. The Constitution provides that the approval of both houses is necessary for the passage of legislation.

    D. All the above are true.

48. Which of the following is NOT a requirement to be the president of the United States?

    A. over 35 years old

    B. natural-born citizen

    C. resident for at least 15 years

    D. All the above are required.

49. For what term are federal judges appointed?

    A. six years

    B. one year

    C. life

    D. 10 years

50. The *Federalist Papers* were signed by "Publius." Historians' consensus says the papers were written by

    A.   Hamilton, Madison, and Jay.

    B.   Jefferson, Hamilton, and Washington.

    C.   Madison, Washington, and Calhoun.

    D.   Hamilton, Madison, and three others.

51. Who wrote the Bill of Rights?

    A.   Hamilton

    B.   Jefferson

    C.   Washington

    D.   Madison

52. How does the Constitution provide for political parties?

    A.   Parties are considered viable if they are on ballots in two-thirds of the states.

    B.   Our bicameral system is set up for two parties.

    C.   Political parties are not mentioned in the Constitution.

    D.   Political parties are mentioned as an area of state authority.

53. Which of the following items are the primary responsibility of the states?

    A.   public safety, administering and certifying elections, and recording birth and death certificates

    B.   interstate commerce and regulating television and radio

    C.   regulating immigration and naturalization

    D.   national defense and creating money

54. How is a local government chartered?

    A.   according to the state constitution

    B.   through application to the federal government

    C.   by the county

    D.   by the local government writing a constitution and notifying the next largest government entity of its existence

55. Realism is the theory that

    A.   nations cooperate for their common interest.

    B.   nation-states are the basic governmental unit above which no other government entity has authority.

    C.   real authority is found in the United Nations.

    D.   people are the real authority for all governments.

56. Government by the many is called

    A.   democracy.

    B.   oligarchy.

    C.   monarchy.

    D.   liberalism.

57. Which of the following types of government is closely related to autocracy?

    A.   democracy

    B.   capitalism

    C.   despotism

    D.   tyranny

58. The modern democratic state in which the people do not take a direct role in legislating or governing but elect representatives to express their views and wants is called

    A.   a republic.

    B.   liberalism.

    C.   a constitutional monarchy.

    D.   totalitarianism.

59. Which constitutional amendment included in the Bill of Rights states in part that "Congress shall make no law respecting an establishment of religion"?

    A.   Fourteenth Amendment

    B.   Fifteenth Amendment

    C.   First Amendment

    D.   Tenth Amendment

60. Define the term *prehistoric* as it relates to world history.

    A.   before the use of fire

    B.   before the use of tools

    C.   before the appearance of the written word

    D.   during the age of the dinosaur

61. The time early in the development of human cultures, before the use of metals, is called

    A.   ancient times.

    B.   the Stone Age.

    C.   the Horse Age.

    D.   the Bronze Age.

62. The Paleolithic, Mesolithic, and Neolithic periods are part of the

    A.   Copper Age.

    B.   Bronze Age.

    C.   Iron Age.

    D.   Stone Age.

63. Which of the following statements is true?

    A.   The use of the term *age* does not refer to the same dates in all parts of the world because cultures developed differently.

    B.   Archaeological discoveries since 1960 have confirmed traditional theories concerning the origins of copper and bronze technologies.

    C.   Regular imports of tin from Cornwall in Britain during the first millennium B.C.E. made the wider use of copper possible.

    D.   The Bronze Age started at the same time in Greece and China.

64. What is considered the cradle of Western civilization?

    A.   the Holy Roman Empire

    B.   ancient Greece

    C.   Christianity

    D.   the Enlightenment and the Age of Reason

65. Which of the following items is NOT considered one of the three pillars of Western culture?

   A.   Roman law

   B.   Greek philosophy

   C.   Catholic and Protestant Christianity

   D.   the *Iliad* and the *Odyssey*

66. The ancient Greek period is said to have ended with

   A.   the first Olympic Games.

   B.   the death of Alexander the Great.

   C.   both A and B.

   D.   neither A nor B.

67. The ancient Greeks considered the Trojan War as the first moment in history when

   A.   all Greeks came together as one people with a common purpose.

   B.   their weaknesses as a military power became evident.

   C.   they were embarrassed by the affluent nature of their society.

   D.   None of the above occurred.

68. Rome was founded by

   A.   the Catholic Church.

   B.   Romulus and Remus.

   C.   Plato and Aristotle.

   D.   Julius Caesar.

69. Rome was first ruled by kings. Then, about 500 BCE, the Roman Republic was established, with two annually elected consuls at its head, guided by a senate. What happened next?

   A.   Rome was ruled by this system until its ultimate fall.

   B.   Rome was ruled by a succession of emperors.

   C.   Local governors ruled the many elements of the empire after it split apart.

   D.   Christianity forced the pope into the ultimate authority.

70. Which of the following is NOT generally accepted as a reason for the fall of the Roman Empire?

    A. decline in morals and values

    B. public health and environmental issues

    C. political corruption and no clear way to choose a new emperor

    D. lack of an education system

71. Which of the following statements about the Han Dynasty is false?

    A. The boundaries established by the Qin and maintained by the Han have more or less defined the nation of China to the present day.

    B. Poetry, literature, and philosophy flourished.

    C. Confucianism was established as the basis for correct official and individual conduct and for the educational curriculum.

    D. The Western Han capital was a relatively small city because of the agricultural nature of the society.

72. Which statement about Africa is false?

    A. Mount Kilimanjaro remains capped with snow year round.

    B. The Sahara is the largest and the hottest desert on the earth.

    C. Africa has primarily two languages with many dialects.

    D. Africa has rain forests.

73. Which of the following statements about China is true?

    A. The Chinese writing system is the oldest continuously used writing system in the world.

    B. Because China has one language, all Chinese can easily speak to each other. This is the reason for the country's size and stability over time.

    C. Chinese characters represent a set of letters that has remained unchanged throughout China's history.

    D. Confucianism, Buddhism, Chinese characters, and other Chinese cultural influences have minimized diversity among the various regions of the country.

74. Which of the following nations share an ethnic background and have similar cultures?

    A. Tibet, India, and Nepal

    B. India, Pakistan, and Bangladesh

    C. Pakistan, Afganistan, and Turkey

    D. Tibet, Nepal, and China

75. What four religions were founded in the region known today as India?

    A. Hinduism, Buddhism, Jainism, and Sikhism

    B. Islam, Hinduism, Buddhism, and Sikhism

    C. Christianity, Buddhism, the Baha'i faith, and Jainism

    D. Hinduism, Buddhism, Taoism, and Sikhism

76. What caused the many small Mayan village populations to grow and city-states to emerge?

    A. sophisticated, organized government

    B. improved farming practices

    C. climate changes

    D. advanced architectural designs that allowed for better building

77. Which of the following was the focus of Mayan cities?

    A. ceremonial centers

    B. governmental headquarters

    C. central market places

    D. festivals and celebrations

78. Which of the following statements about the Silk Road is false?

    A. The Silk Road was not a trade route that existed solely for the purpose of trading in silk; many other commodities were also traded.

    B. Because the Silk Road was composed of a single route, security along it was tight and the trading posts large.

    C. Movement of traders along the Silk Road is related to the spread of religion and the development of languages.

    D. Gold, ivory, and even exotic animals and plants were traded on the Silk Road.

79. What was unique about the Hammurabi Code?

    A. It was the earliest-known example of a ruler proclaiming publicly to his people an entire body of laws.

    B. It was written in books that citizens could reference.

    C. It had a court system as part of it.

    D. None of the above is a unique feature of the code.

80. Which of the following statements about the Middle Ages is false?

    A. Modern European states owe their origins to the Middle Ages.

    B. Modern European states and their political boundaries as we know them are essentially the result of the military and dynastic achievements made in the Middle Ages.

    C. The Middle Ages are commonly dated from the first century until the end of the fifteenth century.

    D. Science, technology, agricultural production, and social identity changed drastically during the Middle Ages.

81. Which of the following did NOT occur in the Renaissance?

    A. the revival of learning based on classical sources

    B. the decline of courtly and papal patronage

    C. the development of perspective in painting

    D. advancements in science

82. Who would be considered a Renaissance man?

    A. Leonardo da Vinci

    B. Michelangelo

    C. both A and B

    D. neither A nor B

83. Which of the following statements is false?

   A.   The Renaissance lasted roughly from the fourteenth through the seventeenth centuries.

   B.   The Carolingian Renaissance was a period in the late eighth and ninth centuries.

   C.   The Protestant Reformation was a movement in the twelfth century.

   D.   The Enlightenment was an eighteenth-century European and American philosophical movement.

84. In which of the following periods did Immanuel Kant live?

   A.   Enlightenment

   B.   Age of Reason

   C.   Renaissance

   D.   Protestant Reformation

85. Who would NOT be considered part of the Protestant Reformation?

   A.   Martin Luther

   B.   John Wycliffe

   C.   Jan Hus

   D.   René Descartes

86. How did the nature of colonialism change in the seventeenth century?

   A.   European nations had become dependent on the trade and resources of their New World colonies.

   B.   Europeans had a desire to conquer the known world.

   C.   Explorers had a desire to find the end of the earth.

   D.   All the above are true.

87. Which of the following is NOT commonly believed to be one of the results of colonialism?

    A. Knowledge gained from exploration yielded a new interest in studying the world.

    B. Explorers carefully catalogued the various plants, animals, crops, and peoples in the lands they explored.

    C. New "natural sciences" such as biology and geology became popular pastimes for Europeans.

    D. A new level of peace settled on the world.

88. What was the first major colonial stronghold in North America?

    A. New Amsterdam

    B. Massachusetts Bay Colony

    C. Louisiana

    D. New South Wales

89. Which of the following is NOT considered one of the devastating effects of colonialism on the native populations of Africa and the Americas?

    A. spread of European diseases among indigenous peoples whose immune systems could not fight the infections

    B. development of mercantile trade

    C. procurement of African slaves

    D. displacement of Native American populations

90. Which of the following pairings is NOT correct?

    A. James Cooke and modern maps

    B. John Harrison and longitude navigation

    C. Thomas Malthus and classification of peoples by region and racial characteristics

    D. Charles Lyell and maritime charts

91. Among the Jamestown settlers were

    A. artisans.

    B. soldiers.

    C. surgeons.

    D. all the above.

92. After eight months in Jamestown, how many of the original 120 pioneers were still alive?

    A. 100

    B. 67

    C. 45

    D. 38

93. Which of the following pairings is NOT correct?

    A. Captain John Smith and adventurer, explorer

    B. John Rolfe and tobacco farmer

    C. John Rolfe and Pocahontas

    D. Samoset and chief of the Cherokee near Jamestown

94. Sir George Carteret and Lord Berkeley settled what area?

    A. New York

    B. New Jersey

    C. Massachusetts

    D. Virginia

95. What agreement served as the official constitution of the Plymouth Colony for many years?

    A. Exeter Compact

    B. Jamestown Agreement

    C. Mayflower Compact

    D. Pilgrim Constitution

96. In the French and Indian War (also known as the Seven Years' War), the British fought against

    A. the French.
    B. the Austrians.
    C. the Spanish.
    D. all the above.

97. In 1764 the British for the first time imposed a series of taxes designed specifically to raise revenue from the colonies. What was this tax called?

    A. Sugar Act
    B. Stamp Act
    C. Quartering Act
    D. Tea Act

98. Which of the following does NOT apply to the Sons of Liberty?

    A. resorted to coercion to force stamp agents to resign their posts
    B. were prominent citizens
    C. was an organization with branches throughout the colonies
    D. publicly proclaimed their membership

99. The British parliament gave its speedy assent to a series of acts that became known as the Coercive Acts. In the colonies, the acts were known as the

    A. American Revenue Acts.
    B. Intolerable Acts.
    C. Hutchinson Acts.
    D. special taxes on lead, paint, paper, glass, and tea.

100. Which of the following statements about the First Continental Congress is false?

    A. It met in Philadelphia.
    B. Every colony was represented.
    C. The representatives gathered to discuss their response to the British Intolerable Acts.
    D. Its purpose was not to seek independence from Britain.

101. Which of the following statements about the Second Continental Congress is false?

    A.   The members decided that the colonies should completely break away from Great Britain.

    B.   The members decided to form an army called the American Continental Army.

    C.   The members officially appointed George Washington as commander in chief.

    D.   The Second Continental Congress met on May 10, 1770.

102. The Articles of Confederation was the first governing document of the United States. Which of the following was a major problem with the articles?

    A.   It did not give the central government the authority to levy taxes.

    B.   Each state had one vote in the Congress of the Confederation, which large states considered unfair because they were expected to contribute more to the management of the confederation than were small states.

    C.   Neither A nor B was a problem.

    D.   Both A and B were problems.

103. Which of the following statements about the *Federalist Papers* is false?

    A.   It consists of 85 essays.

    B.   The essays serve as a primary source for interpreting the Constitution.

    C.   Each essay was written by a different signer of the Declaration of Independence.

    D.   The authors of the essays wanted to influence the vote in favor of ratification and shape future interpretations of the Constitution.

104. Which of the following statements about Manifest Destiny is false?

    A.   It is a doctrine used to rationalize U.S. territorial expansion.

    B.   The term was coined by the journalist John L. O'Sullivan.

    C.   The term was initially used in regard to Mexican and Indian land in Texas and the Southwest.

    D.   It was the rationale for removing the Spanish from Florida.

105. The Northwest Ordinance of 1787 accomplished which of the following?

    A.   It provided the means by which new states would be created out of the western lands and then admitted into the Union.

    B.   It made clear that the original states would always have more power and authority than new states.

    C.   It provided for immediate election of government officials in new territories.

    D.   It counted all citizens as equal.

106. Which of the following statements about the Treaty of Guadalupe is false?

    A.   It was inaccurate with regard to boundaries.

    B.   It marked the end of the Mexican-American War.

    C.   It signaled the immediate admission of Texas into the Union.

    D.   It led to the Gadsden Purchase.

107. Which of the following was NOT a characteristic of the antebellum period?

    A.   sectional differences between the North and South

    B.   massive foreign immigration from Ireland and Germany, which greatly increased the size of cities in the North

    C.   the issue of whether slavery would be allowed to expand into the western territories

    D.   subsistence agriculture replacing commercial agriculture

108. Which of the following statements about the antebellum period is false?

    A.   Free southern blacks were able travel and assemble freely.

    B.   The *Dred Scott* decision eliminated possible compromise solutions to the sectional conflict.

    C.   John Brown's raid on Harpers Ferry convinced many Southerners that most Northerners wanted to free the slaves and incite race war.

    D.   The Compromise of 1850 was an attempt to solve the problem of slavery in the territories by admitting California as a free state but permitting slavery in the rest of the Southwest.

109. Which of the following was an almost perfect crop for the lower South because it was easy to grow and its demands were met by the region's climate and soil?

   A.   corn

   B.   cotton

   C.   wheat

   D.   potatoes

110. How many lives were lost during the American Civil War?

   A.   more than 600,000

   B.   less than 500,000

   C.   about 300,000

   D.   198,300

111. Which of the following states was NOT one of the first seven states to secede from the Union just before the Civil War began?

   A.   Florida

   B.   Alabama

   C.   North Carolina

   D.   Texas

112. Who was president when the first states left the Union?

   A.   Abraham Lincoln

   B.   James Buchanan

   C.   Robert E. Lee

   D.   Jefferson Davis

113. Who was the first president of the Confederacy?

   A.   Abraham Lincoln

   B.   James Buchanan

   C.   Robert E. Lee

   D.   Jefferson Davis

114. Which of the following was NOT a strength of the Union?

   A.   Its sea power was vastly superior to that of the Confederacy.

   B.   Britain never formally recognized the Confederacy.

   C.   The Emancipation Proclamation helped win popular support for the Union in England and France.

   D.   The Union army had an unlimited supply of funds.

115. After the North defeated the South in the Civil War, politicians faced the task of putting the divided country back together. Which of the following made former slaves citizens?

   A.   Reconstruction Acts of 1867

   B.   Fourteenth Amendment

   C.   Fifteenth Amendment

   D.   individual state laws

116. Which president announced the restoration of the Union and on what date?

   A.   Andrew Johnson on December 6, 1866

   B.   Abraham Lincoln on March 20, 1865

   C.   Abraham Lincoln on December 1, 1866

   D.   A formal announcement of restoration was never made.

117. What was the primary impact of the Black Codes?

   A.   effectively tied freed slaves to the land on which they lived and worked

   B.   brought southern blacks together and assisted their efforts to run for office

   C.   abolished slavery

   D.   gave blacks equal rights in all southern states

118. What were the approximate dates of the Progressive Era?

   A.   1890 to 1917

   B.   1920 to 1929

   C.   1868 to 1900

   D.   1939 to 1945

119. In the early 1900s, which country(ies) did most immigrants to the United States come from?

    A.   Germany, Ireland, and England

    B.   Japan, China, and Korea

    C.   Romania

    D.   Russia

120. What is considered the first important movement of black artists and writers?

    A.   Roaring Twenties

    B.   Harlem Renaissance

    C.   Lost Generation

    D.   Jazz Age

121. The analysis of the effect of immigration on Miami's school system, clean water supply, and social services is an example of

    A.   the interrelationships among social science disciplines.

    B.   the challenges of a major city.

    C.   a fact of life in modern America.

    D.   the reason for immigration legislation.

122. What is the definition of *sociology*?

    A.   a science of humankind

    B.   the study of how we become members of groups, how we move among groups, and how being in different groups affects us and the groups in which we participate

    C.   study of the earth and its features

    D.   the study of interpreting the past and how it affects our views of the present and of understanding trends or the lack thereof in the past

123. What is the definition of *history*?

    A.   a science of humankind

    B.   the study of how we become members of groups, how we move among groups, and how being in different groups affects individuals and the groups in which they participate

    C.   the study of the earth and its features

    D.   the study of the past and how it affects our views of the present

124. Primary sources are

    A.   actual records that have survived from the past, such as letters, photographs, and articles of clothing.

    B.   accounts of the past created by people writing about events some time after they happened.

    C.   both A and B.

    D.   neither A nor B.

125. Which of the following policies is (are) necessary when asking students to do historical research in a school computer lab?

    A.   Require that students stay on one site like the Library of Congress or any site that has an internal search engine.

    B.   Be sure to explore any site yourself prior to allowing your students to use that site.

    C.   Monitor Google searches by students to avoid problems and off-task behavior.

    D.   All the above are good policies.

PRACTICE TEST 1 ANSWER KEY

Question	Answer	Competency
1	A	Knowledge of Geography
2	B	Knowledge of Geography
3	A	Knowledge of Geography
4	D	Knowledge of Geography
5	A	Knowledge of Geography
6	B	Knowledge of Geography
7	A	Knowledge of Geography
8	C	Knowledge of Geography
9	D	Knowledge of Geography
10	D	Knowledge of Geography
11	B	Knowledge of Geography
12	B	Knowledge of Geography
13	C	Knowledge of Geography
14	C	Knowledge of Geography
15	B	Knowledge of Geography
16	C	Knowledge of Geography
17	C	Knowledge of Geography
18	A	Knowledge of Geography
19	C	Knowledge of Economics
20	D	Knowledge of Economics
21	C	Knowledge of Economics
22	B	Knowledge of Economics
23	C	Knowledge of Economics
24	C	Knowledge of Economics
25	A	Knowledge of Economics
26	D	Knowledge of Economics
27	A	Knowledge of Economics

Question	Answer	Competency
28	B	Knowledge of Economics
29	D	Knowledge of Economics
30	B	Knowledge of Economics
31	A	Knowledge of Economics
32	A	Knowledge of Economics
33	D	Knowledge of Economics
34	A	Knowledge of Economics
35	B	Knowledge of Economics
36	A	Knowledge of Economics
37	A	Knowledge of Economics
38	B	Knowledge of Economics
39	D	Knowledge of Economics
40	D	Knowledge of Economics
41	D	Knowledge of Political Science
42	A	Knowledge of Political Science
43	D	Knowledge of Political Science
44	A	Knowledge of Political Science
45	D	Knowledge of Political Science
46	A	Knowledge of Political Science
47	D	Knowledge of Political Science
48	C	Knowledge of Political Science
49	C	Knowledge of Political Science
50	A	Knowledge of Political Science
51	D	Knowledge of Political Science
52	C	Knowledge of Political Science
53	A	Knowledge of Political Science
54	A	Knowledge of Political Science
55	B	Knowledge of Political Science

Question	Answer	Competency
56	A	Knowledge of Political Science
57	C	Knowledge of Political Science
58	A	Knowledge of Political Science
59	C	Knowledge of Political Science
60	C	Knowledge of World History
61	B	Knowledge of World History
62	D	Knowledge of World History
63	A	Knowledge of World History
64	B	Knowledge of World History
65	D	Knowledge of World History
66	B	Knowledge of World History
67	A	Knowledge of World History
68	B	Knowledge of World History
69	B	Knowledge of World History
70	D	Knowledge of World History
71	D	Knowledge of World History
72	C	Knowledge of World History
73	A	Knowledge of World History
74	B	Knowledge of World History
75	A	Knowledge of World History
76	B	Knowledge of World History
77	A	Knowledge of World History
78	B	Knowledge of World History
79	A	Knowledge of World History
80	C	Knowledge of World History
81	B	Knowledge of World History
82	C	Knowledge of World History
83	C	Knowledge of World History

Question	Answer	Competency
84	A	Knowledge of World History
85	D	Knowledge of World History
86	A	Knowledge of World History
87	D	Knowledge of World History
88	B	Knowledge of American History
89	B	Knowledge of American History
90	D	Knowledge of American History
91	D	Knowledge of American History
92	D	Knowledge of American History
93	D	Knowledge of American History
94	B	Knowledge of American History
95	C	Knowledge of American History
96	D	Knowledge of American History
97	A	Knowledge of American History
98	D	Knowledge of American History
99	B	Knowledge of American History
100	B	Knowledge of American History
101	D	Knowledge of American History
102	B	Knowledge of American History
103	C	Knowledge of American History
104	D	Knowledge of American History
105	A	Knowledge of American History
106	C	Knowledge of American History
107	D	Knowledge of American History
108	A	Knowledge of American History
109	B	Knowledge of American History
110	A	Knowledge of American History
111	C	Knowledge of American History

Question	Answer	Competency
112	B	Knowledge of American History
113	D	Knowledge of American History
114	D	Knowledge of American History
115	B	Knowledge of American History
116	A	Knowledge of American History
117	A	Knowledge of American History
118	A	Knowledge of American History
119	A	Knowledge of American History
120	B	Knowledge of American History
121	A	Knowledge of Social Science and Its Methodology
122	B	Knowledge of Social Science and Its Methodology
123	D	Knowledge of Social Science and Its Methodology
124	A	Knowledge of Social Science and Its Methodology
125	D	Knowledge of Social Science and Its Methodology

PRACTICE TEST 1 PROGRESS CHART

Knowledge of Geography ———/18

1	2	3	4	5	6	7	8	9

10	11	12	13	14	15	16	17	18

Knowledge of Economics ———/22

19	20	21	22	23	24	25	26	27	28	29

30	31	32	33	34	35	36	37	38	39	40

Knowledge of Political Science ———/19

41	42	43	44	45	46	47	48	49	50

51	52	53	54	55	56	57	58	59

Knowledge of World History ———/28

60	61	62	63	64	65	66	67	68	69	70	71	72	73

74	75	76	77	78	79	80	81	82	83	84	85	86	87

Knowledge of American History ———/33

88	89	90	91	92	93	94	95	96	97	98

99	100	101	102	103	104	105	106	107	108	109

110	111	112	113	114	115	116	117	118	119	120

Knowledge of Social Science and Its Methodology ———/5

121	122	123	124	125

DETAILED EXPLANATIONS FOR PRACTICE TEST 1

(For further review, refer back to the chapter noted at the end of each explanation.)

1. **A.**

   Longitude and latitude are part of the location theme of geography. See Chapter 2.

2. **B.**

   Continentality is the idea that continental locations—those not near the sea—experience temperature extremes across the seasons. Land heats and cools faster than does the sea. Therefore, coastal areas have narrower temperature ranges than do inland areas. On the coast, winters are mild and summers are cool. In inland areas, temperatures are high in the summer and low in the winter. Because Clearwater Beach is on the Gulf of Mexico, its summers are cooler than those in Orlando, which is a continental location. See Chapter 2.

3. **A.**

   Climate can be displayed on a graph. A climate graph contains two pieces of information about an area: the amount of rainfall and the temperature. The temperature is shown as a line, and the rainfall is displayed as bars. The numbers shown on the graph are usually averages calculated over a number of years. See Chapter 2.

4. **D.**

   People are central to geography and make up the component of geography known as human systems. Humans are involved in all the answer choices. See Chapter 2.

5. **A.**

   The world has about 200 different nations and more than 6,000 distinct languages. Because language is a basic part of a culture, the world also has more than 6,000 cultures. See Chapter 2.

6. **B.**

   The number of female prisoners is depicted in the black portion of the graph. The largest increase appears to have occurred between 1994 and 1995; another possibility is between 1993 and 1994. Doing the math confirms that the increase of 606 female prisoners that occurred between 1994 and 1995 is the largest. See Chapter 6.

7. **A.**

   The number of male prisoners is depicted by the lighter color and represents the largest portion of each bar in the graph. The largest increase appears to have occurred between 1994 and 1995; another possibility is between 1993 and 1994. The increases in those two periods are close, but the 5,334-person rise in male prisoners that happened from 1994 to 1995 is greater than the 5,198-person rise from 1993 to 1994. See Chapter 6 for questions 7–9.

8. **C.**

   The total prison population is the number above each column. Between 1993 and 1994, this number rose 5,449, but between 1994 and 1995, the increase was 5,940.

9. **D.**

   Both A and D are statements regarding the smallest increase in prisoners; thus, one of them must be false. Therefore, you can ignore answer choices B and C and simply do the math to find that D is the false statement.

10. **D.**

    Movement of people or products, beach erosion, and hurricanes all relate to geography. See Chapter 2.

11. **B.**

    Florida borders Alabama in the Panhandle. See Chapter 2.

12. **B.**

    Humans have learned to use things like air-conditioning to modify the environment. See Chapter 2.

13. **C.**

    Answer choices A, B, and D are true statements. *Deep South* is a term used during the antebellum and Civil War periods in reference to the southern states whose culture depended on the institution of slavery; today the term is used loosely and often pejoratively to refer to states in that general cultural region. Therefore, it is a vernacular region, not a functional region. See Chapter 2.

14. **C.**

> Florida is a flat state in which high altitudes do not exist. At 345 feet above sea level, Britton Hill is the highest point in Florida and the lowest high point of any U.S. state. See Chapter 2.

15. **B.**

> This question may seem simplistic, but FTCE map questions will be simple if you read the map legends and use them to interpret the maps. On maps see Chapter 1.

16. **C.**

> Each city on the map is indicated by a circle or black dot. The most northern circle on the west coast indicates the city of Pensacola.

17. **C.**

> Four bodies of water are shown on the map.

18. **A.**

> Although the Dry Tortugas are south of Key West, they are not shown on the map.

19. **C.**

> Economics is the science that deals with the production, allocation, and use of goods and services. See Chapter 3.

20. **D.**

> Answer choices A, B, and C are the three basic questions of economics. As you take the FTCE, be sure to notice key words in the questions like *not, false, true, always, never,* and *sometimes.* Misreading a question could result in your losing valuable points. See Chapter 3.

21. **C.**

> Opportunity cost is the cost of giving up something to get something else. In this case, the teacher sacrifices extra income for the sake of the more desired alternative of a relaxing summer vacation. See Chapter 3.

22. **B.**

> Market economies typically are free of government control and offer individuals the freedom to have the careers of their choice. See Chapter 3.

23. **C.**

   Market forces determine how resources are allocated when everyone is free to make choices in their purchases. See Chapter 3.

24. **C.**

   Germany, France, and Australia, like the United States, have market economies. In contrast, Japan, especially since World War II, has planned much of its economy, especially the steel and automotive industries. See Chapter 2.

25. **A.**

   Resources that are readily abundant are called free goods. However, most goods and services are considered scarce because individuals desire more of them than they already possess (scarcity is maintained by demand). See Chapter 3.

26. **D.**

   All the answer choices are considered scarce today. Scarcity occurs when a limited supply of goods or services coincides with an ever-increasing demand. When facing scarcity, an economy must make every effort to ensure the proper utilization and distribution of goods and services so as to avoid inefficiency. See Chapter 3.

27. **A.**

   As long as people demand goods or services, economies will have to contend with scarcity. See Chapter 3.

28. **B.**

   The four factors of production are labor, capital, land, and entrepreneurship. See Chapter 3.

29. **D.**

   Government intervention is one aspect of a planned economy. Quotas, license fees, and subsidies are examples of government intervention. Although taxes are a sign of government influence, they are not normally considered a sign of government control or intervention. See Chapter 3.

30. **B.**

   Macroeconomics studies the elements of economics on the national level. It is possibly the largest branch of economics and includes the concepts of output, consumption, investment, government spending, and net exports. See Chapter 3.

31. **A.**

    Microeconomics is the study of the economic behavior of small groups like firms and families. See Chapter 3.

32. **A.**

    The automotive industry always has a high barrier to entry. Sporting goods in some areas may have a relatively high barrier to entry, but it is possible for someone to start a retail business without a lot of barriers. See Chapter 3.

33. **D.**

    Obviously, if a child can start a lemonade stand, it has the lowest barrier to entry. See Chapter 3.

34. **A.**

    Because nothing is perfect, the concept of perfect competition is a theoretical extreme. Under perfect competition, products are relatively identical, sellers have no control over prices, and there are no barriers to entry. The agricultural industry is thought to function under perfect competition. See Chapter 3.

35. **B.**

    Answer choices A and D are not correct because they are extreme answers (the clues are the words *everyone* and *no one*). In a monopoly, one firm controls prices, making the firm equal to the industry. See Chapter 3.

36. **A.**

    Monopolistic competition is a very common market form that includes the markets for restaurants, books, clothing, and the film and service industries in large cities. The characteristics of a monopolistically competitive market are many producers and many consumers, heterogeneous products, few barriers to entry, and a degree of control over price. See Chapter 3.

37. **A.**

    An oligopoly is a market form in which a market or industry is dominated by a small number of sellers, called oligopolists. See Chapter 3.

38. **B.**

    Monopolistic competition is characterized by few barriers to entry and exit. See Chapter 3.

39. **D.**

   The four broad sectors of a macroeconomics are consumers, businesses, government, and the foreign sector. See Chapter 3.

40. **D.**

   The Fed does not have the authority to establish tariffs, taxes, or fees. See Chapter 3.

41. **D.**

   The Declaration of Independence and the Constitution define the basic elements of the U.S. government. See Chapter 4.

42. **A.**

   The critical word in this question is *civil*, which refers to citizens. See Chapter 4.

43. **D.**

   Among the issues the framers of the Constitution faced were slavery, defining the power of president, and conflicts between large and small states. Another major issue was how the president should be elected. See Chapter 4.

44. **A.**

   The three-branch system created checks and balances so that no branch had the power to override the others, protecting the people from an oppressive form of government. See Chapter 4.

45. **D.**

   Political science deals with the structure and policies of government. The term *political* in answer choice B is a hint that it is also part of political science. See Chapter 4.

46. **A.**

   Article I establishes the legislative branch of the U.S. government as a bicameral body, consisting of two houses. See Chapter 4.

47. **D.**

You may not be aware of the historical detail that state legislatures originally selected members of the U.S. Senate. However, you probably know that both B and C are true, so you could safely conclude that D is the correct answer. See Chapter 4.

48. **C.**

A presidential candidate must have resided in the United States for at least 14 years. See Chapter 4.

49. **C.**

Federal judges are appointed for life by the president. See Chapter 4.

50. **A.**

Jefferson, Washington, and Calhoun were not involved in the writing of the *Federalist Papers*. Alexander Hamilton wrote 52 of the essays in the book, James Madison wrote 28, and John Jay contributed the remaining 5. See Chapter 4.

51. **D.**

Initially drafted by James Madison in 1789, the Bill of Rights was written at a time when ideological conflict between Federalists and Antifederalists, dating from the Philadelphia Convention in 1787, threatened to prevent ratification of the Constitution. The Bill of Rights was largely a response to the Constitution's opponents, including prominent Founding Fathers, who argued that it failed to protect the basic principles of human liberty. See Chapter 4.

52. **C.**

The Constitution does not mention political parties. In fact, "factions" with "jealousies and false alarms" were feared as damaging to the country. Political parties were thought to merely search for profit, not provide for the common good. See Chapter 4.

53. **A.**

Answer choices B, C, and D refer to activities that take place across state borders, making them the responsibility of the federal government. See Chapter 4.

54. **A.**

A local government is chartered according to the constitution of the state in which the government is located. Just as the policies enacted by the state government must not conflict with federal law, a local government is subject to the legal environment created by the state's constitution and statutes. See Chapter 4.

55. **B.**

Realism has been one of the dominant forces guiding international relations theory and influencing foreign policy, especially since the end of World War II. As an international theory, realism holds that nation-states are the basic governmental unit and there is no authority above individual nations. See Chapter 4.

56. **A.**

Government by the many, once called a polity, is now called a constitutional democracy. See Chapter 4.

57. **C.**

Another related term for autocracy, more commonly used in the past, is despotism, or rule by a despot. See Chapter 4.

58. **A.**

The United States is a republic. The modern democratic state is usually a republic, in which the people do not take a direct role in legislating or governing but elect representatives to express their views and wants. A democratic government exists when these representatives are freely chosen by the people, whose demands are then recognized by the duly elected government. See Chapter 4.

59. **C.**

Most people remember the First Amendment to the Constitution, which is included in the Bill of Rights, as the "free speech" amendment. However, in its entirety, the amendment defines other freedoms: "Congress shall make no law respecting an establishment of religion, or prohibiting the free exercise thereof; or abridging the freedom of speech, or of the press; or the right of the people peaceably to assemble, and to petition the government for a redress of grievances." See Chapter 4.

60. **C.**

Prehistoric means the time in the development of human culture before the appearance of the written word. See Chapter 5.

61. **B.**

The Stone Age is the time early in the development of human cultures, before the use of metals, when tools and weapons were made of stone. The dates of the Stone Age vary considerably for different parts of the world. In Europe, Asia, and Africa, it began about 2 million years ago. See Chapter 5.

62. **D.**

Throughout the immense time span of the Stone Age, vast changes occurred in climate and in other conditions affecting human culture. Humans themselves evolved into their modern form during the latter part of it. The Stone Age has been divided into three periods: Paleolithic, Mesolithic, and Neolithic. See Chapter 5.

63. **A.**

Discoveries made since 1960 have upset rather than confirmed theories about copper and bronze. Imports of tin took place in the second millennium B.C.E., and the Bronze Age began at distinctly different times in Greece and China. See Chapter 5.

64. **B.**

Ancient Greece was the most sophisticated Western society of its time, had a lasting impact on Western culture, and predates the Roman Empire and Christianity. See Chapter 5.

65. **D.**

The origins of Western culture are often referred to as "three pillars": ancient Greece (specifically, Greek philosophy); the Roman Empire (specifically, Roman law); and Catholic and Protestant Christianity. Broadly, these foundations are referred to as the Greco-Roman and Judeo-Christian roots of Western culture. See Chapter 5.

66. **B.**

Traditionally, the ancient Greek period was thought to begin with the date of the first recorded Olympic Games in 776 B.C.E., but many historians now extend its origins back to about 1000 B.C.E. The traditional date for the end of the ancient Greek period is the year Alexander the Great died, 323 B.C.E. See Chapter 5.

67. **A.**

Whether the Trojan War was real or mere myth is a matter of dispute. However, the ancient Greeks considered the Trojan War as the first moment in history when the Greeks came together as one people with a common purpose. See Chapter 5.

68. **B.**

   According to legend, Rome was founded in 753 B.C.E. by the brothers Romulus and Remus. See Chapter 5.

69. **B.**

   The Roman republic eventually weakened, and the rule of Rome passed to one man—first Julius Caesar, who was assassinated in 44 B.C.E., and then to Augustus. Over the next few centuries, a succession of emperors ruled. See Chapter 5.

70. **D.**

   Following are some generally accepted reasons for the fall of the Roman Empire:

   • Decline in morals and values

   • Public health and environmental issues

   • Political corruption and no clear way to choose a new emperor

   • Unemployment resulting from wealthy landowners taking over small farms

   • Inflation caused by an insufficient flow of gold to use for coins

   • Urban decay

   • Inferior technology

   • Military spending

   • Civil war in Italy that brought many soldiers home from battling outside invaders

   See Chapter 5.

71. **D.**

   The Western Han capital of Xi'an, in present-day Shaanxi Province—a monumental urban center laid out on a north–south axis with palaces, residential wards, and two bustling market areas—was one of the two largest cities in the ancient world (Rome was the other). See Chapter 5.

72. **C.**

The peoples on the continent of Africa speak hundreds of languages, and if dialects spoken by various ethnic groups are also included, the number is much higher. See Chapter 5.

73. **A.**

China has one language, but the dialects make it impossible to communicate verbally for many. Writing is their common bond. Chinese characters are not letters but represent complete words or ideas. China is very diverse. See Chapter 5.

74. **B.**

The nations of India, Pakistan, Bangladesh, Bhutan, Nepal, and Sri Lanka share an ethnic background and have similar cultures. See Chapter 5.

75. **A.**

Hinduism, Buddhism, Jainism, and Sikhism, the four major world religions founded in the region that is modern-day India, are spread throughout the subcontinent. See Chapter 5.

76. **B.**

As farming practices improved, the many small Mayan villages could support larger populations, and that allowed city-states to emerge. Some city-states, such as Tikal, had populations approaching 40,000. See Chapter 5.

77. **A.**

The cities the Maya built were ceremonial centers. A priestly class lived in the cities, but for the most part, the Maya population lived in small farming villages. The priestly class would carry out daily religious duties, particularly sacrifices, and the peasants would periodically gather for religious ceremonies and festivals. See Chapter 5.

78. **B.**

Despite what the name suggests, the Silk Road was not a single route. Crossing Central Asia, several branches developed, passing through various oasis settlements. See Chapter 5.

79. **A.**

It is important to understand the importance of the Hammurabi Code. It was the earliest known example of a ruler proclaiming publicly to his people an entire body of laws, arranged in orderly groups, so that all men might read and know what was required of them. The code was carved on a black stone monument 8 feet high and clearly was intended to be placed in public view. See Chapter 5.

80. **C.**

The Middle Ages are commonly dated from the fifth-century fall of the Western Roman Empire until the end of the fifteenth century. See Chapter 5.

81. **B.**

The Renaissance witnessed the revival of learning based on classical sources, the rise of courtly and papal patronage, the development of perspective in painting, and advancements in science. See Chapter 5.

82. **C.**

Leonardo Da Vinci was an artist, inventor, and scientist, and Michelangelo was a sculptor, painter, and architect of the Renaissance. See Chapter 5.

83. **C.**

The Protestant Reformation was a sixteenth-century movement to reform the Catholic Church in western Europe. See Chapter 5.

84. **A.**

Immanuel Kant is regarded as one of the most influential thinkers of modern Europe and the last major philosopher of the Enlightenment. See Chapter 5.

85. **D.**

Martin Luther was building on work done by John Wycliffe and Jan Hus, and other reformers joined the cause. René Descartes was a prominent figure in the Age of Reason. See Chapter 5.

86. **A.**

Trade was the key motivator for colonization. European ships traveled around the world in search of new trading routes and partners to feed burgeoning capitalism in Europe. See Chapter 5.

87. **D.**

   Peace was seldom part of the colonization process. For example, consider the effect that colonialism had on Native Americans. See Chapter 5.

88. **B.**

   While the Massachusetts Bay Colony was not the first successful settlement in the New World, it was the first major stronghold in North America. See Chapter 6.

89. **B.**

   Answering this question is a process of elimination, because answer choices A, C, and D refer to devastating events, but the development of trade would not be considered a problem. See Chapter 6.

90. **D.**

   The English geologist Charles Lyell published his *Principles of Geology*. See Chapter 6.

91. **D.**

   Half of the Jamestown settlers were artisans, craftsmen, soldiers, and laborers, including a tailor, a barber, and two surgeons. The other half comprised "gentlemen," men of wealth who did not have professions. See Chapter 6.

92. **D.**

   After eight months, only 38 of the 120 pioneers were still alive. See Chapter 6.

93. **D.**

   The Native Americans near Jamestown were Algonquian Indians. Powhatan was their chief. See Chapter 6.

94. **B.**

   In 1664, after obtaining control of Dutch holdings lying between Virginia and New England, the Duke of York made a proprietary grant to Sir George Carteret and Lord Berkeley of the land between the Hudson and the Delaware rivers. These men intended to profit from real estate sales. The new grant was named New Jersey for Carteret, who was governor of the Isle of Jersey. See Chapter 6.

95. **C.**

When the Pilgrims arrived, they anchored off the tip of modern-day Cape Cod, in an area now known as Massachusetts. Before they set foot on shore, however, they wrote, and all the men signed, an agreement called the Mayflower Compact, setting the rules that would guide them through the early hard times of establishing a new community. The compact, which was signed on November 21, 1620, served as the official constitution of the Plymouth Colony for many years. See Chapter 6.

96. **D.**

The French and Indian War (also known as the Seven Years' War) saw the British pitted against the French, the Austrians, and the Spanish. This war raged across the globe. See Chapter 6.

97. **A.**

In 1764 the British for the first time imposed a series of taxes designed specifically to raise revenue from the colonies. The American Revenue Act, which became popularly known as the Sugar Act, raised the tariff on sugar. The act was combined with a greater attempt to enforce existing tariffs. See Chapter 6.

98. **D.**

One reaction to the Stamp Act was the creation of secret organizations throughout the colonies, known as the Sons of Liberty. See Chapter 6.

99. **B.**

The British parliament gave its speedy assent to a series of acts that became known as the Coercive Acts; in the colonies, the acts were called the Intolerable Acts. Among other things, the acts closed the Port of Boston until the East India Company received compensation for the tea dumped into the harbor. See Chapter 6.

100. **B.**

Representatives from each colony except Georgia met in Philadelphia. The royal governor in Georgia succeeded in blocking delegates from being sent to the congress. See Chapter 6.

101. **D.**

Soon after the battles of Lexington and Concord, on May 10, 1776, the Second Continental Congress met in Philadelphia's State House, now called Independence Hall. The delegates decided the colonies should make a complete break from Great

Britain and be officially put in a state of defense. The congress formed the American Continental Army and appointed George Washington as commander in chief. See Chapter 6.

102. **B.**

One major issue with the Articles of Confederation was that it did not grant taxing authority to the central government; the federal government had to request funds from the states. A second concern was the one-state, one-vote provision. See Chapter 6.

103. **C.**

The *Federalist Papers* consist of 85 essays about the philosophy and motivation of the new American government. Although all the essays were signed "Publius" and the authors real identities are a matter of some dispute, the general consensus is that the writers were Alexander Hamilton, James Madison, and John Jay. See Chapter 6.

104. **D.**

Manifest Destiny is a doctrine used to rationalize U.S. territorial expansion in the 1840s and 1850s. It asserted that expansion of the United States throughout the American continents was both justified and inevitable. The phrase was coined by the U.S. journalist John L. O'Sullivan, and was initially used in regard to Mexican and Indian land in Texas and the Southwest. The concept was invoked later in a dispute with Great Britain over Oregon and in relation to territory controlled by the United States as a result of the Spanish-American War. The Spanish had left Florida long before the concept of Manifest Destiny was promulgated. See Chapter 6.

105. **A.**

The Northwest Ordinance of 1787 provided the means by which new states would be created out of the western lands and then admitted into the Union. See Chapter 6.

106. **C.**

After gaining independence from Mexico, Texas wanted to join the United States immediately. However, Congress voted against Texas joining the Union. See Chapter 6.

107. **D.**

Between 1790 and 1860, commercial agriculture replaced subsistence agriculture in the North, and household production was replaced by factory production. Massive foreign immigration from Ireland and Germany greatly increased the size of cities. In the South, slavery impeded the development of industry and cities and discouraged technological innovation. See Chapter 6.

108. **A.**

Even blacks who were free lived under the shadow of slavery in the South, unable to travel or assemble as freely as those in the North. It was also more difficult for them to organize and sustain churches, schools, and fraternal orders such as the Masons. See Chapter 6.

109. **B.**

Cotton was an almost perfect crop for the lower South because it was easy to grow and its demands were met by the region's climate and soil. Between the cotton South and the wheat North was a middle ground in which the main crop was corn. Cattle, hemp, and tobacco were produced in the vicinity of Lexington, Kentucky; Nashville and Knoxville, Tennessee; and what is now Charleston, West Virginia. Corn was also widely planted in those hilly regions. See Chapter 6.

110. **A.**

The American Civil War (1861–65) was one of the most devastating conflicts in U.S. history, with a death toll exceeding 600,000 men. More lives were lost in that one war than in all the wars and conflicts the United States has been involved in since. See Chapter 6.

111. **C.**

Lincoln's election was the signal for the secession of South Carolina (December 20, 1860), and that state was followed out of the Union by six other states: Mississippi, Florida, Alabama, Georgia, Louisiana, and Texas. See Chapter 6.

112. **B.**

When the first seven states seceded from the Union, the outgoing president, James Buchanan, a northern Democrat, was pursuing a vacillating course, sometimes conceding to the proslavery wing of his part and at other times sincerely attempting to avert war. See Chapter 6.

113. **D.**

The Confederacy's first and only president, Jefferson Davis, was determined to oust the Federals. See Chapter 6.

114. **D.**

Almost no one ever has an *unlimited* supply of anything. That was certainly true for the Union army. See Chapter 6.

115. **B.**

The Fourteenth Amendment to the Constitution provided former slaves with national citizenship and gave federal protection to freed slaves whose rights could not be limited by state governments. It passed Congress on June 13, 1868, and was submitted to the states for ratification. See Chapter 6.

116. **A.**

By December of 1865, every Confederate state except Texas had taken the required steps toward rejoining the Union. Texas conformed on April 6, 1866, and on December 6, President Johnson announced to Congress that the Union was restored. See Chapter 6.

117. **A.**

Some states enacted Black Codes to effectively tie the freed slaves to the land on which they lived and worked. The federal government established the Freedmen's Bureau on February 19, 1866, to protect freed slaves from the harsh Black Codes. See Chapter 6.

118. **A.**

In the late nineteenth century, wealthy families like the Carnegies, Mellons, Rockefellers, and Morgans began building mansions on the edges of the cities. Housing developments of similar-looking single- or multiple-family dwellings, built by speculators, also sprouted on the edges of cities. These often catered to a new middle class of white-collar employees in business and industry. By 1900 more than a third of urban dwellers owned their own homes, one of the highest rates in the world at the time. This "progress" led the period from 1890 to 1917 to be labeled the Progressive Era. See Chapter 6.

119. **A.**

Immigrants in the early 1900s were primarily white and came from Germany, Ireland, and England—the principal sources of immigration before the Civil War. That would change drastically in the next three decades. See Chapter 6.

120. **B.**

The Harlem Renaissance is considered the first important movement of black artists and writers in the United States. Centered in the Harlem neighborhood of New York, the movement dispersed to other urban areas during the 1920s and promoted the publication of more black writers than ever before. See Chapter 6.

121. **A.**

The various disciplines within the social sciences are not isolated but blended together and interrelated. See Chapter 7.

122. **B.**

Sociology is the study of how we become members of groups, how we move among groups, and how being in different groups affects us and the groups in which we participate. See Chapter 7.

123. **D.**

History is the study of the past and how it affects our views of the present. See Chapter 7.

124. **A.**

Primary source documents allow you to get closer to the subject matter. To get the most information from a document, you must examine who wrote it and why, the intended audience, the author's motives or intentions, and what information is being presented. See Chapter 7.

125. **D.**

Technology can be a major source of interesting material or a major problem. Be sure to coach your students in the proper use of the Internet. See Chapter 7.

Practice Test 2

FTCE Social Science

ANSWER SHEET FOR PRACTICE TEST 2

1 _____   2 _____   3 _____   4 _____   5 _____

6 _____   7 _____   8 _____   9 _____   10 _____

11 _____   12 _____   13 _____   14 _____   15 _____

16 _____   17 _____   18 _____   19 _____   20 _____

21 _____   22 _____   23 _____   24 _____   25 _____

26 _____   27 _____   28 _____   29 _____   30 _____

31 _____   32 _____   33 _____   34 _____   35 _____

36 _____   37 _____   38 _____   39 _____   40 _____

41 _____   42 _____   43 _____   44 _____   45 _____

46 _____   47 _____   48 _____   49 _____   50 _____

51 _____   52 _____   53 _____   54 _____   55 _____

56 _____   57 _____   58 _____   59 _____   60 _____

61 _____   62 _____   63 _____   64 _____   65 _____

66 _____   67 _____   68 _____   69 _____   70 _____

71 _____   72 _____   73 _____   74 _____   75 _____

76 _____   77 _____   78 _____   79 _____   80 _____

81 _____   82 _____   83 _____   84 _____   85 _____

86 _____   87 _____   88 _____   89 _____   90 _____

91 _____   92 _____   93 _____   94 _____   95 _____

96 _____   97 _____   98 _____   99 _____   100 _____

101 _____ 102 _____ 103 _____ 104 _____ 105 _____

106 _____ 107 _____ 108 _____ 109 _____ 110 _____

111 _____ 112 _____ 113 _____ 114 _____ 115 _____

116 _____ 117 _____ 118 _____ 119 _____ 120 _____

121 _____ 122 _____ 123 _____ 124 _____ 125 _____

1. You are interested in finding peer-reviewed research on teachers' opinions on the best way to present world religions to twelfth-graders. What type of data are you looking for?

   A. Qualitative

   B. Quantitative

   C. Mixed methods

   D. Teachers' lounge conversations

2. In theory the League of Nations was a good idea and did have some early successes, but ultimately it was a failure. Why?

   A. Russia and Germany were intentionally not invited.

   B. Trade with member states could not be controlled.

   C. China invaded Japan.

   D. The economic boom of the time created a disinterest in the league's decisions.

3. Which of the following pairings is NOT correct?

   A. Lost Generation and Ernest Hemingway

   B. Harlem Renaissance and Zora Neale Hurston

   C. Algonquin Round Table and Harpo Marx

   D. Algonquin Round Table and F. Scott Fitzgerald.

4. Which of the following pairings is correct?

   A. Franklin D. Roosevelt and the New Deal

   B. Hitler and economic prosperity

   C. Black Codes and freedom for slaves

   D. Charles de Gaulle and the Tehran Conference

5. Which of the following is NOT considered a necessary element of a democratic society?

   A. free elections

   B. capitalism

   C. freedom of speech

   D. peaceful and orderly transfer of political power

6. Which of the following pairings is NOT like the others?

    A. realism and liberalism

    B. market economy and planned economy

    C. quantitative and qualitative

    D. Congress and bicameral legislature

7. Which of the following pairings is NOT like the others?

    A. Hinduism and Buddhism

    B. Jainism and Sikhism

    C. Christianity and Islam

    D. Confucianism and Emperor Wudi

8. Which of the following does NOT belong with the others?

    A. Anne Hutchinson

    B. Exeter Compact

    C. John Wheelwright

    D. George Calvert

9. Which of the following was NOT one of the purposes of the First Continental Congress?

    A. discuss the colonies' relationship with Britain but not seek independence

    B. establish a Continental Army

    C. compose a statement of colonial rights

    D. provide a plan that would convince Britain to restore colonial rights

10. Which of the following leaders had a far different strategy for expanding civil rights for African Americans than the others?

    A. Malcolm X

    B. Martin Luther King

    C. Rosa Parks

    D. James Meredith

11. Which of the following statements about the Vietnam War is false?

    A. More than 58,000 Americans were killed.

    B. Waged from 1959 to 1975, it is consider the longest-lasting conflict in which the United States has participated.

    C. The U.S. fought the North Vietnamese with no assistance from allies.

    D. More than 3 million Vietnamese were killed.

12. Which of the following statements about Florida is true?

    A. Florida became a state in 1845 with almost 50 percent of its population composed of slaves.

    B. The United States accepted the surrender of the Seminoles in 1842.

    C. Florida's first theme parks opened in 1960.

    D. Most of Florida's immigrants come from eastern Europe.

13. Which of the following New Deal programs was (were) designed to reduce unemployment?

    A. Public Works Administration

    B. Works Progress Administration

    C. neither A nor B

    D. both A and B

14. Which of the following is considered a major cause of the Great Depression?

    A. military unrest in Europe

    B. the Cold War

    C. extensive stock market speculation

    D. weak unions

15. Which country chose not to join the League of Nations?

    A. Britain

    B. France

    C. United States

    D. Germany

16. When did the United States first decide to form a militia?

   A.   after the First Continental Congress

   B.   after the Second Continental Congress

   C.   after Great Britain's retaliation against the Boston Tea party

   D.   after enactment of the Stamp Act

17. Which of the following pairings is correct?

   A.   Coercive Acts and Intolerable Acts

   B.   General Oglethorpe and North Carolina in 1758

   C.   William L. Yancey and abolitionist

   D.   P. G. T. Beauregard and Union commander

18. In which of the following countries did acts of genocide occur?

   A.   Srebrenica

   B.   South Africa

   C.   Rwanda

   D.   both A and C

19. Which of the following is a negative result of nationalism?

   A.   war

   B.   national pride and self-determinism

   C.   cultural advancement

   D.   technological advancement

20. Which of the following pairings is NOT correct?

   A.   republic and the United States

   B.   totalitarianism and fascist Italy

   C.   absolute monarchy and modern Russia

   D.   democracy and ancient Greece

21. Which of the following pairings is NOT correct?

    A.   Eighth Amendment and excessive bail

    B.   Seventh Amendment and trial by jury

    C.   Fourth Amendment and unreasonable searches and seizures

    D.   Tenth Amendment and the right to a speedy and public trial

22. What is the discount rate?

    A.   the interest rate a Federal Reserve Bank charges eligible financial institutions to borrow funds on a short-term basis

    B.   the interest rate a Federal Reserve Bank charges eligible financial institutions to borrow funds on a long-term basis

    C.   the percentage rate of deposits required by banks

    D.   the interest rate relative to the prime rate

23. Which statement about GDP is correct?

    A.   The GDP is the monetary value of all the finished goods and services produced within a country's borders in a specific period.

    B.   GDP is usually calculated on a three-year average.

    C.   It includes all public consumption and government outlays.

    D.   It does not include investments and exports less imports.

24. Which of the following is antithetical to a capitalist economy?

    A.   mixed economy

    B.   socialist economy

    C.   inflationary economy

    D.   depression

25. Which of the following is NOT considered a means of economic control?

    A.   government ownership

    B.   taxes

    C.   product dumping in another country

    D.   All of the above are controls.

26. Under which of the following conditions does the federal government have a certain amount of control over a program that normally is the responsibility of the state?

   A.   The program requires reinterpretation of the constitution.

   B.   The program requires federal funds to operate.

   C.   The program is subject to political pressure.

   D.   The federal government has no control over programs run by the states.

27. The constitution specifically gives the responsibility for education to the states. Which of the following is an example of federal intervention in education?

   A.   America's Promise

   B.   Read 180

   C.   No Child Left Behind

   D.   Phonics

Use the following chart to answer questions 28 through 30.

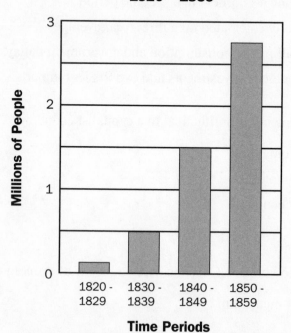

**Immigration to the United States
1820 – 1859**

28. How many people immigrated to the United States from 1830 to 1839?

    A. 50,000

    B. 100,000

    C. 500,000

    D. 1,000,000

29. In which decade did 1.5 million immigrants come to the United States?

    A. 1820s

    B. 1830s

    C. 1840s

    D. 1850s

30. Based on the graph, where did these immigrants come from?

    A. Ireland, because of the potato famine

    B. eastern Europe

    C. China

    D. The chart does not indicate any country of origin.

31. Which of the following is NOT delegated to states in the U.S. Constitution?

    A. establishing state-sponsored colleges and universities

    B. administering and certifying elections, including elections for federal officials

    C. administering publicly funded health, housing, and nutrition programs for low-income and disabled residents

    D. commanding the state National Guard when called up to serve in Iraq

32. Which of the following sequence of eras is NOT in chronological order?

    A. Paleolithic, Mesolithic, Neolithic

    B. antiquity, Middle Ages, modern times

    C. Renaissance, Protestant Reformation, Age of Enlightenment

    D. Age of Reason, Renaissance, Age of Enlightenment

33. Nation-states use the state as an instrument of

 A. national unity.

 B. economic life.

 C. cultural life.

 D. all the above.

Use the following charts to answer questions 34 through 37.

Orlando, FL   Latitude: 28° 26' N   Longitude: 81° 20' W

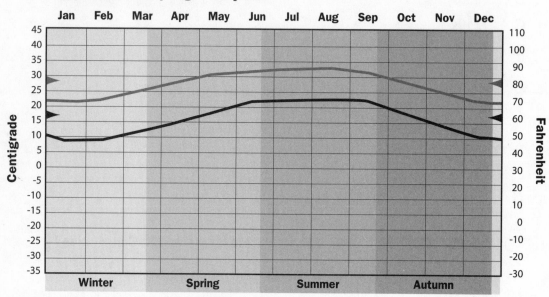

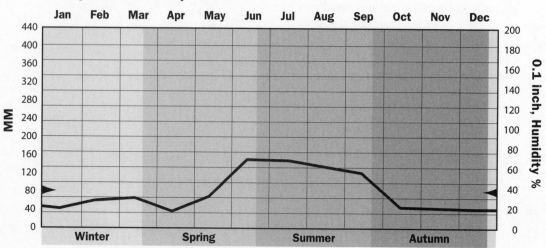

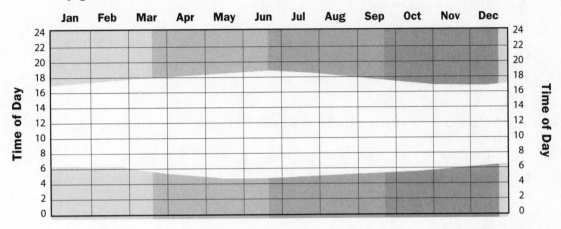

34. In what month would you vacation in Orlando to have the least potential for rain?

    A. April

    B. June

    C. September

    D. March

35. Which of the following statements is true?

    A. The average low temperature in December is about 50 degrees.

    B. The most amount of daylight is in May.

    C. According to the chart, the average humidity in June is very high.

    D. The average high temperature in July is about 95 degrees.

36. Which of the following is NOT indicated on the charts?

    A. sunrise

    B. sunset

    C. temperature in June

    D. humidity

37. What information is presented directly above the top chart?

    A. longitude and latitude

    B. elevation in yards

    C. origin of the information

    D. all the above

38. What was the form of government in Russia before the Revolution of 1917?

    A. democracy

    B. autocracy

    C. monarchy

    D. none of the above

39. This Age of Revolution was the period from about 1750 to 1800, when most European countries changed their form of government to

    A. absolutist or constitutional states.

    B. democratic or socialist states.

    C. aristocracy- or peasant-run states.

    D. none of the above.

40. Which of the following was NOT a result of the Industrial Revolution?

    A. important developments in transportation, including the steam locomotive, steamship, automobile, and airplane

    B. important developments in communication, including the telegraph and radio

    C. agricultural improvements that made possible the provision of food for a larger nonagricultural population

    D. a decline in the application of science to industry

41. Which of the following is the largest of the world's religions?

    A. Christianity

    B. Islam

    C. Taoism

    D. Buddhism

42. Labor unions have lost strength and membership in recent years. When was the growth period of labor unions?

    A.   1880 to 1950

    B.   1900 to 1950

    C.   1933 to 1950

    D.   1945 to 1975

43. A relatively large number of Chinese immigrated to the United States in one period in our history. When was that?

    A.   between the start of the California gold rush in 1849 and 1882

    B.   during the Industrial Revolution, from 1900 to 1925

    C.   after the Civil War, from 1870 to 1920

    D.   during the Roaring Twenties

44. From a sociological standpoint, what is one difference between Asian immigrants and South American immigrants?

    A.   Most South Americans are Catholic, whereas most Asians are Buddhist.

    B.   Most South American immigrants are seeking political asylum, whereas most Asian immigrants are seeking job opportunities.

    C.   Most South Americans speak Spanish, whereas immigrants from various Asian countries have no common language.

    D.   Asian and South American immigrants are basically the same from a sociological point of view.

45. The Treaty of Versailles ended World War I. What happened to the treaty in the United States?

    A.   President Woodrow Wilson signed it.

    B.   The Senate refused to ratify it.

    C.   President Franklin D. Roosevelt signed it.

    D.   None of the above occurred.

46. What happened to U.S. foreign policy after World War I?

    A.   Quotas for all immigrants were established.

    B.   The United States and its people turned inward.

    C.   The United States became a global economy.

    D.   Both A and B are correct.

47. What was the result of the Eighteenth Amendment?

    A.   All Americans became eligible to vote.

    B.   Prohibition heightened criminal activity.

    C.   The Great Depression was eased.

    D.   Presidents were limited to two terms of four years each.

48. Adolf Hitler became the chancellor of Germany in 1933. What was one of his first acts?

    A.   He began secretly building up Germany's army and weapons.

    B.   He established government policies to ease the effects of the Great Depression.

    C.   He established alliances with Italy and Czechoslovakia.

    D.   He met with France and Britain to work out treaties.

49. Which of the following is an element of the Civil Rights Act of 1964?

    A.   It prohibited discrimination on the basis of color, race, religion, or national origin in places of public accommodation covered by interstate commerce.

    B.   It desegregated public schools.

    C.   It ensured equal voting rights.

    D.   It prohibited housing and real estate discrimination.

50. Which of the following statements about Martin Luther King Jr. is true?

    A.   In 1963 King became *Time* magazine's "Man of the Year."

    B.   All African Americans united behind him.

    C.   He was the pastor of Ebenezer Baptist Church in Birmingham, Alabama.

    D.   He was assassinated on Christmas Day in 1969.

51. The Internet has made the world into a global society. This has both negative and positive consequences. Which of the following is one positive consequence?

    A. Worldwide corporations can become more powerful than some countries.

    B. Global awareness has brought advanced medicine and major philanthropic work to many parts of the world.

    C. Environmental regulations have improved.

    D. The chance of achieving world peace is greater.

52. The Twenty-sixth Amendment was passed during the Vietnam War. What is the focus of the amendment?

    A. It set 18 years as the legal drinking age across the United States.

    B. It ended the draft.

    C. It made the voting age 18 years.

    D. None of the above is the focus of the amendment.

53. Which of the following statements about the Han Dynasty is true?

    A. The boundaries established by the Qin and maintained by the Han have more or less defined the nation of China to the present day.

    B. The Han Dynasty ended before the birth of Christ.

    C. The Han relied on Buddhism as the philosophical basis for government.

    D. China was relatively unsophisticated during the Han Dynasty, with little poetry, literature, or philosophy.

54. Which of the following statements about geography is (are) true?

    A. GIS uses computer-assisted cartography.

    B. About 50 percent of the earth's surface is water.

    C. Slopes facing the sun are cooler than those that are not.

    D. All the above are true.

55. Temperatures in cities on the coast of Great Britain are more moderate than those in other cities at the same latitude. Why?

    A.   The altitude along the British coast is very low.

    B.   The British coast is on the end of the Gulf Stream and therefore gets a flow of warmer water.

    C.   Both A and B are true.

    D.   Neither A nor B is true

56. What type of economy finds market forces to allocate resources and goods, and to determine prices and quantities of each good that will be produced?

    A.   managed

    B.   socialist

    C.   market

    D.   planned

57. Which of the following is NOT one of the four factors of production?

    A.   labor

    B.   capital

    C.   entrepreneurship

    D.   scarcity

58. Which of the following is NOT a part of political science?

    A.   media

    B.   candidate behavior

    C.   election reform

    D.   All of the above are part of political science.

59. How can the federal government influence a state in an area that the Constitution defines as a state responsibility?

    A.   The federal government can use executive privilege.

    B.   Leaders within the federal government can pressure state leaders.

    C.   The federal government can threaten to withhold funding for projects administered by the states.

    D.   The states can ignore the federal government.

60. Which of the following did NOT live in Greece?

    A.   Aristotle

    B.   Plato

    C.   Socrates

    D.   Giotto

61. Which of the following people from the Renaissance and Reformation is out of place?

    A.   Shakespeare

    B.   Chaucer

    C.   Boccaccio

    D.   Galileo

62. Which of the following is NOT part of human–environment interaction?

    A.   Humans adapt to the environment.

    B.   Humans modify the environment.

    C.   Humans depend on the environment.

    D.   All the above are part of it.

63. Which of the following is NOT an example of a functional region in geography?

    A.   cell phone service area

    B.   newspaper delivery area

    C.   New York City

    D.   Chinatown in New York City

64. Which of the following is unique to the geography of Australia?

    A.   It is very large.

    B.   It has drastic changes in climate.

    C.   It is both a continent and a country.

    D.   It has a large desert region.

65. Which of the following relates to macroeconomics?

    A. government spending

    B. checking accounts

    C. home budgets

    D. popular car purchases

66. Which of the following relates to microeconomics?

    A. family spending

    B. exports

    C. investment

    D. tariffs

67. The Federal Open Market Committee (FOMC) sets the Federal Reserve's monetary policy, which is carried out

    A. at the trading desk of the Federal Reserve Bank of New York.

    B. in Washington, D.C., inside the FOMC office building.

    C. through brokers.

    D. in none of the above locations.

68. Who sets the discount rate for the Federal Reserve?

    A. a member of the president's cabinet

    B. the boards of directors of all the Federal Reserve Banks

    C. the chairman of the Federal Reserve

    D. the president of the United States

69. The Federal Reserve sets reserve requirements for all commercial banks, savings banks, savings and loans, credit unions, and U.S. branches and agencies of foreign banks. Depository institutions use their reserve accounts at Federal Reserve Banks for

    A. processing check and electronic payments.

    B. currency and coin services.

    C. neither A nor B; the reserves cannot be touched.

    D. both A and B.

70. Which of the following is the only federal agency to have both consumer protection and competition jurisdiction in broad sectors of the economy?

    A. Federal Reserve

    B. Federal Open Market Committee

    C. Federal Trade Commission

    D. Federal Consumer Protection Committee

71. How many judges are on the federal Supreme Court?

    A. 5

    B. 7

    C. 9

    D. 11

72. Who was one of the authors of the *Federalist Papers* and wrote the Bill of Rights?

    A. Alexander Hamilton

    B. James Madison

    C. John Jay

    D. Thomas Jefferson

73. Primaries are used in determining U.S. presidential candidates. Who decides the rules of the primaries?

    A. Congress

    B. the chief of elections in each state

    C. the national committee of each party

    D. state legislatures

74. Primaries can be open or closed. What is one benefit of a closed primary?

    A. On the day of the election, each individual is allowed to choose the party primary in which to participate.

    B. Voters must register with a party in advance of the election.

    C. Candidates are chosen freely by all people.

    D. Candidates are not able to focus their campaign funds entirely on partisans; instead, they must canvass the entire electorate.

75. Thomas Jefferson was elected in 1800. What was unusual about that election?

    A. Thomas Jefferson and Aaron Burr had an equal number of electoral votes.

    B. Jefferson won all the electoral votes.

    C. Many electoral voters broke from their original promises and voted for Jefferson, negating the popular vote.

    D. Jefferson ran with a vice president from the other party.

76. Which of the following is a disadvantage of the electoral college?

    A. It weakens the status of minority groups.

    B. It can include "faithless" electors—that is, electors who will not stay loyal to their parties or candidates.

    C. It maintains the federal system of government and representation.

    D. It requires a distribution of popular support to be elected president.

77. Which of the following is an advantage of the electoral college?

    A. It strengthens the status of minority groups because the votes of small minorities within a state can make the difference between winning all or none of the state's electoral votes.

    B. The electoral college increases voter turnout.

    C. The electoral college guarantees that the candidate with the most popular votes is elected president.

    D. None of the above is an advantage.

78. Which of the following statements about Mussolini is true?

    A. At age 39, he became the youngest prime minister in Italian history.

    B. Mussolini came to power after Hitler.

    C. Mussolini ruled as a dictator for only 10 years.

    D. His father was a doctor and his mother a nurse.

79. Which of the following accurately describes Adolf Hitler?

    A. charismatic

    B. true to his word

    C. the son of a Jewish father and Protestant mother

    D. none of the above

80. Which of the following statements about Winston Churchill is true?

    A.   He was followed in office by Neville Chamberlain.

    B.   He was never in the military.

    C.   He lost the election of 1945.

    D.   He was not an exceptional speaker.

81. Which of the following statements about the Cuban missile crisis is false?

    A.   It was a major incident during the Cold War.

    B.   The crisis began in 1961.

    C.   Russians refer to the event as the Caribbean crisis.

    D.   It would never have escalated into a war.

82. Which of the following statements about the Korean War is false?

    A.   It began as a civil war.

    B.   China entered the conflict.

    C.   The United States declared war in December 1950.

    D.   Outside Korea, the war is sometimes referred to as the forgotten war.

83. What is the correct chronological order of the following events?

    I.   President Andrew Johnson faces possible impeachment

    II. President Lincoln makes the Emancipation Proclamation

    III. James Buchanan is elected president

    IV. Sherman is victorious in Atlanta

    A.   III, II, IV, I

    B.   I, II, IV, III

    C.   II, IV, I, III

    D.   IV, II, I, III

84. Which of the following lists the wars in chronological order?

    A. French and Indian War, Revolutionary War, War of 1812

    B. Revolutionary War, War of 1812, French and Indian War

    C. War of 1812, French and Indian War, Revolutionary War

    D. War of 1812, Revolutionary War, French and Indian War

85. When was the U.S. Navy created?

    A. 1770

    B. 1775

    C. 1790

    D. 1800

86. Who wrote *Common Sense*?

    A. James Madison

    B. Thomas Paine

    C. John Jay

    D. George Washington

87. What was the purpose of *Common Sense*?

    A. encouraged citizens to adventure westward

    B. encouraged Americans to give up slavery

    C. argued that the time had come to sever colonial ties with Great Britain

    D. argued that Americans should befriend Indians, not attack them

88. Which of the following statements about the French and Indian War is true?

    A. It is also known as the Thirty Years' War.

    B. George Washington fought to help the British.

    C. Native Americans fought with the British against U.S. and French troops.

    D. The war was part of a larger conflict that involved several European countries but was fought only in France.

89. Which of the following was NOT associated with the Cold War?

    A.   military coalitions

    B.   espionage

    C.   space race

    D.   All the above were part of the Cold War.

90. Which of the following is the world's most populated continent?

    A.   North America

    B.   Australia

    C.   South America

    D.   Asia

91. The branch of geography that is the study of the earth's surface is

    A.   cartography.

    B.   ethnography.

    C.   hydrology.

    D.   climatology.

92. Which of the following is NOT related to sociology?

    A.   class structure

    B.   race

    C.   gender

    D.   industrial technologies

93. Which of the following is considered a key influence on the development of the nation-state?

    A.   World War I

    B.   Peace of Westphalia

    C.   Thirty Years' War

    D.   Trojan War

94. Which of the following is the best definition of *apartheid*?

    A. desegregation

    B. equality

    C. segregation

    D. violence

95. Which of the following was the earliest cause of World War II?

    A. Treaty of Versailles

    B. rise of Hitler to power

    C. alliance of Hitler and Mussolini

    D. Japan's success in China

96. Which of the following does not belong with the others?

    A. Benito Mussolini

    B. Joseph Stalin

    C. Mao Zedong

    D. Harry Truman

97. Define *wealth*.

    A. total assets

    B. the ability to do what you want, when you want

    C. total assets minus liabilities

    D. the ability to make purchases using cash rather than credit

98. *Inflation* is defined as

    A. a general rise in prices measured against a standard level of purchasing power.

    B. the difference between the cost of a computer now and five years ago.

    C. a government program to keep the economy growing.

    D. a period when prices are always increasing.

99. *Interest rate* is defined as

 A. a bank's profit from lending money.

 B. the percentage of the principal paid as a fee.

 C. a means for the government to control borrowing.

 D. a means for the government to control inflation.

100. Which of the following statements about Christ and Buddha is true?

 A. Buddha came before Christ.

 B. Christ came before Buddha.

 C. They lived at the same time in different parts of the world.

 D. They met and discussed mutual beliefs.

101. Animism includes all the following except

 A. the god of the heavens.

 B. the god of the sea.

 C. Almighty God the Father.

 D. the god of the harvest.

102. To spark students' interest in history, you could use which of the following in your classroom, in addition to the textbook?

 A. primary source documents

 B. secondary source documents

 C. both A and B

 D. neither A nor B

103. Which of the following is not a primary source?

 A. letters sent home during World War II

 B. newspaper articles from 1900

 C. a guest speaker on Auschwitz

 D. letters from grandparents to students about the Great Depression

104. Which of the following statements about Florida since World War II is false?

    A.   Florida's economy has become more diverse.

    B.   The citrus industry continues to prosper, despite occasional winter freezes.

    C.   The university and community college system has expanded rapidly.

    D.   High-technology industries have avoided Florida.

105. The Manhattan Project developed

    A.   ideas for the second Industrial Revolution.

    B.   the airplane.

    C.   the first nuclear weapon during World War II.

    D.   the Sherman tank.

106. Which of the following worked to develop the atomic bomb?

    A.   J. Robert Oppenheimer

    B.   General Leslie R. Groves

    C.   both A and B

    D.   neither A nor B

107. Which of the following is the world's longest human-made structure?

    A.   Panama Canal

    B.   Great Wall of China

    C.   Wailing Wall

    D.   Grand Canal of China

108. Which of the following pairings is NOT correct?

    A.   Japan, Hirohito

    B.   Greece, Alexander the Great

    C.   Vietnam, Ho Chi Minh

    D.   France, Winston Churchill

109. During the Vietnam War, the Viet Minh took over the government from

    A.   the French.

    B.   Emperor Bao Dai.

    C.   Prime Minister Ngo Dinh Diem.

    D.   the Khmer Rouge.

110. Which of the following is NOT a reason the United States entered World War II?

    A.   Nazi Germany was sinking American supply ships.

    B.   Japan attacked the U.S. naval base at Pearl Harbor.

    C.   Italy and Germany declared war on the United States.

    D.   All the above are reasons the United States entered the war.

111. Which country was not part of the Potsdam Declaration ending World War II?

    A.   United States

    B.   Britain

    C.   China

    D.   France

112. Which of the following statements about Florida since World War II is (are) true?

    A.   Population growth has been steady.

    B.   Job growth has slowed.

    C.   Florida has become the tenth most populous state in the nation.

    D.   All the above are true.

113. Which of the following statements about early Florida history is false?

    A.   Written records about life in Florida began with the arrival of the Spanish explorer and adventurer Juan Ponce de León in 1513.

    B.   Ponce de León waded ashore on the northeast coast of Florida, possibly near present-day Saint Augustine.

    C.   In 1539, Hernando de Soto began another expedition in search of gold and silver.

    D.   Spanish conquistadors who explored Florida found great treasures near Tallahassee, which led to significant expansion of Spanish exploration.

114. Which of the following correctly matches the location or name and date of the worst hurricane in Florida history with the death toll from that hurricane?

    A. Key West, 1919; more than 800 killed

    B. Lake Okeechobee, 1928; almost 2,000 killed

    C. Hurricane Andrew, 1992; 176 killed

    D. Hurricane Betsy, 1965; 293 killed

115. Ellis Island was the main entry facility for immigrants arriving in the United States in the late nineteenth and early twentieth centuries. Which of the following statements about Ellis Island is true?

    A. It was within the boundaries of Massachusetts.

    B. About 12 million immigrants were inspected there.

    C. It was one of only 10 processing stations opened by the federal government.

    D. About one-third of all immigrants who came to Ellis Island were denied admission to the United States and sent back to their countries of origin.

116. Which of the following is not related to the Roman Empire?

    A. Julius Caesar

    B. Augustus

    C. Mark Antony

    D. Lysander

117. Which of the following statements about Vietnamese immigrants is false?

    A. Vietnamese immigration to America has been almost exclusively a by-product of the United States' involvement in the Vietnam War.

    B. Fewer than 10,000 Vietnamese were living in America in 1970.

    C. By 1980 the number of Vietnamese living in America had risen to almost a quarter of a million.

    D. The largest concentration (approximately 40 percent) of Vietnamese immigrants is in Miami, predominantly in Little Saigon, near Liberty City.

118. Which of the following statements about General George S. Patton Jr. is false?

   A.   He was the senior commander of a tank corps.

   B.   He commanded major military units in North Africa, Sicily, and the European theater of operations.

   C.   He was the first military man in his family.

   D.   His record was marred by insubordination and some periods of apparent instability.

119. Which of the following statements about George Washington is false?

   A.   He was one of the Virginia delegates to the Second Continental Congress.

   B.   He lived in the area around Mount Vernon.

   C.   He assisted in the formation of the nation's first two political parties.

   D.   When the U.S. Constitution was ratified, the electoral college unanimously elected him president.

120. Which of the following pairings is NOT correct?

   A.   Eisenhower, West Point graduate

   B.   Nimitz, Naval Academy graduate

   C.   John F. Kennedy, Naval Academy graduate

   D.   Ulysses S. Grant, West Point graduate

121. What do presidents George Washington, Andrew Jackson, William Henry Harrison, and Teddy Roosevelt have in common?

   A.   All were members of the Progressive Party.

   B.   None was a vice president.

   C.   All were distinguished military leaders.

   D.   All were senators.

122. Which of the following presidents was not assassinated?

   A.   Abraham Lincoln

   B.   James A. Garfield

   C.   William McKinley

   D.   William Howard Taft

123. The Presidential Succession Act of 1947 established the line of succession should the president of the United States die while in office. Who is first in line to succeed the president if the vice president is killed at the same time?

    A. speaker of the House

    B. president pro tempore of the Senate

    C. secretary of state

    D. secretary of the Treasury

124. Which of the following statements about the ancient Olympic Games is true?

    A. Women were equal to men in some events.

    B. Running was not included.

    C. Only free men who spoke Greek could compete.

    D. The games united Greece with the world outside its borders.

125. Which of the following might be found in a communist country?

    A. state-owned airlines

    B. bicameral legislature

    C. reasonable health insurance premiums

    D. extensive tourism

PRACTICE TEST 2 ANSWER KEY

Question	Answer	Competency
1	A	Knowledge of Social Science and Its Methodology
2	A	Knowledge of American History
3	D	Knowledge of American History
4	A	Knowledge of American History
5	B	Knowledge of Political Science
6	D	Knowledge of Economics
		Knowledge of Political Science
		Knowledge of American History
		Knowledge of Social Science and Its Methodology
7	D	Knowledge of World History
8	D	Knowledge of American History
9	B	Knowledge of American History
10	A	Knowledge of American History
11	C	Knowledge of American History
12	A	Knowledge of American History
13	D	Knowledge of American History
14	C	Knowledge of American History
15	C	Knowledge of American History
16	B	Knowledge of American History
17	A	Knowledge of American History
18	D	Knowledge of World History
19	A	Knowledge of Political Science
20	C	Knowledge of Political Science
21	D	Knowledge of Political Science
22	A	Knowledge of Economics
23	A	Knowledge of Economics

Question	Answer	Competency
24	B	Knowledge of Economics
25	B	Knowledge of Economics
26	B	Knowledge of Economics
27	C	Knowledge of Economics
28	C	Knowledge of Geography
29	C	Knowledge of Geography
30	D	Knowledge of Geography
31	D	Knowledge of Political Science
32	D	Knowledge of World History
33	D	Knowledge of Political Science
34	A	Knowledge of Geography
35	A	Knowledge of Geography
36	D	Knowledge of Geography
37	A	Knowledge of Geography
38	B	Knowledge of World History
39	A	Knowledge of World History
40	D	Knowledge of World History
41	A	Knowledge of World History
42	B	Knowledge of American History
43	A	Knowledge of American History
44	C	Knowledge of American History Knowledge of Geography
45	B	Knowledge of American History
46	D	Knowledge of American History
47	B	Knowledge of American History
48	A	Knowledge of American History
49	A	Knowledge of American History
50	A	Knowledge of American History

Question	Answer	Competency
51	B	Knowledge of Economics
52	C	Knowledge of Political Science
		Knowledge of American History
53	A	Knowledge of American History
54	A	Knowledge of Geography
55	B	Knowledge of Geography
56	C	Knowledge of Economics
57	D	Knowledge of Economics
58	D	Knowledge of Political Science
59	C	Knowledge of Political Science
60	D	Knowledge of American History
61	D	Knowledge of World History
62	D	Knowledge of Geography
63	C	Knowledge of Geography
64	C	Knowledge of Geography
65	A	Knowledge of Economics
66	A	Knowledge of Economics
67	A	Knowledge of Economics
68	B	Knowledge of Economics
69	D	Knowledge of Economics
70	C	Knowledge of Economics
71	C	Knowledge of Political Science
72	B	Knowledge of American History
		Knowledge of Political Science
73	C	Knowledge of Political Science
74	B	Knowledge of Political Science
75	A	Knowledge of American History
76	B	Knowledge of Political Science

Question	Answer	Competency
77	A	Knowledge of Political Science
78	A	Knowledge of American History
79	A	Knowledge of American History
80	C	Knowledge of American History
81	D	Knowledge of American History
82	C	Knowledge of American History
83	A	Knowledge of American History
84	A	Knowledge of American History
85	B	Knowledge of American History
86	B	Knowledge of American History
87	C	Knowledge of American History
88	B	Knowledge of American History
89	D	Knowledge of American History
90	D	Knowledge of Geography
91	A	Knowledge of Geography
92	D	Knowledge of Social Science and Its Methodology
93	B	Knowledge of World History
94	C	Knowledge of World History
95	A	Knowledge of American History
96	D	Knowledge of World History
97	C	Knowledge of Economics
98	A	Knowledge of Economics
99	B	Knowledge of Economics
100	A	Knowledge of World History
101	C	Knowledge of World History
102	C	Knowledge of Social Science and Its Methodology
103	B	Knowledge of Social Science and Its Methodology
104	D	Knowledge of American History

Question	Answer	Competency
105	C	Knowledge of American History
106	C	Knowledge of American History
107	B	Knowledge of World History
108	D	Knowledge of American History
109	B	Knowledge of American History
110	D	Knowledge of American History
111	D	Knowledge of American History
112	A	Knowledge of American History
113	D	Knowledge of American History
114	B	Knowledge of American History
115	B	Knowledge of American History
116	D	Knowledge of World History
117	D	Knowledge of American History
118	C	Knowledge of American History
119	C	Knowledge of American History
120	C	Knowledge of American History
121	C	Knowledge of American History
122	D	Knowledge of American History
123	A	Knowledge of Political Science
124	C	Knowledge of World History
125	A	Knowledge of Political Science

PRACTICE TEST 2 PROGRESS CHART

Knowledge of Geography —/15

28	29	30	34	35	36	37	44

54	55	62	63	64	90	91

Knowledge of Economics —/19

6	22	23	24	25	26	27	51	56	57

65	66	67	68	69	70	97	98	99

Knowledge of Political Science —/18

5	6	19	20	21	31	33	52	58

59	71	72	73	74	76	77	123	125

Knowledge of World History —/16

7	18	32	38	39	40	41	61

93	94	96	100	101	107	116	124

Knowledge of American History —/58

2	3	4	6	8	9	10	11	12	13	14	15	16	17	42

43	44	45	46	47	48	49	50	52	53	60	72	75	78	79

80	81	82	83	84	85	86	87	88	89	95	104	105	106	108

109	110	111	112	113	114	115	117	118	119	120	121	122

Knowledge of Social Science and Its Methodology —/5

1	6	92	102	103

DETAILED EXPLANATIONS FOR PRACTICE TEST 2

(For further review, refer back to the chapter(s) noted at the end of each explanation.)

1. **A.**

    Qualitative data is varied in nature but consists primarily of information that is not numerical, including data derived from interviews and written documents. See Chapter 7.

2. **A.**

    Russia was not invited to join the League of Nations because of a fear of communism. Germany was not invited because it was held responsible for World War I. See Chapter 6.

3. **D.**

    F. Scott Fitzgerald was part of the group of writers known as the Lost Generation. See Chapter 6.

4. **A.**

    The reforms enacted under Roosevelt's New Deal gave the government more power and helped ease the Depression. Hitler rose to power because of the economic misery most Germans were experiencing. The Black Codes tied slaves to the land on which they worked. De Gaulle was not at the Tehran Conference; Stalin, Roosevelt and Churchill were. See Chapter 6.

5. **B.**

    Capitalism is not a requirement of a democracy. It may follow, but a society with many socialist elements can still be a democracy. See Chapter 4.

6. **D.**

    Each answer choice is a pairing of opposites except D, in which both elements are the same. See Chapters 3, 4, 6, and 7.

7. **D.**

    Each answer choice is a pair of world religions except D, which matches a religion with its founder. See Chapter 5.

8. **D.**

Answer choices A, B, and C relate to Exeter, a settlement in New Hampshire. In 1632 King Charles I of England granted the Maryland Charter to George Calvert, whose son eventually led the group of settlers who founded a colony there. See Chapter 6.

9. **B.**

The members of the First Continental Congress had no intention of separating the colonies from Great Britain, but they wanted to peacefully establish their rights. See Chapter 6.

10. **A.**

Malcolm X did not follow the strategy of nonviolent resistance that the other civil rights leaders listed had adopted from India's Mahatma Ghandi. See Chapter 6.

11. **C.**

The United States had many allies, with Australia, Korea, the Philippines, and other countries providing troops. See Chapter 6.

12. **A.**

The Seminoles were never defeated; Florida's first themes parks opened in 1930 and most of its immigrants are from South America. See Chapter 6.

13. **D.**

Both programs were instituted to reduce unemployment during the Great Depression. See Chapter 6.

14. **C.**

The stock market crash was one major cause of the Great Depression. See Chapter 6.

15. **C.**

Germany was not invited into the League of Nations. Although the league was proposed by President Woodrow Wilson, Congress voted not to join it. See Chapter 6.

16. **B.**

   None of the members of the First Continental Congress wanted to break away from Great Britain. By the Second Continental Congress, however, military conflict seemed inevitable. See Chapter 6.

17. **A.**

   The laws that the colonists called the Intolerable Acts were called the Coercive Acts in Great Britain. Oglethorpe went to Georgia in 1738; Yancey was one of the proslavery extremists known as fire-eaters; and Beauregard was a Confederate general. See Chapter 6.

18. **D.**

   Srebrenica was the site of genocide in Bosnia, and Rwanda was the site of genocide in Africa. South Africa had apartheid and war but not genocide. See Chapter 5.

19. **A.**

   The only negative among the answer choices is war. See Chapter 4.

20. **C.**

   Russia is ruled by more than one person, so it cannot be a monarchy. See Chapter 4.

21. **D.**

   The right to a speedy and public trial is stated in the Sixth Amendment. The Tenth Amendment states, "The powers not delegated to the United States by the Constitution, nor prohibited by it to the states, are reserved to the states respectively, or to the people." See Chapter 4.

22. **A.**

   The discount rate is an element of federal monetary policy. It affects the cost of money to banks and subsequently the cost to borrow by consumers. See Chapter 3.

23. **A.**

   The GDP is the monetary value of all the finished goods and services produced within a country's borders in a specific period, usually one year. It includes all private and public consumption, government outlays, investments, and exports minus imports that occur within a defined territory. See Chapter 3.

24. **B.**

 Capitalist economies are market economies free of government control, whereas socialist economies are managed economies with a great deal of government control. See Chapter 3.

25. **B.**

 Although taxes are a form of government influence they are not considered control. See Chapter 4.

26. **B.**

 Working with the states, the federal government creates certain laws and programs that are funded federally but administered by the states. Education, social welfare, assisted housing and nutrition, homeland security, transportation, and emergency response are key areas in which states deliver services using federal funds and are subject to federal guidelines. See Chapter 4.

27. **C.**

 No Child Left Behind is a federal program with massive influence on the states. See Chapter 4.

28. **C.**

 The horizontal lines are in increments of 500,000. The bar that reaches the first line, or 500,000, is labeled 1830–1839.

29. **C.**

 The bar that reaches the 1.5 million mark is labeled 1840–1849.

30. **D.**

 Answering this question correctly requires you to read carefully and base your answer only on the information presented in the graph.

31. **D.**

 The state commands the National Guard except when the troops are called to national service. See Chapter 4.

32. **D.**

 The Renaissance came before the Age of Reason. See Chapter 5.

33. **D.**

> Nation-states use the state as an instrument of national unity in economic, social, and cultural life. See Chapter 4.

34. **A.**

> The chart shows a drop in precipitation in April to the lowest point of the year.

35. **A.**

> The average high temperature in July is below 95 degrees, and the most amount of daylight is in June or July.

36. **D.**

> The chart specifically states that no data on humidity are included.

37. **A.**

> Elevation is given in meters, not yards, and the source of the data is not given.

38. **B.**

> The February Revolution of 1917 led directly to the fall of the autocracy of Tsar Nicholas II of Russia, the last tsar of Russia. Instead of having one ruler with absolute power, the revolutionaries sought to establish a democratic republic. See Chapter 5.

39. **A.**

> The Age of Revolution was the period from about 1750 to 1800, after most European countries changed their forms of government to absolutist states or constitutionalist states. The Age of Revolution specifically includes the American, French, and Russian revolutions. See Chapter 5.

40. **D.**

> Science was increasingly used in industry during the Industrial Revolution. See Chapter 5.

41. **A.**

> More than 2 billion people are Christians. Islam is the only other religion with more than a billion followers, at 1.2 billion. See Chapter 5.

42. **B.**

Labor unions helped raise wages and benefits for many U.S. workers, particularly the most skilled, from 1900 to 1950. See Chapter 6.

43. **A.**

A relatively large number of Chinese immigrated to the United States between the start of the California gold rush in 1849 and when federal law stopped their immigration in 1882. See Chapter 6.

44. **C.**

Asian immigrants do not have a universal language. Koreans, Chinese, Japanese, Cambodians, and Vietnamese all speak different languages. See Chapters 2 and 6.

45. **B.**

At the end of World War I, the United States retreated into isolation. The Senate refused to ratify the Treaty of Versailles that ended World War I. Additionally, the U.S. failed to join the League of Nations, the international organization that was the less successful predecessor of the United Nations. See Chapter 6.

46. **D.**

More than 1.2 million immigrants came to the U.S. in 1914. However, once the immigration restrictions of the 1920s took effect, the overall total was fixed at only about 160,000 immigrants a year. Moreover, different quotas were set for different nationalities. The quotas for immigrants from northern and western Europe were more than ample for the demand, but the quotas for immigrants from southern and eastern Europe were very small. The United States tried to pretend that the rest of the world did not really exist. Its people turned inward. See Chapter 6.

47. **B.**

The Eighteenth Amendment, effective in 1920, made the sale of alcohol illegal, thus establishing the period known as Prohibition. Lasting until 1933, when ratification of the Twenty-first Amendment repealed the eighteenth, Prohibition had the unintended effect of increasing organized crime in America, because manufacturing, importing, and selling illegal alcohol provided a financial windfall for gangs of criminals in the cities. The money was used to expand the influence of organized crime into gambling, prostitution, narcotics, and some legitimate businesses. See Chapter 6.

48. **A.**

Almost immediately after assuming the office of chancellor, Adolf Hitler began secretly building up Germany's army and weapons. In 1934, he increased the size of the army, began building warships, and created a German air force. Compulsory military service was also introduced. See Chapter 6.

49. **A.**

The Civil Rights Act of 1964 prohibited discrimination on the basis of color, race, religion, or national origin in places of public accommodation covered by interstate commerce—for example, in restaurants, hotels, motels, and theaters. Besides dealing with the desegregation of public schools, the act, in Title VII, forbade discrimination in employment. Title VII also prohibited discrimination on the basis of sex. In 1965, the Voting Rights Act was passed, which placed federal observers at polls to ensure equal voting rights. The Civil Rights Act of 1968 dealt with housing and real estate discrimination. See Chapter 6.

50. **A.**

King moved to Atlanta, Georgia, to co-pastor with his father at Ebenezer Baptist Church. In 1963 *Time* magazine named King its "Man of the Year," and he received the Noble Peace Prize in 1964. Radical African Americans did not agree with King's method of nonviolent resistance. Further, as the black power movement became stronger and Malcolm X's message of black nationalism became more accepted by northern urban blacks, King became an increasingly controversial figure. On April 4, 1968, while standing on the balcony of a motel in Memphis, Tennessee, he was shot. He was 39 years old. Two months later James Earl Ray was arrested in London, England. Ray pled guilty to King's assassination and was sentenced to 99 years in prison. See Chapter 6.

51. **B.**

In today's global society, with information spread quickly and widely, the humanitarian needs of people in one country are more likely to be known by people in other countries who can possibly help fill those needs. However, globalization also means that major companies can produce their goods in countries with fewer environmental regulations, like China and Vietnam. Without government supervision, these corporations may focus solely on profit and care little if at all about the lives of the people working in their factories. Thus, globalization has not made our world more peaceful. See Chapter 3.

52. **C.**

Congress passed the Twenty-sixth Amendment in 1971. It states, "The right of citizens of the United States, who are 18 years of age or older, to vote shall not be denied or abridged by the United States or by any State on account of age."

53. **A.**

China was reunited under the rule of the Han Dynasty, which is divided into two major periods: the Western or Former Han (206 B.C.E–9 C.E.) and the Eastern or Later Han (25–220 C.E.). The boundaries established by the previous Qin Dynasty and maintained by the Han have more or less defined the nation of China to the present day. The Western Han capital of Xi'an, in present-day Shaanxi Province—a monumental urban center laid out on a north–south axis with palaces, residential wards, and two bustling market areas—was one of the two largest cities in the ancient world (Rome was the other). Poetry, literature, and philosophy flourished during the reign of Emperor Wudi (141–86 B.C.E.). The monumental *Shiji*, written by Sima Qian (145–80 B.C.E.), set the standard for later government-sponsored histories. Among many other things, it recorded information about the various peoples, invariably described as "barbarian," who lived on the empire's borders. Wudi also established Confucianism as the basis for correct official and individual conduct and for the educational curriculum. The reliance of the bureaucracy on members of a highly educated class grounded in Confucian writings and other classics defined China's statecraft for many centuries. See Chapter 6.

54. **A.**

The technology of a geographic information system (GIS) combines the advantages of computer-assisted cartography with those of spatial database management. The earth's surface is 70 percent water, and slopes facing the sun are warmer than those that are not. See Chapter 2.

55. **B.**

The Gulf Stream wraps around the Keys and then moves north and east toward Great Britain. See Chapter 2.

56. **C.**

A market economy relies largely on market forces to allocate resources and goods and to determine prices and quantities of each good that will be produced. Capitalist economies are market economies. Socialist economies, on the other hand, are managed or planned economies that rely less on market forces and more on government control. See Chapter 3.

57. **D.**

Economics is the science that deals with the production, allocation, and use of goods and services. Resources relate to the four factors of production: labor, capital, land, and entrepreneurship. The supply of these four factors is finite. See Chapter 3.

58. **D.**

Even if you did not know that the media are part of political science, if you knew that both answer choices B and C are, you would know to pick answer choice D. See Chapter 4.

59. **C.**

Working with the states, the federal government creates certain laws and programs that are at least partially funded by the federal government but administered by the states. Education, social welfare, assisted housing and nutrition, homeland security, transportation, and emergency response are key areas where states deliver services using federal funds and are subject to federal guidelines. This gives the federal government the power to influence the states. For example, in the 1970s the federal government wanted to lower highway speed limits to reduce energy consumption. Rather than simply legislate a lower speed limit, the federal government threatened to withhold money for road projects from states that did not lower the speed limit on their highways. In many cases, the states must also partially fund the programs to qualify for federal funds. See Chapter 4.

60. **D.**

You may not know where Giotto lived, but you probably know that Aristotle, Plato, and Socrates were Greek. Giotto was an Italian painter and architect from Florence. He is generally considered the first in a line of great artists who contributed to the Italian Renaissance. See Chapter 6.

61. **D.**

Answer choices A, B, and C are literary figures, and answer choice D is a scientist. See Chapter 5.

62. **D.**

The concept of human–environment interaction holds that people adapt to, modify, and depend on the environment. See Chapter 2.

63. **C.**

   Answer choices A, B, and D are functional regions because they are defined by their purpose (Chinatown offers services unique to the Chinese population of New York City). See Chapter 2.

64. **C.**

   Although answer choices A, B, and D correctly describe features of Australia, they may be correct for other countries as well. However, only Australia is both a country and a continent. See Chapter 2.

65. **A.**

   Macroeconomics studies the elements of economics on the national level. See Chapter 3.

66. **A.**

   Microeconomics is the study of the economic behavior of small economic groups such as firms and families. See Chapter 3.

67. **A.**

   The FOMC sets the Fed's monetary policy, which is carried out through the trading desk of the Federal Reserve Bank of New York. If the FOMC decides that more money and credit should be available, it directs the trading desk in New York to buy securities from the open market. See Chapter 3.

68. **B.**

   The discount rate is the interest rate a Federal Reserve Bank charges eligible financial institutions to borrow funds on a short-term basis. Unlike open-market operations, which interact with financial market forces to influence short-term interest rates, the discount rate is set by the boards of the Federal Reserve Banks, and it is subject to approval by the Fed's board of governors. Under some circumstances, changes in the discount rate can affect other open-market interest rates in the economy. Changes in the discount rate also can have an announcement effect, causing financial markets to respond to a potential change in the direction of monetary policy. A higher discount rate can indicate a more restrictive policy, while a lower rate may be used to signal a more expansive policy. See Chapter 3.

69. **D.**

Depository institutions use their reserve accounts at Federal Reserve Banks not only to satisfy reserve requirements but also to process many financial transactions through the Federal Reserve, such as check and electronic payments and currency and coin services. See Chapter 3.

70. **C.**

The Federal Trade Commission deals with issues that touch the economic life of every American. It is the only federal agency with both consumer protection and competition jurisdiction in broad sectors of the economy. See Chapter 3.

71. **C.**

The number of Supreme Court justices is determined by Congress rather than the Constitution, and since 1869 the Court has been composed of one chief justice and eight associate justices. See Chapter 4.

72. **B.**

The general consensus is that Alexander Hamilton wrote 52 of the essays in the *Federalist Papers,* James Madison wrote 28, and John Jay contributed the remaining 5. Initially drafted by James Madison in 1789, the Bill of Rights was written at a time when an ideological conflict between Federalists and Antifederalists, dating from the Philadelphia Convention in 1787, threatened the Constitution's ratification. See Chapters 4 and 6.

73. **C.**

The Democratic National Committee and the Republican National Committee decide with separate rules for each party. See Chapter 4.

74. **B.**

The closed primary is often favored by the parties for a number of reasons. First, voters must register with a party in advance of the election. This is favorable for the party because it generates a list of loyal partisans. Closed primaries also ensure that the voters in each party's primary truly support the party and do not mean to undermine its success. The chief criticism of the closed primary is that voters must openly declare partisanship. Consequently, not everyone is involved in the choice of candidates for the general election. See Chapter 4.

75. **A.**

In the presidential election of 1800, the electors of the Democratic Republican Party gave Thomas Jefferson and Aaron Burr an equal number of electoral votes. The tie-breaking decision was made in the House of Representatives, resulting in the election of Thomas Jefferson. See Chapter 6.

76. **B.**

In its more than 200-year history, the electoral college has received its share of criticism and praise. Following is a list of the most frequently cited disadvantages of the electoral college:

- Enables a person receiving less than a majority of the votes to be elected president; one way for that to happen would be if the country was so deeply divided politically that three or more presidential candidates split the vote and no one obtained the necessary majority.

- Can include "faithless" electors—that is, electors who will not stay loyal to their parties or candidates.

- Can depress voter turnout. Because each state is only entitled to a certain number of electoral votes regardless of voter turnout, states have no incentive to encourage voter participation.

- Does not accurately reflect the national popular will because it does not elect a candidate by a direct popular vote.

See Chapter 4.

77. **A.**

Following is a list of the most frequently cited advantages of the electoral college:

- Requires a distribution of popular support to elect a president; the winning candidate must demonstrate both a sufficient popular support to govern as well as a sufficient distribution of that support.

- Strengthens the status of minority groups because the votes of small minorities within a state can make the difference between winning all or none of a state's electoral votes.

- Enhances the political stability of the nation by promoting a two-party system, protecting the presidency from impassioned but transitory third-party movements, and forcing the major parties to absorb the interests of minorities.

- Maintains the federal system of government and representation.

See Chapter 4.

78. **A.**

   Mussolini's father was a blacksmith and his mother a teacher. He became prime minister of Italy in 1922 and in 1924 changed his title to "head of the government." He was no longer responsible to the parliament, only Mussolini could determine the parliament's agenda; and only the king could depose the dictator. Hitler became Germany's chancellor in 1933. See Chapter 6.

79. **A.**

   Hitler broke many treaties. His parents were Roman Catholic. See Chapter 6.

80. **C.**

   Churchill became Britain's prime minister after Neville Chamberlain resigned. Churchill served in the army, and his speeches were considered inspirational. Although his role in World War II garnered him much support, many people in Britain did not agree with his domestic policies, especially his opposition to national health care and educational reforms. As a result, he was defeated in the 1945 election. Churchill resumed the office of prime minister in 1951 and retired in 1955. See Chapter 6.

81. **D.**

   As part of the Cold War, the Soviet president Nikita Khrushchev thought about placing nuclear missiles in Cuba to counter the emerging lead of the United States in developing and deploying strategic missiles. He also presented the scheme as a means of protecting Cuba from another U.S.-sponsored invasion, such as the failed attempt at the Bay of Pigs in 1961. This brought on what is known as the Cuban Missile Crisis, which is generally regarded as the time when the Cold War came closest to escalating into a nuclear war. See Chapter 6.

82. **C.**

   The Korean War is known as a "police action" because it was never officially declared a war.

83. **A.**

Buchanan was president before Lincoln. Lincoln made the Emancipation Proclamation before Sherman's defeat of Atlanta, which was near the end of the war. After the war, Lincoln was assassinated and Johnson assumed the presidency. Johnson was nearly impeached in 1868 on charges that included allegedly violating the Tenure of Office Act and the Command of the Army Act and bringing disgrace on the U.S. Congress; however, the resolution for impeachment did not receive the necessary two-thirds of the votes in Congress. See Chapter 6.

84. **A.**

The French and Indian War was fought from 1754 to 1763, the Revolutionary War lasted from 1775 to 1783, and the War of 1812 ended in 1815. See Chapter 6.

85. **B.**

On November 28, 1775, the Continental Congress authorized the establishment of the American navy. Although the navy was to play only a minor role in the war, the success of American privateers in interrupting British trade was an important factor aiding the patriot cause. You may not know the details, but you might be able to guess that the navy was created in Revolutionary War times. See Chapter 6.

86. **B.**

In *Common Sense,* Thomas Paine argued that the time had come to sever colonial ties with England and that it was in the American interest to do so. This pamphlet sold 120,000 copies in the three months after its first printing and was instrumental in convincing many colonists that the time had come for independence. See Chapter 6.

87. **C.**

Published in 1776, *Common Sense* challenged the authority of the British government and the royal monarchy. The plain language that Paine used spoke to the common people of America and was the first work to openly ask for independence from Great Britain. See Chapter 6.

88. **B.**

The French and Indian War was the North American part of the Seven Years' War, which was fought across Europe among all the most powerful nations of the period. In North America, Native Americans fought with the French against the British and American armies. George Washington led a contingent of troops to help establish British control in the West, and when he heard of the surrender of Fort Prince George in Pennsylvania, he set up camp in Great Meadows, southeast of Fort Duquesne (present-day Philadelphia). Washington received a report that a nearby French contingent intended to attack, so he launched a preemptive strike against the French camp. This was the first engagement of the yet undeclared French and Indian War. Although Washington won that engagement, he was soon defeated by a superior force sent out from Fort Duquesne, leaving the French in command of the entire region west of the Allegheny Mountains. See Chapter 6.

89. **D.**

The Cold War was the period of conflict, tension, and competition between the United States and the Soviet Union and their respective allies from the mid-1940s until the early 1990s. Throughout the period, the rivalry between the two superpowers was played out in multiple arenas: military coalitions; ideology, psychology, and espionage; military, industrial, and technological developments, including the space race; costly defense spending; a massive conventional and nuclear arms race; and many proxy wars. See Chapter 6.

90. **D.**

Asia is the world's largest and most populous continent. It covers 8.6 percent of the earth's total surface area (or 29.4 percent of its land area); and with almost 4 billion people, it has more than 60 percent of the world's population. See Chapter 2.

91. **A.**

Cartography (mapmaking) is the study of representations of the earth's surface with abstract symbols. Although other subdisciplines of geography rely on maps for presenting their analyses, the actual making of maps is abstract enough to be regarded as a separate field of study. Cartography has grown from a collection of drafting techniques into an actual science. See Chapter 2.

92. **D.**

Sociology is the study of society and human social interaction. See Chapter 7.

93. **B.**

The history of international relations is often traced back to the Peace of Westphalia of 1648, where the modern state system was developed. Before that, the European medieval organization of political authority was based on a vaguely hierarchical religious order. The Peace of Westphalia instituted the legal concept of sovereignty, which essentially meant that rulers, or the legitimate sovereigns, would recognize no internal equals within a defined territory and no external superiors as the ultimate authority within the territory's sovereign borders. See Chapter 5.

94. **C.**

Apartheid is an Afrikaans word meaning "separateness." It was a legal system established in South Africa whereby people were classified into racial groups: white, black, Indian, and colored. Separate geographic areas existed for each racial group. Apartheid laws were part of South Africa's legal framework from 1948 to 1994.

95. **A.**

When judging the terms of the peace treaties—in particular, the Treaty of Versailles—it is important to keep in mind the atmosphere in Europe and the attitude toward Germany in the period just after World War I. Obviously, anti-German feeling was strong in 1919. President Woodrow Wilson wanted to secure a peace based on his 14 points. He wanted a peace that would be based on justice, have liberal principles at its core, and be maintained by a new international organization (the League of Nations). Wilson did agree that Germany needed to be punished for starting the war, but he wanted the punishment to be fair. However, Europe took the punishment to the extreme, setting up the next conflict. See Chapter 6.

96. **D.**

Answer choices A, B, and C are dictators. See Chapter 5.

97. **C.**

Any definition of wealth must include both assets and liabilities. See Chapter 3.

98. **A.**

In mainstream economics, *inflation* refers to a general rise in prices measured against a standard level of purchasing power. See Chapter 3.

99. **B.**

Interest is a fee paid on borrowed money. The fee is a compensation to the lender for foregoing other useful investments that could have been made with the loaned money. The amount lent is called the principal. The percentage of the principal that is paid as fee (the interest) over a certain period is called the interest rate. See Chapter 3.

100. **A.**

Buddhism was founded around the fifth century B.C.E. by Siddhartha Gautama, commonly referred to as the Buddha. See Chapter 5.

101. **C.**

Animists do not believe in one all-powerful God. See Chapter 5.

102. **C.**

Both primary and secondary source documents can provide a closer look at history. See Chapter 7.

103. **B.**

Newspapers present observations and points of view and thus are secondary source documents. See Chapter 7.

104. **D.**

Since World War II Florida's economy has become more diverse. Tourism, cattle, citrus, and phosphate have been joined by a host of new industries that have greatly expanded the number of jobs available to residents. Electronics, plastics, construction, real estate, and international banking are among the state's more recently developed industries. Several major U.S. corporations have moved their headquarters to Florida. An interstate highway system exists throughout the state, and Florida is home to major international airports. The university and community college system has expanded rapidly, and high-technology industries have grown steadily. The U.S. space program executes its historic launches from Cape Canaveral, bringing significant media attention to the state. The citrus industry continues to prosper, despite occasional winter freezes, and tourism also remains important, bolstered by large capital investments. Florida attractions, such as the large theme parks in the Orlando area, bring millions of visitors to the state from across the U.S. and around the world. See Chapter 6.

105. **C.**

The intent of the Manhattan Project was to develop the first nuclear weapon (atomic bomb) during World War II by the United States, the United Kingdom, and Canada. See Chapter 6.

106. **C.**

From 1941 through 1946, the Manhattan Project was under the control of the U.S. Army Corps of Engineers, under the administration of General Leslie R. Groves. The scientific research was directed by the American physicist J. Robert Oppenheimer. See Chapter 6.

107. **B.**

The Great Wall is the world's longest human-made structure, stretching across roughly 4,000 miles and visible from outer space. See Chapter 5.

108. **D.**

Winston Churchill was the British prime minister from 1940 to 1945 and again from 1951 to 1955. See Chapter 6.

109. **B.**

On August 25, 1945, Emperor Bao Dai abdicated when the communist Viet Minh seized power. He lived for a time in exile in Hong Kong, returned to Vietnam in 1949 to act in an advisory role, was restored to rule in 1950, abdicated again in 1955, and lived the rest of his life in exile in Paris. See Chapter 6.

110. **D.**

Many factors led to American troops joining the war effort, including Nazi Germany's sinking of American supply ships because the United States was providing financial and military support to the Allied troops (England, France, China, and Russia). Most importantly, Japan attacked the U.S. naval base at Pearl Harbor, Hawaii, on December 7, 1941, without a declaration of war or any warning that hostilities were being commenced, sinking most of the battle fleet. The day after the attack, President Roosevelt went before the U.S. Congress and asked for a formal declaration of war against Japan; he did not ask Congress to formally declare war against Italy or Germany. Instead, a few days later, Italy and Germany declared war on the United States. See Chapter 6.

111. **D.**

On July 26, 1945, the United States, Britain, and China released the Potsdam Declaration, announcing the terms for Japan's surrender, with the warning, "We will not deviate from them. There are no alternatives. We shall brook no delay." See Chapter 6.

112. **A.**

One of the most significant trends of the postwar era in Florida has been steady population growth, resulting from large migrations to the state from within the United States and from countries throughout the Western Hemisphere, most notably Cuba and Haiti. Florida is now the fourth most populous state in the nation. See Chapter 6.

113. **D.**

No great treasure troves awaited the Spanish conquistadors who explored Florida. However, their stories helped inform Europeans about Florida and its relationship to Cuba, Mexico, and Central and South America, from which Spain regularly shipped gold, silver, and other products. See Chapter 6.

114. **B.**

When the hurricane roared ashore at Palm Beach on September 16, 1928, many coastal residents were prepared. But inland, along Lake Okeechobee, few conceived the disaster that was brewing. The storm struck first in Puerto Rico, killing 1,000 people, and then hit Florida with 125 mph winds. Forty miles west of the coast, rain filled Lake Okeechobee to the brim and the dikes crumbled. Water rushed onto the swampy farmland, and homes and people were swept away. Almost 2,000 people perished. See Chapter 6.

115. **B.**

The federal immigration station was closed in November 12, 1954, but not before 12 million immigrants passed through its doors. Ellis Island was one of 30 processing stations opened by the federal government. It was the major processing station for immigrants traveling third class or steerage to arrive in the United States in 1892; it processed 70 percent of all immigrants in that year. Located at the mouth of the Hudson River in New York Harbor, Ellis Island is within Jersey City, New Jersey, but is legally part of New York under the 1834 treaty setting the boundary between the two states. See Chapter 6.

116. **D.**

Lysander was the commander of the Spartan fleet that was victorious against the Athenians at Aegospotami in 405 B.C.E. The following year he took Athens itself, bringing the Peloponnesian War to an end. See Chapter 5.

117. **D.**

   Vietnamese immigration to America has been almost exclusively a by-product of the Vietnam War. Although probably fewer than 10,000 Vietnamese lived in America in 1970, by 1980 that figure had risen to almost a quarter of a million as a result of the defeat of the South Vietnamese and subsequent refugee flows. Today, these and subsequent immigrants from Vietnam, along with their descendants, number well over half a million. Although Vietnamese Americans reside nationwide, the largest concentration (approximately 40 percent) is in California, predominantly in Orange County, just south of Los Angeles. See Chapter 6.

118. **C.**

   Patton descended from a long line of soldiers, including General Hugh Mercer of the American Revolution. A great-uncle, Waller T. Patton, perished of wounds received in Pickett's charge during the Battle of Gettysburg. Another relative, Hugh Weedon Mercer, was a Confederate general. Patton's paternal grandparents were Colonel George Smith Patton and Susan Thornton Glassell. Patton's grandfather, born in Fredericksburg, graduated from Virginia Military Institute. See Chapter 6.

119. **C.**

   Logically, a person cannot be involved in the formation of two parties. In fact, George Washington was disappointed that two parties were developing by the end of his first term as president. Weary of politics, feeling old, he retired at the end of his second term. In his farewell address, he urged his countrymen to forswear excessive partisan spirit and geographical distinctions. In foreign affairs, he warned against long-term alliances. See Chapter 6.

120. **C.**

   Kennedy was a Harvard graduate as well as a naval military hero. See Chapter 6.

121. **C.**

   Washington, as America's first president, could not have been a Progressive Republican (the Progressives split off from the Republican Party in 1912), vice president, or senator. The common element in the lives of these men is their military careers. Every war except Vietnam has produced military leaders who later became presidents. See Chapter 6.

122. **D.**

Four presidents have been killed in office: Abraham Lincoln, James A. Garfield, William McKinley, and John F. Kennedy. Taft, the twenty-seventh president, died in 1930, 17 years after leaving office. See Chapter 6.

123. **A.**

The line of succession after vice president is speaker of the House of Representatives, president pro tempore of the Senate, secretary of state, and secretary of the Treasury. See Chapter 4.

124. **C.**

All the participants in the ancient Olympic Games were male citizens of the city-states from every corner of the Greek world, coming from as far away as Iberia (Spain) in the west and the Black Sea (Turkey) in the east. A separate competition for young unmarried girls was held in honor of Hera. Foot races were originally the only events in the Olympic Games, but the marathon race was not introduced until the 1896 Olympics held in Athens. See Chapter 5.

125. **A.**

In a communist country, the government owns businesses like airlines. It also typically provides health care, education, and housing assistance. See Chapter 4.

Index

G